TO THE VICTOR

There was no hope now for the Forty Fort. Its garrison surrendered on British Colonel John Butler's promise to spare their lives. But the amnesty did not apply to the Indians' prisoners taken in the battle.

That night they met their dreaded fate. Fugitives in the woods and people of the farms saw the heaps of dried brush flame up around the torture stakes in the clearings and along the river bank, and heard the screams of the victims. Others, the stakes having burned down, were flung onto the hot embers and held down with pitchforks until they died . . .

Of those who escaped, many perished of starvation and exhaustion in the swamps. Relief regiments found few survivors in the ravaged countryside . . .

Here is only one of the dramatic true episodes recounted in this exciting chronicle of the early Indian Wars.

AUTHOR'S PROFILE

Rated as one of the nation's top experts on guns, warfare and Americana as well as horses and dogs, Fairfax Downey is the author of 37 books. He has written extensively in the fields of history, biography and fiction and some of his best known books include INDIAN-FIGHTING ARMY, THE GUNS AT GETTYSBURG and STORMING OF THE GATEWAY; CHATTANOOGA, 1863.

Mr. Downey was born in Salt Lake City, Utah, and is a graduate of Yale University. A veteran of both World Wars, he holds a Silver Star citation and is a distinguished member of the Company of Military Historians.

He now lives with his wife in West Springfield, New Hampshire.

FROM THE REVIEWS

"This is the 16th history book Fairfax Downey has written and, like the earlier offerings, rates top consideration . . . Recommended highly for history students. It's brilliantly chronicled and reflects the temper of the times when young America fought in what may well have been the strangest wars of any nation's baptism."

Utica *Observer Dispatch*

"Downey's style is vivid, his presentation arresting. He makes the reader see the engagements and understand them. Writing with a soldier's point of view, he compares the campaigns and battles, the equipment and the men, with armies of other days, from the legions of Roman times to present day battle groups."

Charleston *Evening Post*

"This is a succinct, precise account of American participation in wars against the Indians, from the time of the Revolution to the last campaign in the West . . . Consistently interesting."

Madison (Wisc.) *Capital Times*

"This is not dry history. Downey is one of the nation's most accomplished and prolific writers and he does not fail the reader here."

Houston *Chronicle*

"Interestingly and graphically presented, INDIAN WARS OF THE U. S. ARMY is a valuable contribution to the American history bookshelf."

Anniston (Ala.) *Star*

"Mr. Downey's story is enlivening and interesting and he emphasizes the dramatic, romantic, and heroic aspects of his subject. He indulges in some tradition and verified reports, but he gives them exactly for what they are, while he shows a very full knowledge of his subject and a conscientious desire to make his biography true to history. It is fortunate that such a book as this by Fairfax Downey is offered to the reading public."

St. Louis *Post Dispatch*

A Monarch Americana Book

INDIAN WARS OF THE U.S. ARMY

(1776-1865)

Fairfax Downey

Author of INDIAN-FIGHTING ARMY

Illustrated Edition

MONARCH BOOKS, INC.

Derby, Connecticut

Charles N. Heckelmann • President
Allan Adams • Executive Vice President

INDIAN WARS OF THE U.S. ARMY

(1776-1865)

A Monarch Americana Book

Published in July, 1964 by special arrangement
with Doubleday & Company, Inc.

Library of Congress Catalog Card Number 63-11228

Cover Photo: Massacre at Fort Mims (Alonzo Chappel)
Courtesy of The Chicago Historical Society

To The Gallant Memory Of The Old Army
Of The Indian Wars

Monarch Books are published by MONARCH BOOKS, INC., Capital Building, Derby, Connecticut, and represent the works of outstanding novelists and writers of non-fiction especially chosen for their literary merit and reading entertainment.

Printed in the United States of America

Contents

Foreword

THE AMERICAN INDIAN WARS of the middle period have been overshadowed by those that followed the Civil War and to some extent by those of Colonial times. Yet the wars from 1776 to 1865 were as fiercely fought as their predecessors and successors and more critical in the development of the country. They spread over a vast area, widened by the outthrusting frontier. Few years passed without a campaign or an action, large or small. Indian hostilities formed a second front for the U. S. Army during the conflicts with Great Britain and Mexico and throughout the Civil War.

The intermediate Indian Wars helped make three Presidents of the United States: Jackson, Harrison, and Taylor. Abraham Lincoln's brief service in the Black Hawk War of 1832 proved significant. Many a Civil War general had won his spurs in Indian combat. Battle honors are proudly borne by descendants of regiments that fought on hotly contested fields from Fallen Timbers onward.

The U. S. Army is the protagonist in this book as in the author's *Indian-Fighting Army*, dealing with the later wars. Here is portrayed the American soldier in garrison and on campaign—in victory or defeat—his bravery and endurance of almost incredible hardships—his faults and failures—his rigorous service at a pay for privates of $4 a month, rising no higher than $13 in the 1860s. Exploration, the great reconnaissances of Lewis and Clark, Pike, and others; resettlement of conquered tribes; such are among achievements that stand to the Army's credit along with its battle record.

Being military history, this work is chiefly a chronicle of passages-at-arms, in the medieval phrase. Justification or condemnation of the Indian Wars is not its province. The Army was the instrument, not the instigator, of conquest.

In line of duty it opened the way for the westward course of empire.

Tribes that sought to bar that path across the continent fought a savage warfare, sometimes matched by their adversaries. By every means in their power they strove to defend their hunting grounds. History repeating itself, nomadic people, in spite of valiant resistance, lost their lands to a strong industrial nation. Wars, smallpox, tuberculosis, and whiskey reduced the Indian population, estimated at 850,000 on the discovery of America, to 250,000. By 1960 it had increased to 500,000, with remaining tribes on the road to recovery.

Soldier and warrior met as worthy foemen or fought side by side as allies. The Old Army of the Indian Wars left as its legacy to armies that came after it a valorous tradition.

A writer of history must pay grateful tribute to his sources in the form of a bibliography and by mention of the repositories of material. Research for this book was chiefly accomplished in the following libraries. That of Dartmouth College where many needed volumes were available, with those not on the shelves obtained through the efficient inter-library loan service of the reference department. The Yale University Library, particularly its Western Americana section. The New York Public Library and that of the University Club, New York City. My own small collection of military books was useful. As with earlier works, the Company of Military Collectors & Historians served as a valuable source of data and illustrations, notably so in help given by fellow members.

Chapters in advance of book publication appeared in the following magazines: *Army, Civil War Times,* and *Montana.*

Sincere thanks for generous and valued aid are offered Bruce Lancaster for authoritative advice on the Revolutionary period and to Southworth Lancaster; also to others of the Company: Harold L. Peterson, Dr. James G. Hazlett, Lee A. Wallace, Jr., A. McC. Craighead, W. Ogden McCagg, and Godfrey L. Olsen. I am deeply indebted to H. Charles McBarron, Jr., for his permission and that of the Company to reproduce a number of his drawings in the Military Uniforms in America series. Other illustrations are credited where they appear to sources whose courtesy allowed their use. Staff members of the National Park Service, notably Franklin G. Smith and Robert M. Utley, obligingly checked several chapters, enabling correction of errors. Mrs. Archibald M. Richards lent a copy of a letter written by her grandfather, General A. B. Dyer; permission to republish excerpts was kindly given by the *New Mexico Historical Review.*

I was fortunate in the supervision of George Shively, senior editor, Doubleday & Company, and in the services of my literary agent, Oliver G. Swan of Paul R. Reynolds & Son. Again, as for all my other books, a benison upon my wife, Mildred Adams Downey, for criticism, typing, and tolerance of the abstraction of one who was present in the flesh but otherwise "away off somewhere a century or so ago fighting Indians."

FAIRFAX DOWNEY

West Springfield
New Hampshire
1963

I

The Scalp

THE INDIAN flourished a scalp of long black hair, still lustrous with life, from its texture and length plainly a white woman's. He held it high beside his own roached scalp lock, jutting challengingly from shaven skull. With savage pride and rum-warmed bravado the Wyandot warrior called Panther dared display his trophy in the midst of the British camp at Skenesboro, New York, on that twenty-seventh day of July 1777. Despite all General Burgoyne's stern words forbidding scalping of wounded enemy or prisoners and any harm whatever to noncombatants, especially women and children, the Wyandot sought a sale for his prize and finally found it—to the most unlikely buyer.

But the scalp of Jane McCrae, who was to have been the bride of a Tory officer with Burgoyne, exacted an incomparably greater price than was paid for it. Its image in the minds of men was one of the most compelling stimulants to recruiting the American army ever knew. Nothing except the hiring of Hessian mercenaries by the British matched it in fanning the flames of the Revolution.

Jenny McCrae was only one of the thousands of frontier women, along with children and many men, whose scalps had been taken since the days of the early settlements. It was the circumstances surrounding her tragedy that set it apart—that caused it to exert such widespread influence when the United States faced the Indians, as British allies, in the first of a long series of conflicts which would not cease until the last decade of the next century.

Jenny's brother had tried hard to persuade her to sail down the Hudson with him to the safety of Albany. The countryside was dangerous, burning with war fever. Burgoyne's army was marching down from captured Fort Ticonderoga, and the Rebels in retreat before it. Indians with the invading force and those waiting to join it might be expected not to molest Tories like the McCraes, British partisans. However, on the warpath they sometimes failed to make distinction between white settlers.

Jenny, with all the independence of her twenty-three years, refused to leave. She believed she was safe as a loyalist—doubly so, for she was affianced to Lieutenant David Jones serving in one of Burgoyne's Tory contingents mustered in Canada. Any day now the young officer, with whom she had grown up in this neighborhood, would return. She might have met him later in Albany when Burgoyne, as confidently anticipated, drove through to link with Clinton and cut off New England from Washington's army in the middle states. Jenny, being deeply in love, would not wait. She bade farewell to her brother and went to live with fat, garrulous Widow McNeil in her house near ruinous Fort Edward, still garrisoned by a few American militiamen.

The morning Indians broke into the cabin Jenny had put on her best dress "as for a bridal." The four raiders were not of the Six Nations of the Iroquois but Wyandots, kin to the Hurons. Ominous though they looked in full war paint, they did no injury to the two women but hustled them out, making them understand that they were being taken to the newly pitched British camp. Jenny's eyes must have lit up. Burgoyne's army had arrived, and David Jones would be with it. Mrs. McNeil, puffing as she was hurried along, still had breath enough to scold her captors. British General Simon Fraser was her cousin, she told them, and she would have plenty to say to him for having sent rascally Indians for her.

To hasten the pace the Wyandots led up two horses they had caught. They put Jenny on one, but united efforts failed to hoist ponderous Mrs. McNeil onto the other. Jenny, flanked by two guards, rode ahead, out of sight of the lagging fat woman, prodded along by her escorts. The widow saw nothing of what happened though she heard shooting. A hovering American militiaman reported he caught a glimpse of Indians with a captive on horseback and fired at them, but it was a distant view and a long shot. He was understandably cautious; his captain had been killed and two of his comrades captured in a recent Indian attack on a Fort Edward picket. While the militiaman's shot may have prompted what followed, it was improbable that the fast-moving raiders would have been alarmed by a lone soldier. A far more likely version of what took place was generally accepted.

A quarrel arose between the two warriors as to whose prisoner Jenny was. Who had first laid hands on her in the cabin and was due the reward for bringing her into camp—more of the white man's rum they had been drinking—surely a jug at least? They must share it if both turned her in. Angry words ended with muskets leveled, not at each other but at the girl rider. If one could not claim her, the other should not.

Underneath the branches of a lofty oak, which stood for many years as a memorial, the muskets rang out. Jenny slid, moaning, from the back of her mount. First to leap on her was the big Wyandot, Panther, described as "of gigantic stature." He whipped out his scalping knife. As sunlight glinted on it, it illuminated, perhaps, letters graven on the blade. Such articles of coveted trade goods, betraying their source, were often marked with the initials of Brittanic Majesty, G.R.— *Georgius Rex.*

What Jane McCrae suffered was familiar enough to frontiersmen. Dr. James Thacher, from Barnstable in Massachusetts, described it in his journal where he also recorded Jenny's story. Surgeon with General Schuyler's American army, its retreat halted and slowing the British advance, Dr. Thacher had recently attended a captain scalped, tomahawked, shot, and left for dead. His dog had led rescuers to him, and under the surgeon's care the officer recovered.

"The Indian method of scalping their victims is this," Dr. Thacher wrote. "With a knife they make a circular cut from the forehead quite round, just above the ears, then taking hold of the skin with their teeth, they tear off the whole hairy scalp in an instant, with wonderful dexterity. Then they carefully dry and preserve it as a trophy, showing the number of their victims, and have a method of painting on the dried scalp, different figures and colors, to designate the sex and age of the victim, and also the manner and circumstances of the murder."

The Wyandots, more thorough than the assailants of the American captain, gave Jenny no chance to survive her mutilation. A local tradition declares they raped her. Then a tomahawk was sunk deep in her head. Her body was stripped of wedding gown, further mangled, and thrown aside.

When Mrs. McNeil reached the British camp, her captors, impatient from her scoldings and slowness, had torn off all her clothing except her chemise. Taken to General Fraser's tent, the furious widow gave her cousin a tongue-lashing. There were moments of embarrassingly comic relief while a vain search was made for women's clothing large enough. Finally the general wrapped her in his great-coat. Only then did they begin to wonder what had become of Jenny McCrae.

The appearance of Panther with the scalp furnished the answer. For those who knew Jenny there was no mistaking her long tresses. Unbound, they had fallen to the ground, and she was tall. Mrs. McNeil instantly recognized them. So did Lieutenant David Jones. Only General Burgoyne's quick action in ordering the arrest and execution of the Wyandot could have restrained the frantic young officer from taking vengeance on the murderer.

Enter now Louis St. Luc de La Corne, seventy-year-old nobleman of France, an unexcelled leader of Indians since he had marshaled tribes against the British in the French and Indian War. Now he was commanding them for his former enemy against rebel Americans. Renowned for his strength and endurance despite his age and for his wood-craft, St. Luc lived, spoke, and thought like an Indian and was as merciless. Throughout the frontier he was known to settlers as a devil incarnate. *"Il faut brutalizer les affaires,"* was the advice he had been dinning in the ears of Gentleman Johnny Burgoyne. One must get tough, particularly in warfare using Indians. Now that his advice had been followed in the instance of Jenny, he retracted not a bit of it. Furthermore he warned that if the Panther was condemned and hanged, all of Britain's Indian allies would immediately desert.

That was more than General Burgoyne, deep in enemy territory, dared risk. A dismaying dispatch, which he kept to himself for the time being, had reached him. No strong force would march north to form a junction with him, as he understood had been arranged, but all the British main army in the east would remain to face General Washington. He would have to push his way through to Albany with only the help of St. Leger's small reinforcing expedition coming east down the Mohawk Valley.

Gentleman Johnny Burgoyne, the polished and debonair man of the world—Burgoyne, fighting a war in the American wilderness encamped with such comforts of civilization as a mistress and a plentiful supply of champagne—Burgoyne, the dramatic general—like many another, good or bad—Burgoyne, the playwright, was confronted by a situation of high drama, hinging on a girl's scalp. Nor did he see how he could resolve its dilemma, either as a commander or a dramatist, if he gave the cue for exit of his Indian allies.

Genuinely distressed though he was by the fate of Jane McCrae, he saw no course open to him under the circumstances but to pardon and release the Panther.

Neither Burgoyne nor perhaps at the moment anyone else foresaw the far-reaching effect of the scalping and slaughter of a single frontier girl and of the failure to punish it. Ripples of outrage slowly widened. That same day Indians had wiped out a whole family: man, wife, three children, and three Negro slaves. Yet that deed fell, little noted, into a familiar pattern. As General Fraser observed of a similar occurrence, "It is a conquered country, and we must wink at such things."

But there was to be no ignoring the slaying of Jenny McCrae. Tories were shocked and alarmed, their loyalty shaken, by the massacre, without retribution, of one of their own people. As for grief-stricken Lieutenant David Jones, he could do no more than buy the scalp of his fiancée. Better that than let it hang at the Panther's belt and be triumphantly flaunted at war dances. The young officer offered his resignation. Though it was refused, he was allowed to return to Canada as unlikely to be of further use to the British Army. Heartbroken he spent the rest of his life as a melancholy figure to whom none ever dared mention the Revolution, shutting himself in his room every year on the anniversary of Jenny's death.

The story of Jenny, losing none of its tragic poignancy, spread through Burgoyne's ranks and it was not good for morale. Soldiers who kept journals, Lieutenants Digby and Anburey, Sergeant Lamb, and others, wrote with pity of "the unfortunate young lady whose death must be universally lamented"—"her family loyal to the King"—the victim of "our Indians (I may well now call them Savages)." In England the story rekindled flames lit in Parliament to brand British use of Indians in the American war as inhuman. On learning of Burgoyne's speech forbidding his Indians to commit atrocities the eloquent Edmund Burke had poured out bitter irony. "Suppose there was a riot on Tower Hill. What would the keeper of his Majesty's lions do? Would he not fling open the dens of the wild beasts and then address them thus: 'My gentle lions—my humane bears—my tender-hearted hyenas, go forth! But I exhort you, as you are Christians and members of civil society, to take care not to harm any man, woman or child.' "

It was of little use for British apologists to point out that the Americans had made the first move to make allies of the Indians. As early as April 1775, the Provincial Congress appealed to the Christian Stockbridge tribe "to take up the hatchet in the cause of liberty," offering a bonus of blankets, ribbons, and money. After an attempt for a year to keep the Indians neutral at least, General Washington was authorized by Congress to enlist 2000 for an attack on Canada. Only a few responded, and with the repulse of the invasion, most tribes turned toward the winning side.

Besides, it was a natural for the Indians to form an alliance with the British as earlier with the French. From the outset the red men's true enemies were the settlers, whether as British subjects or citizens of rebellious states. These were the people, not content with trading posts, whose axes bit steadily encroaching clearings out of the forest for cabins and crops. Slayers of deer, the Indian's livelihood, as later of the buffalo. Hewers of roads through the wilderness, as patent a threat as the steel rails for the Iron Horse of the future. Conquerors who had engulfed and rendered impotent tribe after tribe in the East and were thrusting others steadily westward.

"Take up the hatchet for liberty." Whose liberty? Not the Indians'. Too many of them had long lost it.

American inducements for Indian support were scarcely more persuasive than their exhortations. It was the British who were generous with guns, powder, blankets, and clothing the rebels could ill spare—with knives, trinkets, and greatly craved rum. Tribes attempting to blackmail Congress for bribes achieved little.

Yet the American government kept trying to win over the Indians. An official message on the victory at Trenton was sent the Six Nations of the Iroquois, and an attempt made to seduce even the Mohawks, stanchest of British allies. Only one success crowned American zeal and that was due to the work of the missionary, Samuel Kirkland. Respect and love for that remarkable man severed two of the powerful Six Nations from British allegiance. Because of Kirkland, the Tuscaroras remained neutral, while the Oneidas became active partisans of the Americans.

When the murder of Jane McCrae focused attention on the savage custom of scalping, it was as futile for the British to protest that they were generally powerless to prevent it as it was for them to retort that Americans were by no means guiltless of lifting Indian hair. There were, for instance, numbers like Timothy Murphy, the Virginia rifleman, who would boast twenty scalps taken before the war was over. And how about the Oneida Indians, American allies, who brought in British and Hessian scalps and were doubtless paid for them? But the glaring fact remained that there was no counterpart to the case of Jane McCrae, although there might have been if Indians on the American side had wielded knives on the Hessian commander's wife, blond, petite Baroness Riedesel who followed the army with three little daughters, often under the escort of a single Jaeger.

As the word of Jenny's massacre filtered through the countryside, American anger, smoldering from similar slayings, flamed up. General Horatio Gates, who had intrigued the abler Schuyler out of the army's command, promptly seized upon the occasion. That "old granny of a feller," as his troops called him, surpassed himself in a letter blasting Burgoyne. Gentleman Johnny's reply, deploring the event and stating that the murderer had been arrested and lectured —but pardoned—was far more damaging than silence. General Washington, receiving a report, saw to it that the story of Jenny was kept alive. For the main army tragedy was remote, but its propaganda value was as high as that of atrocities in past and future wars. From New York town a versifier, probably Francis Hopkinson, sped a shaft at Burgoyne.

I will let loose the dogs of Hell,
Ten thousand Indians, who shall yell
And foam and tear, and grin and roar,
And drench their moccasins in gore;
To these I'll give full scope and play
From Ticonderog to Florida;
They'll scalp your heads . . .

At the seat of war in central and eastern New York the first result of Indian forays had been to spur the flight of refugee families. But soon their men started to drift back and others to assemble. Militia rallied to the support of the Continental regiments of the northern army, demoralized by retreat and defeat since Ticonderoga. Without these militiamen the forthcoming Battles of Bennington and Saratoga could have had a different outcome—as might the war of which Saratoga has been justly termed the turning point.

Along Burgoyne's defense lines dead British and Hessian sentries were increasingly found by their reliefs. On their bodies, as well as on those of Indians, were found scraps of paper. Scrawled across them was "*For Jane McCrae.*"

The name on the bits of paper was a symbol for many others etched in memories, written in family Bibles and other records, or on graveboards such as the fresh-marked one at Crown Point, New York.

Beneath this humble sod
Lie Cap^{n} Adams, Lieut. Culbertson and 2 privates of
the 2^{d} Pennsylvania regt.
Not hirelings but Patriots
who fell, not in battle,
but unarmed,
who were barbaroously murdered and inhumanely scalped
by the emissaries of the once just but
now abandoned Kingdom of Britain.
Sons of America rest in quiet here.
Britannia blush, Burgoyne let fall a tear,
And tremble Europe's Sons with savage race.
Death and revenge await you with disgrace.

Scalping and torture—those baleful prospects a soldier or a settler and his family faced. Greater than the terror they struck was the resistance they steeled.

Now, as often before, the scalping knife had made that indelible cut that runs like a scarlet thread through the history of the Indian Wars.

II

Siege and Ambush

THE WALLS OF FORT STANWIX rose above cleared ground, confronting the surrounding forest. That little stronghold (on the site of the present city of Rome, New York) dominated a portage the Indians called the Great Carrying Place. Its bastions were bars in a land gate athwart the vital water route from Lake Ontario via the Mohawk River and thence on through tributaries to the Hudson and the Atlantic Ocean. Hold Stanwix, and the gate stood closed. Yield it, and all the Mohawk Valley settlements would lie at the mercy of raiding redskins and Tories. A vital source of beef cattle and grain would be lost to the American army. That part of it which was defending New York State would be trapped between Burgoyne and a force under Lieutenant Colonel Barry St. Leger, marching down from Canada via Oswego to storm Stanwix and clamp the second jaw of the vise. Then the enemy's path to Albany would be cleared—New England severed from the rest of the Union—last resistance under General Washington hemmed in by land and sea. Seldom have such great potentialities pivoted on one little frontier fort.

Fort Stanwix, built in 1758, had been rechristened Fort Schuyler in 1776, but the old name clung. It was none too soon that Colonel Peter Gansevoort's regiments arrived to raise its garrison to 750 men and plunge into the work of strengthening the crumbling stockade. Hard, exhausting work, all the digging and tree felling, and the rank and file grumbled loudly, as soldiers will, when their officers and noncoms drove them at it with urgency. What was the use of it? They'd soon have to pull out anyway and give up the fort to heavy odds under Burgoyne or some other Britisher. Even more effective than profane language spurring on the fatigue parties was the Bible quotation (Joel 2:20) prophetically declaimed by Lieutenant Colonel Marinus Willett, second in command: "But I will remove far off from you the northern army, and will drive him into a land barren and desolate, with his face turned toward the eastern and his hinder parts toward the utmost sea."

Shortly the garrison was glad of its backbreaking labor. The Indians, forerunners of the coming invasion, were closing in. Settlers had been warned and all but a few, reluctant to leave their homes until the last moment, had fled. Bitter in the memory of the garrison was the pitiful spectacle of three little girls, who had strayed away from their late-staying families, running toward the fort. A sally had been unable to save two of them, caught and scalped by pursuing braves, but the third had escaped, bleeding from a wound in her breast. Shortly afterward she and the other children and women in the fort, all but a few soldiers' wives who refused to leave their men, were escorted to a safer place than Stanwix.

Time gave grace for the arrival of a string of batteaux, sailing down the Mohawk with a precious cargo of ammunition and provisions. The batteaux men managed to fight off the Indians with only a few losses, while the garrison rushed to the rescue and unloaded the crafts.

Stanwix was on its own now. Vigilant sentries peered over parapets between the blockhouse bastions at the four corners. Sod-banked walls of logs pointed at the top were loopholed for flintlocks and pierced above with embrasures for a few small cannon. Within the stockade a parade ground spared space for barracks for enlisted men and small huts which were officers' quarters. Stanwix was typical of the little forts that stood in perilous isolation defending key points on wide stretches of the frontier. Throughout the Indian Wars its like would move westward with the course of empire.

Holding a fort when the prospect of relief was none too bright demanded resolute commanders, and Stanwix was fortunate in that respect. Both Gansevoort and Willett, already veterans, would serve through the rest of the Revolution. The former's portrait by Stuart shows a handsome face which could set in stern lines as quickly as his engaging personality could turn tough. Steel in the level gaze of tall, wiry Willett betokened a man who was supremely daring without rashness. His war record stretched back to service against the French, the early revolts of the Sons of Liberty, and Montgomery's invasion of Canada. A highly able officer in any type of campaigning, his particular flair for fighting Indians would be signalized by a reckoning with the redoubtable Chief Brant of the Mohawks.

Gansevoort and Willett inspected the garrison, its backbone their own 3rd New York and the 9th Massachusetts Regiment. Troops of the Continental Line, Regulars, they were founding a proud tradition in the United States Army. Already, with the Revolution still young, crack units had made a name for themselves. Glover's Marbleheaders, Haslett's Delaware Blues, Smallwood's Marylanders, Morgan's Virginia Riflemen, Greene's Rhode Islanders, and Wayne's light infantry. Knox's artillery and the cavalry of Light-Horse Harry Lee. The men of the Line enlisted for a year or more in contrast to the militia who signed up for a few months and like as not would turn back before a battle if they toted up their time and found it was about to expire. "They let others strike for their country while they struck for home."

Ten dollars a month was the pay of volunteers for the Line—when they got anything—and that pay would soon dwindle from hard money to depreciated paper currency "not worth a Continental." It was the militia who, along with higher pay, drew bounties without which many refused to enlist. General Washington had sadly written Congress: "There must be some other stimulus, besides love for their country, to make men fond of the service." Of course a militiaman fought on his own ground for his family and home and to save his skin. Those imperatives had called men to arms since the days of the first train bands. But to make a soldier willing to fight far away from his own hearthstone there must be a less immediate demand—an abstract idea, patriotism—defense of a nation struggling for independence. Without that inspiration Washington would have lacked an army. It gave him the Continental Line, below 10,000 men at all times, never more than 3000 in the northern contingent. Barely enough, with the aid of France, to win the war. And toward gaining that vital alliance the holding of Fort Stanwix would become a link in the chain finally forged at Saratoga.

The Continental Line. It must plead guilty to not a few

faults and failures: refusal to re-enlist, desertion, even mutiny by units hungry and long unpaid. Too often its troops resented discipline as strongly as militiamen. They considered it *was* theirs to reason why and disobeyed orders they thought didn't make sense. Nevertheless the Line was beginning to learn the profession of arms from hard experience, their better leaders, and foreign drillmasters such as Steuben, Lafayette, Kosciusko, and Febiger. The pride that comes to soldiers who prove worthy of the name was born and grew.

That pride showed in the regiments marshaled for the defense of Fort Stanwix. What if their uniforms were nondescript? Battered tricorns, faded blue coats, crossbelts, waistcoats, breeches, and gaiters that may once have been white or buff. They were still uniforms, badges of distinction. Faces were shaven, hair tied in queues, and men tried to keep themselves and their weapons clean, polishing their cartridge boxes, musket barrels, and bayonets. Even in rags, their soldier's pride remained. They mounted guard and drill as if the eyes of the world were upon them. Smartly they handled muskets, going through the nineteen motions of loading and firing until they could count on getting off one or two shots a minute. They strove to bear themselves like Regulars, not militia. Yet their sense of superiority was somewhat lessened by the knowledge that if the siege reached a desperate point, they must look for relief not to Schuyler's army, with all and probably more than it could handle in Burgoyne, but to militiamen of the countryside. Before the fort should be hemmed in by the advancing British, couriers slipped through the Indian-infested woods with an appeal to the militia of Tryon County for help, help that must come or Stanwix would inevitably be lost. The Regular Army must fight most of the Indian Wars alone, given that mission by a nation indifferent and unconcerned as a whole. Yet at Stanwix, as on other critical occasions, the Regular must make his bow to the citizen soldier and thank the God of Battles for him.

August 3, 1777. Thuds of the blades of Canadian axmen, hewing a road of sixteen miles through the forest, heralded St. Leger's approach. Over that last lap marched a long column in uniforms of scarlet, blue, and green—1000 British, Hessian, and Troy troops. The column fanned out into lines that swung around to inclose the fort.

Then on the ramparts a flag soared up its staff. It was made from an officer's blue cloak, white shirts, and a woman's red petticoat. Its design may have followed that of the banner Washington had unfurled at Cambridge, with the united crosses of St. George and St. Andrew in the canton not yet replaced by a circle of thirteen stars. What mattered was that the national colors floated free over Fort Stanwix in the presence of the enemy.

Lower that rebellious rag up there and surrender, St. Leger demanded. "Deliver up your garrison, and your people shall be treated with every attention that a humane and generous enemy can give." Then he added a menacing postscript in the event capitulation were denied. "The Indians are becoming extremely impatient," he wrote Gansevoort. "I am afraid it will be attended by very fatal consequences, not only to you and to your garrison, but the whole country down the Mohawk River." The American commander's answer was a curt refusal. He would, he declared, defend the fort at every hazard and to the last extremity.

Soldiers manning the walls cocked an ear at the war whoops and quavering howls in the woods and nodded approval of Gansevoort's determination to hold out. Other garrisons had made the mistake of trusting enemy pledges of safety with Indians hovering around. There were a thousand of them out there, warriors of four of the Six Nations of the Iroquois, mostly Mohawks and Senecas. The dispatch St. Leger might well be penning could be foreseen. "After the surrendering Rebels had laid down their arms, every effort by His Majesty's troops proved unable to restrain our savage allies, and a massacre took place."

A man risked wounds and death when he went for a soldier, but to be butchered, defenseless, was another matter. And the lucky ones would be those who died quickly. In store for survivors was the torture stake—squaws jabbing burning pine slivers in their flesh—braves carving and hacking away at their bodies, carefully avoiding vital spots, until it was time to light the heaped brushwood. An invisible no-quarter flag flew in Indian warfare. Honor and duty regardless, it was best for a soldier to fight to the last.

The howling out in the forest redoubled. Copper-colored bodies flitted from behind one tree trunk to another, edging in for a closer sniping shot at sentries. A puff of smoke seeped out from the upper leaves of a tall oak. On a Fort Stanwix bastion a sentinel clutched his chest and slumped dead onto the flooring. He was the third to be killed there in three days. That was one of Chief Brant's warriors in the treetop—a crack shot under such good cover that no return fire had been able to dislodge him.

Fortunes of war. Man the post with another sentry. If Indian muskets and arrows and the short-barreled rifles of the Hessian Jaegers continued to whittle down the garrison and if no relief appeared, the siege could not long be withstood.

That was the way Indians fought, the way a white man must fight them if he wanted to survive. General Washington had known it when he was a young colonel and he and his Virginians, fighting Indian style, covered the retreat of the mortally wounded Braddock and his huddled British Regulars, all but overwhelmed by redskins and Frenchmen in the forests by the Monongahela in 1758. That was the way the settlers and the train bands had learned. Spread out and take all the cover wooded or broken country gave you. None of those close-packed ranks and foolishly gallant massed charges the British had brought from victories on the open fields of Europe. What if the like had won at Bunker Hill—when American powder ran out? Indians must be fought in another fashion. They avoided pitched battles whenever possible. Against them it generally came to man-to-man combat. In the cult of the warrior, and no people ever developed it more highly, the red men waged war as a way of life. Any display of cowardice rendered a tribesman outcast. Scouts without a peer, superb in woodcraft, the Indians fought the total warfare of the barbarian hordes of the past and of the "civilized" nations of the future.

Such was the military legacy of the Indians to the garrison of Fort Stanwix, as to their forefathers before them and to the soldiers who would come after them, an invaluable bequest for all our later wars through Korea. The arts of using cover, of infiltration, of ambush and sudden surprise attack, of mobility. From the last even the British had profited as testified by their organization of light infantry in the French and Indian War to cope with fast-moving redskins. Ranger companies before and during the Revolution practiced Indian tactics to the hilt, as would their counterparts on into the twentieth century. In no small measure the Indian Wars made the American Army the effective fighting force it became.

Along with hard-acquired knowledge of Indian skills gradually came perception of grave weaknesses. Indians rarely set guards at night and they intensely disliked battle in winter. Those failings, duly noted by the white man, led to the staging of pre-dawn attacks and cold weather campaigns which were increasingly employed as the contest stretched over the years and were prime factors in advancing the final conquest.

It was also true that Indians were reluctant to attack a fortified place. Any assault, the Stanwix men knew, would be left to the British while the savage cordon hemmed in the fort closely, ready to deal with a sortie or a relieving force. But there was no denying the warriors' prowess, fighting on their own terms. The Iroquois were well led by Joseph Brant, Thayendanegea, the most formidable Indian chieftain since Pontiac. Educated in Connecticut and given his English name, he had journeyed to England, been lionized at court and painted by Romney. His sister Molly had been the consort of the late Sir William Johnson, proprietor of a feudal estate in the Mohawk country, now headed by his Tory heirs. No wonder Brant's own tribe, the Mohawks, swayed by his influence and eloquence along with the Onondagas, Cayugas, and Senecas, wore war paint for the Great White Father Across the Water.

On the bastion where the third sentry had fallen the guard detail anxiously counted up reliefs. The night tours would be safe enough, but the man who drew the post at daylight would be on a hot spot. Strangely, the private due for duty then only grinned. He spent the intervening time stuffing a uniform with straw to make a dummy to put in his place and in arrangements with a squad of artillerymen. They trained one of the fort's 4-pounder cannon on the treetop, loaded with grapeshot and waited for dawn. At first light a musket cracked, and a bullet pierced the dummy. A gunner checked his laying on the smoke puff and touched a match to the vent. The cannon boomed. A brave screeched and tumbled out of the tree.

The fort's few little guns would check an outright assault which its walls were now strong enough to withstand. St.

Leger's eight pieces, also light, could not open breaches. Yet the odds were weighted for the besiegers, and time was on their side, with the garrison's ammunition and provisions dwindling. A blaze, kindled by a soaring bomb from a coehorn mortar or fire arrows—one barracks had already been burned—then a concerted attack from all quarters, and Stanwix was finished.

No word still from the couriers who had slipped out to beg for help. Surely dependable, old General Herkimer, a stanch patriot, could be counted on to raise the militia and march to the relief.

General Nicholas Herkimer, more than sixty years on him but with plenty of iron still in his spirit and frame, called them out. He gave the word in German and in English almost as badly broken as Steuben was using to train Washington's army at Valley Forge. Though he had been born in New York, the language and customs of his German forebears clung to him and many of his neighbors, as sturdy a stock in the state as their kin, the Pennsylvania Dutch. Promptly the militia answered his call in numbers that might not have responded to a summons by a less respected leader. A veteran of the French and Indian War, the old general, and his was the military heritage of the Teuton that would loyally serve the United States—against its own blood in two great conflicts of the twentieth century.

Eight hundred militiamen mustered for Herkimer. They molded bullets, took down muskets from pegs over cabin fireplaces, slung powder horns and strode off to the rendezvous without a backward glance to betray misgivings over whether their families would manage if they didn't come back. The job had to be done. A Tryon County man might not bother too much about the British and the achievement of American independence, but it was plain enough to him what might happen if Fort Stanwix fell. It would let loose a horde of Indians on his homestead and, no less menacing, a mass of Tories, out to win the fierce feud intensified by the war. The fact that the Tories were the militiaman's neighbors and sometimes members of his own family fanned smoldering embers hotter. There must be not letting Sir John Johnson, high-and-mighty old Sir William's son, get the upper hand in the Valley, nor Colonel John Butler and his

Tory Rangers either. Settlers believed they could expect little more mercy from them in wartime than from Brant's Indians.

They assembled at Fort Dayton in the upper Mohawk Valley and formed up into regiments of sorts under officers elected by the men, that handicap which would continue to plague the leadership of American troops for years, on through most of the Civil War. General Herkimer sat his white horse and gave the order to march. Off they moved—advance guard with Oneida Indian scouts, main body, ox carts with supplies, a rearguard. An old soldier like the general could see to so much proper military organization at least. They pushed on eagerly, impetuously, two days' march ahead of them.

Eight hundred men. A force not strong enough to tackle more than twice as many adversaries. But Herkimer's plan was a pincers attack, with the Stanwix garrison to make a sortie as he approached. The enemy would be crushed in between them, just as Burgoyne and St. Leger meant to do with Schuyler.

The general hurried off the couriers now. The four runners must make their way into the fort, creeping through the siege lines at night, and inform Gansevoort of the plan of attack. By the time they arrived, the militia would have reached Oriskany, only half a dozen miles from Stanwix. Let three shots, easily audible at that distance, be fired by the fort's cannon as acknowledgment and signal. Then as Herkimer's men smashed into the disconcerted enemy's rear, the garrison would burst out and like the Israelites in Herkimer's German Bible smite the Philistines hip and thigh.

The militia thrust onward, driving the slow-paced oxen hard. Far swifter were messengers carrying warning of their coming, messengers sent by Molly Brant, Mohawk widow of Sir William Johnson, to her brother Joseph. Before Herkimer could reach Oriskany or his couriers penetrate into Stanwix, Brant had laid an ambush.

A perfect spot presented itself where the trail to Stanwix threaded through a deep ravine. Feathery boughs of giant hemlocks darkened it with an ominous shade. Swollen by rains, a rivulet cutting across had turned the ground so swampy that only a corduroy of logs made it passable by carts. Troops funneled into the defile must thin out into a long, sluggish, vulnerable trickle.

Brant may well have doubted that the militia would be fools enough to blunder into so obvious a place for ambush. Even if white men were that incautious, the Oneida scouts he knew were accompanying them were not likely to be so. However, the opportunity was too good to be missed. His one thousand warriors, the largest Indian force thus far assembled in the war, hid themselves in the wooded fringes of the tortuous, S-shaped ravine. Several companies of Tories, Royal Greens and Rangers, backed them up by blocking the outlet toward the fort.

In the distance the squealing axles of oncoming oxcarts suddenly ceased. Herkimer had called a halt. He knew the ground ahead and he had not yet heard the signal guns of the fort. Wait, he ordered. Angry militia, officers and men, swirled around the white horse. Wait? Not on your life! Push on fast to the fort!

The general shook his head stubbornly. Voices rose higher, protests turned to taunts. Was the old man afraid? they demanded. Had a brother with the Tories, hadn't he? Maybe he . . . To be branded as a coward and traitor was more than the old soldier could stand. He ought to have damned them in blistering German for an undisciplined, foolhardy mob. Instead, white-faced with wrath he waved them forward.

Along the rims of the ravine the waiting Indians heard the cart axles begin to squeal again. They took more swigs of British rum, poised muskets and bows, and loosened tomahawks in their belts. Now they sighted the Americans rushing down the trail into the mouth of the deadly defile. They had not even sent their Oneidas scouting ahead. There were flankers out but not far enough, and they appeared to be utterly unsuspecting. It was August 6, 1777.

Brant's warriors, firewater burning in their bellies, sprang the ambush a little too soon, for the rearguard of the militia had not yet entered the passage. But its sudden shock paralyzed the full length of the American force.

At once there rose so wild a yell
Within the dark and narrow dell
As all the fiends from Heaven that fell
Had pealed the battle cry of Hell.

So Walter Scott would later write of a Highlands ambush, and it fitted the moment at Oriskany. Amid fierce war whoops a hail of bullets and arrows poured down on the trapped, strung-out column. Men reeled and dropped in heaps, sinking into suffocating mire. Herkimer was one of the first to fall. Why must a commander make a target of himself by riding a white horse, good mount or not? Men dragged the wounded general clear, the bone of one leg splintered by the lead slug that killed his charger. On his insistence they propped him against a beech tree, seated on his saddle. They had tried to carry him to the rear, but he refused. He'd stay and face the enemy, he said. Calmly lighting his pipe, he shouted between puffs for a rally, as a red torrent flooded down into the ravine.

In the face of a surprise so shattering a panic could have been expected but none occurred. The rearguard, shut out of the ravine and harried by yelping Indians, did beat a retreat, its path long marked for two miles by the whitened bones of the slain. But the main body of militia, as brave as they had been rash, formed a circle around the knob where Herkimer sat. Steadily they fought off the onrushes. At the general's command they paired up behind the trees, covering each other. When one had fired, and a warrior, tomahawk upraised, dashed in to finish off a foe with an empty musket, the second militiaman drilled the charging red man while the first reloaded.

In that close and desperate combat there were Homeric episodes. An Oneida girl of fifteen, fighting side by side with her tribesmen, shrilled war cries as she fired her musket again and again. Two men, one white, one red, suddenly recognized each other while they were locked in a struggle on the ground. They were old friends, companions on hunts—one of those attachments which sometimes took place between settlers and the Long House of the Iroquois. Instantly the Indian, who was uppermost, halted his plunging knife and offered to spare his opponent's life. The American's answer was a mighty heave that threw off the other and a fatal stab with his own knife. Up at the farther end of the ravine there were more recognitions as the Tories flung themselves on the Rebel vanguard. Neighbors fought one another to the death with a savagery Indians could not surpass.

Abruptly a downpour of rain silenced the fusillade, drenching the flintlocks' powder pans and making it impossible to fire, loosening taut bowstrings as well. Through most of the field it became an affair of clubbed muskets, knives, and tomahawks now—in all quarters except where the Tories drove in with the fixed bayonets the militia lacked. And from the siege lines reinforcements were coming into the battle, a company of the Royal Greens sent by Sir John Johnson. Though the rain had ceased as quickly as it began, no fire was opened on the oncoming Tories. They had put on their coats inside out, concealing the color, and the Americans mistook them for the first of the sortie from the fort. Only just in time an American captain shouted, "Look at their hats. Those are Tories. Fire!"

The conflict, renewing its fury, took on for a moment a medieval tinge. That captain who had called out the warning carried a spontoon, an officer's half-pike, survival of the sergeants' halberd of yore. As his thrusts killed three of the disguised Tories, another captain faced three more with a captured musket. He brained one with a butt, then reversed his weapon and shot and stabbed the other two.

Ambushed militiamen were still holding their own, but where was the sortie that was to have been made from Stanwix?

Herkimer's runners had had a difficult time penetrating the siege cordon, and arrived late. As soon as their message had been delivered, the signal cannon were fired. By then their reports were drowned by the racket of battle in the ravine. Promptly as it could be organized, a sally under Lieutenant Colonel Willett burst out of the gate. Cheering soldiers swept over a lightly guarded Tory camp. Sir John Johnson in his shirt sleeves ran for his life. His papers, all the baggage—arm, ammunition, and five flags—fell into American hands. So did the Indians' packs which included a tragic memento, the scalps of two little girls, the hair still neatly plaited. Everything that could not be carried back to the fort was destroyed. Willett withdrew in good order before a tardy British counterattack.

Units of the Royal Greens were hastily pulled back from the fight in the ravine to meet the threat in their rear. As pressure relaxed, the militiamen redoubled their fire. Cries of *"Oonah. Oonah!"*—signal for retreat—rose from the red circle around them. It dissolved and faded back into the forest. These white men had not behaved as a hopelessly cornered enemy should, and ever since the first onset failed to throw them into a panic the heart had begun to go out of their assailants. The Indians, especially the Senecas, had taken heavy losses.

Grimly the men of Tryon County scanned their own dead, the high cost of their folly and their valor: from 160 to 200 by a quick count. They patched up their fifty wounded and put Herkimer and others who could not walk on litters. When the bearers filed out of the ravine onto the trail for home, three of Brant's warriors made a last try for the white chief's scalp, a brave man's trophy worth the taking. As they dashed in, snap shots dropped them, and the column, its march thereafter unmolested, reached the safety of Fort Dayton. Herkimer, the amputation of his leg botched by crude surgery, soon died, reading his Bible and puffing his pipe to the end.

Oriskany, among classic ambushes from Cannae to the Little Big Horn, was as bloody a battle, in proportion to the numbers engaged, as any fought in the Revolution. The killed outnumbered the wounded, reversing the usual ratio. It has been called a tactical victory for the Americans; they had held their ground long enough for the making of the sortie from Stanwix and the ransacking of the Tory camp. The Indians were infuriated by their heavy casualties and the loss of their packs. Yet despite their burning thirst for vengeance, to be slaked later, they were demoralized now and could be counted on little for the reduction of the fort.

St. Leger nevertheless tightened the siege lines. He repeated his demand for surrender and his warning of massacre. Gansevoort retorted that the threat was dishonorable and unworthy of a British officer; that it sullied even the subordinate who delivered it. For all the commander's brave defiance the garrison, with no further prospect of help from the militia, was in more desperate straits than ever. The British were digging approach trenches and moving their artillery forward to deliver a heavier and more effective bombardment.

Help could come now only from General Schuyler, and somehow he must spare it or Stanwix would fall, and the two British forces be able to combine against him. Lieutenant Colonel Willett and a Major Stockwell volunteered for the appallingly risky mission of carrying the word. They left the fort at night, reaching the cover of the woods undetected. When an Indian encampment loomed up in front of them, they circled it by crawling through a swamp on hands and knees. Covering their trail by the old frontiersman's trick of walking in stream channels, they guided on the North Star. After their provisions were exhausted, they lived on berries until they safely made Fort Dayton at the end of the second day. Thence Willett went on to Albany to meet General Benedict Arnold.

Not for three years yet would the traitor's evil star blight the career of one of the finest fighting commanders the American Army ever knew. Even after his treason one of his own soldiers would not withhold due tribute. "A bloody fellow he was. He didn't care for nothing; he'd ride right in. It was 'Come on, boys!' 'twasn't 'Go, boys!' There wasn't any waste timber on him. He was a stern-looking man but kind to his soldiers. They [Congress] didn't treat him right—but he ought to have been true."

It was the still true Arnold, the fiery patriot, who now acted at once, with Schuyler in agreement, to organize a relief expedition in spite of the threat of Burgoyne's 7000 troops, only twenty-four miles away. Ahead of him Arnold sent a half-wit Tory, reprieved from hanging on his promise to spread the rumor that a large force was en route to raise the siege. The Tory, whose coat had been taken off and riddled with bullets to make him seem the fugitive he pretended to be and whose brother was held as a hostage, did his work well. St. Leger's Indians, with their superstitious reverence for a demented person, believed the man implicitly. The very name of Arnold, most dreaded of all American leaders, was enough to cause the immediate desertion of several hundred of the Iroquois. The rest rioted and looted British officers' liquor, including the commander's well-stocked traveling wine cellar. St. Leger in consternation abandoned the siege of Stanwix on August 23 before the arrival of Arnold's small force. On his march back to Oswego the tribesmen spread false alarms of American attacks which made the British deploy to meet them. When they returned they found their packs plundered by their allies.

For General Burgoyne, forced to fight the rest of the campaign in the north alone, his Indians were of little use. Many, who would never have left a successful army, followed St. Luc back to Canada.

Indians scouting for the Hessians at Bennington broke and fled into the woods at the start of the battle which saw the rout of the mercenaries by John Stark and his New Hampshire men. Nor did warriors of the Long House and other tribes play any but a very minor part in the encounters grouped as the Battle of Saratoga. It was only when the issue had been decided and the British were falling back toward a final stand and surrender that red men appeared on the outskirts of retreat for the easy taking of scalps of dead and wounded allies.

Bennington and Saratoga had cleared disputed ground in New York State and its marches of British forces except for the Tories and Indians. At Oriskany and Stanwix the frontier had been held. But the borderlands, source of recruits and supplies for the American Army, must not only be protected but rolled back farther to the west. Beyond them lay enemy bases, the "castles" and fertile fields of the hostile nations of the Iroquois, with the British strongholds of Fort Niagara and Detroit their mainstays to the rear, the latter, gateway and guardian of Northwest Territory. On the borders poised a present menace and a future threat so grave that it might eventually slice through to the east and sever the tendons of the Revolution.

It was not long before the menace materialized. From the west a column of copper-colored bodies, streaked with war paint, and green-coated Tories knifed through the forest into the Wyoming Valley of Pennsylvania.

Ask a soldier of the Continental Line or a militiaman which tribe of the Six Nations was the toughest enemy, and he would unhesitatingly answer, "The Senecas." Troops of later generations, who fought the plains Indians, would hesitate between the Comanches, the Sioux, and Cheyennes, or the Apaches.

The Senecas were one of the two westernmost peoples of the confederation of the Iroquois. Their lands thus far had little known the inroads of settlers. They raided from them, their warlike vigor unsubdued, while the Mohawks and more easterly tribes, repeatedly buffeted back, had been somewhat chastened. Moreover, Mohawk savagery was sometimes partly tempered by Chief Joseph Brant. Civilization had rubbed off on the educated Thayendanegea, a member of the Church of England and a Mason, merciful to a foeman who appealed to him by making the Masonic sign. He also sought to spare women and children and was opposed to torture of prisoners. Not so the Senecas. If anything were needed further to inflame their natural ferocity, it was their heavy losses at Oriskany. And Seneca warriors, wild for revenge, formed the bulk of the force of 700 Indians that joined Tories under John Butler from Fort Niagara on Lake Ontario in the summer of 1778 to descend on the Wyoming Valley of Pennsylvania and perpetrate the bloody massacre called "the surpassing horror of the Revolution."

Toward July they swept down on the farms, settlements, and little stockades of the valley, still claimed by Connecticut. Only a few Regulars, including Colonel Zebulon Butler, home on leave, were in the neighborhood. Most of the able-bodied men of the valley were away with Washington's army, and the tragedy about to occur underlined the high price of patriotism. On its altar many of the Continentals, who had marched away to fight the War for Independence, would sacrifice their families and their homes in the Wyoming Valley.

At the first warning of red raiders Colonel Butler rallied the militia, chiefly old men and boys. By June 30 he had strongly manned Forty Fort with 300 of them. They might have held it and borne the brunt of the invasion until help could come. But rife in the fort was the same rash spirit that had prevailed before the ambush of Oriskany. Zeb Butler was not strong enough to withstand it—no more than Herkimer had been. Without reconnaissance which might have informed him that he was outnumbered by close to three to one, he led his scratch force out of the safety of the fort, leaving only a small garrison, and drew up a line of battle.

The veteran Tory commander must have smiled with satisfaction. His plan of campaign seemed bound to work. It would recall regiments from General Washington for the defense of this region as well as cut communications with

American troops in the west. Furthermore the enemy were now delivering themselves into his hands. As the militia advanced, Rangers and Royal Greens were marshaled to meet frontal assault, while the Indians massed in the woods on the American left.

Volleys of musketry wreathed the field in white smoke. Then the Senecas came boiling out from behind the trees to smash into their adversary's flank. Once their guns were emptied, they flung them aside and with brandished tomahawks rushed whooping into close quarters. Stalwartly the Americans faced them. Their courage was at once admirable and pitiable—those white-haired frontiersmen, fighting their final fight, and the frightened youngsters playing the man in their first battle which was the last, too, for most of them. They could not hold. Fall back steadily, their officers shouted, but the retreat soon became precipitate and turned into a panic. The Indians raged through the rout, hacking, stabbing, and scalping.

It was close to annihilation. At slight loss to the invaders —two Rangers and one Indian killed, eight Indians wounded—most of the Americans lay dead, wounded, or bound prisoners on that stricken field. Two hundred and twenty-seven scalps were taken, paid for at $10 apiece at Detroit by its British commandant, Lieutenant Colonel Henry Hamilton, "The Hair-Buyer." Only sixty militiamen escaped; cut off from the fort, they swam the river and melted into the forest. Colonel Zebulon Butler, mounted, was among those to win clear. He galloped to his home, took his wife up behind him on his horse and quit the coming desolation of the valley.

There was no hope now for Forty Fort. Its garrison surrendered on Colonel John Butler's promise to spare their lives. But his amnesty did not apply to the Indians' prisoners of the battle. That night they met their dreaded fate. Fugitives in the woods and people of the farms saw the heaps of dried brush flame up around the torture stakes in the clearings and along the river bank and heard the screams of the victims. Others, the stakes having burned down, were flung onto the hot embers and held down with pitchforks until they died. The most spectacular slaughter was inflicted by a chieftainess of the Senecas by the light on a bonfire around a large boulder thereafter known by her name as Queen Esther's Rock.

She was a half-breed, born Catharine Montour, a daughter, some said, of French Governor Frontenac. Captured as a girl, she had been taken to the Seneca country where she married a sachem after whose death she gained great influence in the tribe. Now she ordered sixteen prisoners to be held by braves in a circle around the rock. Screeching a death song, the witch made the circuit, striking alternately with a tomahawk and a death maul, a bludgeon with a knot of hard maple, about the size of a 3-pounder roundshot, fastened on a handle. Before she was able to complete her murderous round, two of her intended victims wrenched themselves free from warriors' grasps and escaped.

Although the Tories managed to restrain their allies from wholesale killings, the entire valley was laid waste by Butler's "Destructives." One thousand houses were burned, crops destroyed, and cattle driven off. Groups of women and children were carried into captivity, and the lot of those who had fled soon became desperate. Destitute, many perished of starvation and exhaustion in their refuge, a swamp of the Poconos which earned a lasting name, "The Shades of Death." Relief regiments found few survivors in the ravaged countryside.

Through the rest of the summer, late into the fall, and, after a respite for wintering, on into the following spring the frontier reeked of smoke and blood. Brant's Indians and Walter Butler's Tories spread havoc through the Mohawk Valley again. Settlers retaliated by burning an Indian town. The enemy countered with a raid on Cherry Valley, a village about fifty miles west of Albany, near Otsego Lake. Their advance covered by a thick fog, they caught the inept colonel of the 7th Massachusetts off guard. The fort, strongly built by Lafayette, was held, but soldiers billeted outside were wiped out along with farm families—men, women, and children—and every house and barn put to the torch.

New York and Pennsylvania frontiers were being ripped wide, and if the Indian forays continued unchecked, the Hudson River Valley would lie open again to the enemy. Burgoyne had been counted out, but there was a grave threat that another invasion might be mounted from Canada, Detroit, or Niagara. General Washington, hard pressed though he was in the East, recognized that troops must be spared for a smashing counteroffensive against the Iroquois.

The expedition of 1779 was the United States Army's first full-scale, organized campaign against the tribes, and there is none more remarkable in the history of the Indian Wars.

III

Scorched Earth

FOR THE YOUNG UNITED STATES of 1779 to be able to stage the full-scale Sullivan Expedition against the Iroquois Indians rates as an outstanding feat in military annals. The speed and efficiency of its organization was far more than could have been expected from a war in which so many defeats had been suffered. Despite the recent victories of Saratoga and Monmouth, Washington's army in the East was still faced with heavy odds, and it was from straitened resources that men and equipment were spared for an all-out effort to end the Indian menace on the western frontier.

Total destruction and devastation of the towns and territories of the hostile Iroquois—"not to be merely overrun but destroyed"—was directed by General Washington's orders. They read like the relentless demands of Cato on the Roman Senate for the complete ruin of Carthage. If the aide who drew those orders were a classicist, he must have been tempted to head them *Delenda Est Iroquoia.*

Command of the expedition was given handsome Major General Sullivan of New Hampshire. A brave, hot-tempered man, John Sullivan—a good soldier though sometimes an unlucky one—a skillful politician but not a political general like Horatio Gates, a breed perpetuated to tarnish our armies. Sullivan's army numbered 4000, one of the largest forces to operate on the frontier and a sizable one for any theater in the Revolution. It had everything Washington could give it: veteran troops, arms, ammunition, and equipment in good supply. More artillery than was generally furnished for a wilderness campaign. Plenty of horse transport. Big pontoon boats, called batteaux, with wheeled carriages for portages. Colors and fife and drum corps.

A good half of the army's strength consisted of the Continental Line to carry through the mission whether the short-term militia component stuck with it or not. Brigades were led by generals who knew how to handle them: James Clinton, "Scots Willie" Maxwell, Enoch Poor, and Edward Hand. Tried regiments included units from New York, New Jersey, New Hampshire, Massachusetts, Pennsylvania, and Maryland, with a detachment of Morgan's Virginia Riflemen. In regimental command were such able officers as Colonel Peter Gansevoort and Lieutenant Colonel Marinus Willett, wearing laurels for the recent successful defense of Fort Stanwix, besieged by British, Tories, and redskins under the Mohawk chief, Joseph Brant. Among the many capable subalterns was Lieutenant Erkurias Beatty who would fight through the war and stay on in the Army afterwards, becoming one of our early professional soldiers.

Colonel Thomas Proctor, a crack gunner, to serve on with distinction in the War of 1812, commanded the 4th Artillery with a complement of two 6-pounders, two 5½-inch howitzers, and four 3-pounders. Captain John Lamb, 2nd Artillery, added two 3s whose trails were shafts for a one-horse hitch—handy little pieces called grasshopper guns because of their mobility. Rumble of artillery wheels and the tread of infantry were augmented by the thud of hoofs of 1200 pack and draft horses and a herd of 700 beef cattle.

The plan of campaign formed a trident to be thrust deep into the lands and livelihood of the Iroquois. Two of its prongs, Sullivan's and Clinton's columns, would fuse. The third under Colonel Daniel Brodhead was a separate task force of 600 men, striking from Fort Pitt up the Allegheny River, designated ultimately to join the main body.

While Clinton, brother of Governor George Clinton of New York, mobilized his 1500 for a march through the Mohawk Valley and along the upper reaches of the Susquehanna River, Sullivan mustered 2500 at Easton, Pennsylvania. There occurred the only marked failure in logistics. Supplies were late in arriving, and the delay of several weeks would prove a serious setback of the timetable for the campaign. But Sullivan was able to move out in early July—infantry in advance, artillery in file in the center between three columns of pack horses, flanked in turn by brigades with outguards; finally a rearguard. Drums rattled out the cadence, and fifes shrilled such lively tunes as "The Old Continental March," "Yankee Doodle," and perhaps prophetically, "A Successful Campaign." They "played beautiful," a lieutenant wrote appreciatively in his journal. Music lifted marching feet. And flams, rolls, and drags on the drums also sounded all the army's signals—the General, Assembly, Retreat, and Tapsto (later Tattoo), as well as beating firing commands for the artillery. The bugle, except for the cavalry's trumpet, was not yet used.

Order and music were only for the few stretches of open country. Mostly it was rough going, with sweating axmen out in front widening deer trails into roads passable for artillery and wagons. They struggled through dismal, interminable swamps where horses sank in to their bellies or deeper. Carcasses of poor beasts, drowned or dead from exhaustion, marked the army's progress. Sullivan pushed on, sometimes at the admirable rate of fourteen miles a day.

But at night camps there were tents for shelter from the frequent rains, and cook fires blazed. Journals carried grateful entries: "Drawed rum." General Hand, drilling his officers in the sword salute, was greatly pleased with their performance. "In a moment of generosity" he ordered an issue of a keg for each six members of the drill squad. Whereupon he was toasted with "mirth and jollity" and doubtless saluted some more, although not so precisely as the kegs emptied. The Fourth of July was celebrated with cannonades and musketry volleys and suitable sermons by the chaplains. Also in honor of Independence Day the Adjutant General gave a grog party termed "a sociable drink." Oneida scouts, unable to handle their potations as well as a soldier of the line, quickly ranged through stages of intoxication—from blue to swipsy and on to capsized and snug under the table with the dogs, in current terms. Yet how, asked troops wet and weary after a long march, was a man to fight a war without a cheering drop to warm the blood and ease fatigue?

Discipline was sternly maintained nevertheless. When a cannon boomed reveille, soldiers turned out and tumbled into ranks. If any failed to answer to their names at roll call, they were marked down as deserters. Pursuit details were promptly dispatched, and deserters caught faced drastic court-martial punishment; execution by firing squads, one hundred or more stinging, welting lashes, or running the gantlet between long lines of troops wielding clubs and whips. Reduction to the ranks of deserting noncoms was the lightest penalty inflicted.

While Sullivan's column halted at Tioga to build a fort named for him, Clinton bullied his way from Canajoharie on the Mohawk River to Otsego Lake. Heaving four-horse hitches were loosed from the wheeled batteaux, and the bulky, provision-laden craft launched. They bid fair to be stranded when the lake level began to sink, but Clinton raised it by damming the main outlet. The flotilla swept on, a grasshopper gun in the bow of the foremost boat popping away to show what would happen to any Indian canoes which might try to bar the way.

Before Clinton joined, Sullivan overran and burned Chemung, the first of a long series of Indian towns he would leave in smoking ruins. Chemung was undefended. The Iroquois had not yet realized that this was no raid but a deep-penetrating invasion to desolate the lands of the Senecas, Cayugas, and Onondagas, westernmost tribes of the Six Nations.

Now Joseph Brant, reinforced by Tories, rallied the tribesmen to block the advance of the Sullivan-Clinton column. Once more he laid an ambuscade, but the ground was far from being as well adapated for it as Oriskany had been. Yet the position he took at Newtown (the present city of Elmira) was a promising one. He threw up concealed breastworks on a wooded ridge that paralleled the route of the American march. From it the fire of his warriors could sweep the full length of the passing column, with the slope giving them momentum for a charge down on shattered ranks.

But Brant, shrewd commander though he was, had not taken three elements into account. The enemy's scouts were Virginia riflemen. He was about to encounter disciplined, battle-wise troops of the Continental Line. And they were supported by artillery.

Keen-eyed riflemen spotted the breastworks behind the trees on August 29, 1779. At their warning Sullivan's column swung smoothly into line of regiments facing the ridge. Poor's brigade branched off on the double to circle the redmen's left flank and hit their rear. Colonel Proctor's artillerymen unlimbered and prepared for action.

It was one of the comparatively few times artillery was used throughout the Indian Wars. Despite the difficulties of transport in wooded or mountainous country, the neglect of that arm is incomprehensible in the light of its tremendous effect. All tribes dreaded cannon fire—roundshot, grape, or canister, and most of all bursting shells. A few field guns could rout masses of warriors, or light pieces on walls stave off an attack on a burning fort till flames were quenched. Proctor's men were presently to demonstrate with éclat.

Infantrymen sceptically and sourly watched those fellows in blue uniforms with scarlet facings swarm around their guns. The 6-pounders and howitzers were heavy, unwieldy hunks of metal which foot soldiers were always being called on to help shove and hoist here and there, or to tail on to drag ropes and haul with horses when the wheels of the contraptions got mired. Recently a sergeant had written in his diary: "We marched much impeded by the artillery and ammunition wagons through thick wood and difficult defiles. Such cursing, cutting, and digging; oversetting wagons, cannon and pack horses into the river, etc., is not to be seen every day." Now the disgruntled infantrymen heard drums beat orders for the matrosses, the cannoneers. Charge pieces—clear vent—prime. Gunners spun elevating screws until muzzles peered up at the ridge. Fire! and bombardiers touched matches to the vents. In a cannonade, acclaimed by General Sullivan as "elegant," the guns flamed and boomed. Shells burst among Brant's braves in their breastworks.

Indians were convinced by the shells detonating behind them that they were being attacked in the rear—as they shortly would be by Poor's men, charging in with the bayonet. The warriors broke and fled, and Brant's utmost efforts could not stem the panic. Another attack rolled up the Tories on the right. In a brief space the Battle of Newtown was won at the light cost to the Americans of three killed, with enemy losses heavy.

The only stand the Indians would make was over. Except for minor skirmishes and isolated fights, never halting Sullivan's army, the tribal territories lay open to the total destruction and devastation General Washington had ordered, and those orders were about to be fulfilled to the hilt.

Troops from the eastern seaboard and all who had never dared venture into this hostile country stared at the broad, cultivated fields and well-built towns spread out before their line of march. Here the Iroquois had achieved the North American Indian's finest civilization north of Mexico. Acre on acre of tall, tasseled corn. Bountiful apple, pear, and peach orchards. Rich fields of varieties of flourishing vegetables and ground fruits: potatoes, pumpkins, squashes, cucumber, watermelons, peas, and beans. There were barnyard fowl, cows, horses, wagons, farm implements, and tools. That all the planting and farming, disdained by warriors, had been done by squaws and children made it even more of a marvel of accomplishment for a once nomadic people, dependent upon hunting, fishing, and meager scratch crops.

Still more amazing were the towns or "castles" of frame and stone houses and stout log cabins. Many boasted fireplaces, with brick or stone chimneys, and glazed windows. "Those Indians live a lot better than most of the Mohawk River farmers," ran the comment of the rank and file.

But as enemy resources all this industry and plenty was doomed to be scorched earth, frequent fate of invaded land through history. Here was the granary and base of the hostile Iroquois. They could not be defeated until they had nothing to fall back on but smoking ruins and desolation.

As at Chemung all buildings were burned to the ground. The 130 houses of Catharine's Town were kindled with enthusiasm, for this was the castle of Catharine Montour—the Seneca's Queen Esther who had dashed out the brains of victims with her death maul in the Wyoming Massacre. Genesee and other towns were reduced to ashes until the total reached two score. Troops after foraging all the corn they needed—some of the ears two feet long—fired the fine stands. "Never saw so much corn as I had to burn," said one Continental. Cutting down the orchards came hardest; farmers in the ranks knew the time and care it took to grow such splendidly bearing trees. After axes had hewn, and fields were blackened, regiments moved on to the next to be ravaged. Pockets were stuffed with vegetables, and bayonets spiked two or three pumpkins, a sight that annoyed General Hand. "You damned unmilitary set of rascals!" he roared. "What are you going to do? Storm a town with pompions?"

The campaign came close to that, turning vegetarian as meat ran out. One officer was reduced to trying fried rattlesnake "which would have tasted very good if it had not been snake."

Sullivan reported the destruction of forty towns and 160,000 bushels of corn. Brodhead's smaller column, though it failed to make the expected junction, accounted for several hundred houses and 500 acres of corn burned. Washington's orders were complied with fully in all but a minor respect: the capture of Indian prisoners. Only a few were taken to Albany where they were later released. Their value as hostages was doubted by the commanders of the expedition who in any case could not spare men to guard such redskins as they might have rounded up. You couldn't, they said, hunt partridges and wild turkeys on horseback. And in the little clashes that marked the last stages of the campaign few prisoners were being taken by either side.

But prisoners were being recovered by the Americans—Wyoming Valley captives, abandoned or given an opportunity to escape as the tribes retreated before Sullivan's advance. The deplorable condition of the rescued women and children, worn by privations and harsh treatment, provoked some troops into cruel reprisals. Finding an aged squaw and a crippled boy in a hut, they fastened the door and set the building afire. Indian scalps were increasingly taken. One lieutenant in his journal confessed to a barbarity. "At the request of Major P.——, sent out a small detachment to look for some dead Indians—returned without finding them. Toward morning they found them and skinned two of them from their hips down for boot-legs, one pair for the Major, the other for myself."

"Il faut brutaliser les affaires," that leader of Indians, St. Luc, had advised Burgoyne, and the inevitable corrolary was: *Les affaires brutales tous brutalisent.* Soldiers, grown callous, were rendered savage by the terrible death now inflicted on an officer of the army.

Lieutenant Boyd and twenty-six Virginia Riflemen were decoyed into a trap by Indians they were pursuing. Except for a few who escaped, all were killed or made prisoners.

Boyd, questioned by Colonel John Butler, refused information, whereupon the Tory turned him over to his red allies. Next day comrades found the remains of Boyd and a sergeant, their mangled bodies revealing how frightfully they died. They had been stripped and tied to trees. Blade cuts in the bark were evidence that they had served as targets for tomahawks, skillfully thrown to try their nerve by just missing. The sergeant was finished off with knife stabs, the most fiendish tortures being reserved for the officer. His finger and toe nails were pulled out, nose sliced off, one eye gouged, tongue torn out. A slit was cut in his abdomen and the intestines drawn forth and tied around the tree. Then in excruciating agony he was driven around it until the trunk was ringed with his viscera. Finally both victims were beheaded.

Regiments bore grim witness as the bodies were buried "with the honours of war," and half a dozen of the army's diarists penned shocked descriptions of the tortures undergone. Lieutenant Colonel Henry Dearborn, a future Secretary of War, wrote: "This was a most horrid specticle to behold & from which we are taught the necessity of fighting those more than devels to the last moment rather than fall into their hands alive."

The towns and field of the hostile Iroquois had been ruthlessly ravished. Yet unless Sullivan joined up with Brodhead and drove through to take Detroit, he could not write: mission accomplished. That British stronghold stood as a refuge for the shattered tribes. There they could winter and recuperate. In the spring they would return to harry the settlements and take vengeance on the Oneidas and Tuscaroras, American allies, whose spared lands would suffer as property of traitors to the Long House.

Capture of Detroit would have crowned the campaign as a complete triumph, but Sullivan considered the season too far advanced to run the risk. His casualties had been light, but like not a few of his men, the general, though he was not yet forty, had been worn out by the rigors of the expedition. They had so impaired his health that he would shortly be compelled to end his Army career by retirement. After his return to Easton a march of 700 miles would lie behind him, while Brodhead had covered 400.

So the armies that had destroyed the resources of the Iroquois countermarched. Major Jeremiah Fogg, writing up his journal, sadly made a final entry: "The nests have been destroyed, but the birds are still on the wing." It had, he among others realized, been folly to leave Niagara and Detroit unscathed as bases from which the Iroquois could strike back.

In miserable destitution the Indians camped around the British fort and shivered through the terrible winter of 1779-80, one of the severest recorded. It might have finished off the work of the Sullivan expedition if the British had not supplied food and blankets for their allies to survive. The Iroquois, their spirit of revenge kept burning by issues of rum totaling 10,000 gallons, would return to raid into New York and Pennsylvania for two more years, but their power sapped by the wastage of their lands, they would never again be as grave a threat to the frontier.

IV

Conquest of The Northwest

A WEDGE had been driven through the Iroquois lands by the Sullivan Expedition, but other Indian barriers in long succession rose before the American march westward and southward. No more than in the Revolution would the surge to break them be halted by conflicts with other powers. The United States, whether its enemy was Great Britain again in 1812, Mexico, or the Confederacy, fought two-front wars, hostile tribes on the flanks or in the rear of its armies.

After the repulse of the Iroquois the second front became Northwest Territory, that vast stretch of country bordered on the west by the Mississippi, on the north by the Great Lakes, the Alleghanies to the east, and south through Kentucky. Rich in furs, it had been sought as a prize by three nations. Spain still held its outpost at St. Louis. Absorbed settlements were the only relics of France's claim, lost to Britain which now dominated most of the region from Detroit. The challenge by the United States for possession of the Territory was first made in effect when American pioneers, guided by Daniel Boone, independently pushed into Kentucky.

Strife spread from that "dark and bloody ground," as tribes mustering 8000 warriors, notably the formidable Delawares and Shawnees, took the warpath. They welcomed fur traders, but settlers on their hunting grounds were another matter. Incited and armed by the British—Detroit stocked 150 dozen scalping knives with other weapons among its trade goods—the red men raided the frontier.

The campaigns that conquered the Territory were organized and led by an extraordinary man, George Rogers Clark, officer in the service of Virginia. Their record has been well termed "one of the most illustrious chapters in the history of the Revolution, the subject of more song, story, poetry, and painting than almost any other episode except Valley Forge."

Clark was a tall, stalwart man, still in his twenty-fifth year at the outset of his epic feats. Hair red, forehead broad, piercing eyes blue, he came of sturdy stock. His younger brother William, partner of Meriwether Lewis in the forthcoming exploration of the Far West, would display the same iron endurance and calculated daring. Other outstanding qualities of George Rogers Clark were his mastery of strategy, his ability to inspire soldiers in the face of almost incredible hardships, and his complete understanding of Indians. Lacking any of those three, he could never have achieved the conquest.

One must borrow strings of initials from the Second World War to describe Clark's multifarious capacities. He acted as a one-man G-1, G-2, G-3, and G-4, combining personnel, intelligence, plans and operations, and supply. He was his own OSS, CAMG, USO, and OCMH. That is, he handled strategic services, civil affairs and military government, entertainment of troops (he gave them leave to go hunting and staged rousing dances), and finally in his memoirs wrote military history. Such was the commander whose deeds clinched the United States claim to the Northwest, and it was not his fault that the grip was loosened by the failures of lesser leaders, as well as shortages of troops and supplies, and was only ultimately to be made fast when Mad Anthony Wayne won the Battle of Fallen Timbers.

Clark, defending Kentucky as a militia captain, knew that Detroit was the key to the Territory. To storm the

British post the minor strongholds guarding its approaches must be captured: Kaskaskia, some miles above the confluence of the river of that name and the Mississippi; Cahokia, just below modern East St. Louis; Vincennes, on the Wabash in the present state of Indiana. He went to Virginia, to which Kentucky had appealed for protection, and obtained the support of Governor Patrick Henry, along with that of members of the Legislature. Returning with a commission as lieutenant colonel, a war chest of £1200, and permission to raise several companies of riflemen, he launched his great venture.

There were never more than two hundred men, and usually considerably less, in his command. Though the British garrison at Detroit was small, Indian allies could make the odds appalling, but he planned never to allow a combination stronger than one with which he could cope. With Detroit always his chief objective, he singled out the redcoats as the backbone of resistance and severed the red men from them. In fact, George Rogers Clark fought what might have developed into a major Indian War of the Revolution, with the tribes largely neutralized and relegated to the sidelines. Scouts, spies, and emissaries had laid the ground-work for his campaigns.

His speeches at Indian councils were masterpieces of diplomacy and propaganda. "The Big Knives are very much like the red men," he told them. "They do not know well how to make blankets, powder, and cloth; they buy these things from the English (from whom they formerly descended) and live chiefly by raising corn, hunting, and trading as you and your neighbors, the French do . . . Then the English became angry and stationed strong garrisons through all our country (as you see they have done among you on the lakes and among the French) . . . They said we must do as they pleased and they killed some of us to make the rest afraid . . . The whole land was dark . . . At last the Great Spirit took pity on us and kindled a great council fire that never goes out at a place called Philadelphia. He stuck down a post there and left a war tomahawk by it . . .

"You can now judge who is in the right. I have already told you who I am. Here is a bloody belt and a white belt. Take whichever you please."

It was the white belt most of the tribes chose.

On June 26, 1778, Colonel Clark embarked 178 men on the Ohio River to land near the mouth of the Tennessee. Thence he made a grueling four-day march, the last two without food, through the wilderness, surprising and taking Kaskaskia without bloodshed. Cahokia, then Vincennes, and its Fort Sackville proved as easy prey to an officer with thirty men plus an equal number of French volunteers. In all three towns Clark, as persuasive with white men as with red, had won over the French inhabitants from their lukewarm British allegiance—not only to ready acceptance of American rule but as reinforcements for his little army. He was successful in acquiring supplies locally, from American merchants, and even from Spanish sources.

Lieutenant Colonel Henry Hamilton, commanding at Detroit now realized the suddenly developed danger confronting him. He must strike without delay or lose his vital base and control of all the Territory.

Branded as "The Hair-Buyer" and hated throughout the frontier, it was useless for Hamilton to declare that he did not pay Indians for American scalps but for prisoners of war. If, as the Indians claimed, the captured had tried to escape while being brought in and were killed, their scalps had to be accepted as evidence. Hamilton, following orders from London and using funds forwarded from Quebec, paid off though he knew he was often cheated by the substitution of French, Spanish, and even British scalps for American; also by scalps cut in half or alleged ones which in reality were patches of pubic hair.

Barbarous practices aside, Hamilton was a seasoned soldier and a daring one as he now gave proof. In October 1778, he led 170 British and French troops and sixty Indians through the forest in a tremendous seventy-day march and seized Vincennes where Clark had left only one officer with no troops. He then re-established control over the other French settlements and began preparing for a spring offensive.

All Clark's work must be done over, and he dared not wait. "We now saw that we were in a very critical situation, cut off as we were from all intercourse with the home government," he wrote. "We perceived that Governor Hamilton, by the junction of his northern and southern Indians, would be at the head of such a force in the spring that in this quarter nothing could withstand him. Kentucky must fall immediately, and it would be fortunate if the disaster ended here. We saw but one alternative which was to attack the enemy in his stronghold."

Unhesitatingly Colonel Clark made the grim choice of a campaign in the dead of winter. It demanded a long march, with 170 miles to go from Kaskaskia, over country much of which might be flooded. Mustering 180 men on February 6, 1779, he loaded provisions and a few pieces of artillery on a boat, sent up the Ohio and the Wabash to make rendezvous with his overland force. If he reached his goal, he would take the enemy unawares; they would never be expecting him at that season.

Clark took off from Kaskaskia with his overland force of 127 men in a march that matched Hamilton's in epic quality though not in length. At first the going was relatively easy for veteran frontiersmen. But the unseasonably warm weather meant the rivers were rising. As the column forged forward, reaching the banks of the Little Wabash on February 13, Clark hid his dismay at the sight of the wide expanse of "drowned land," from two to four feet under water, that lay before him. It must be crossed—there was no other way. He ordered a pirogue built, ferried over supplies and swam the pack horses from one patch of higher ground to the next. Rifles and powder horns held high, soldiers waded and floundered after them. Clark, aware that he must keep his men in good spirits, encouraged the antics of his drummer boy, a small, merry fourteen-year-old. The lad would launch his drum on the flood and float on it, flourishing his sticks, to the soldiers' great amusement.

The march became one long amphibious operation. A few hastily made canoes ferried the sick. For the rest it was a seemingly endless trek through rising water, ankle- or knee-deep at the best, finally waist- and shoulder-high in a relentless advance that brooked no delay and allowed no return. At night camps on unsubmerged land, dwindling rations were sparingly issued.

A break of good fortune came when five Frenchmen in a canoe, bound downriver on a hunting expedition, were tricked into paddling to the bank and captured. The hunters supplied both provisions and information. It was known in Vincennes, they said, that the Americans were coming. The townsfolk were well disposed, but Hamilton had strengthened the fort and was determined to hold it. However, troops without plenty of boats must wait for days until the waters receded, for it was now impossible to reach Vincennes through the neck-deep floods.

Clark would not, could not wait. Remaining supplies abandoned, he blackened his face with powder, uttered an Indian war whoop and plunged into the water and clinging mud. Gallantly his riflemen followed. As he led, he raised songs, taken up along the line by hoarse, croaking voices. In the deepening water the taller and stronger men helped along the shorter and weaker. Those forced to swim clutched logs and branches to buoy themselves up. Exhausted soldiers, who could not quite make the next piece of higher ground, were hauled ashore by comrades. When there were signs of faltering, Clark ordered Major Bowman and a detail of twenty-five to form a rearguard and shoot anyone who attempted to turn back. Whereupon even the waverers set up a cheer for him and struggled ahead.

It had turned colder, and stretches of the water were covered with ice. Like jetsam in a current upraised arms jutted through it, numbed fingers locked around rifle stocks and powder horns thonged to them. Below bobbed heads of swimmers, with here and there the shoulders of the tallest men emerging. Vivid in the minds of all to the end of their days were the sufferings culminating in that last desperate lap. If they came to speak of them rarely, it was because they were "too incredible for any person to believe." At last dripping figures dragged themselves up onto firm ground and had sight of the houses of Vincennes looming through the trees.

They took time to build a fire and thaw shivering bodies. Then Clark broke out the colors that had come all that weary way, formed up his little army and marched. The drummer boy stretched the damp head of his instrument and beat a spirited cadence. While Indians fled into the forest, and the townsfolk stayed indoors, Clark paraded his men through the streets. Where they could be seen from the parapets of the fort, he doubled back the van into the rear to give the appearance of greater numbers. Shortly a band of British Indians, flourishing American scalps, was decoyed into reach. Clark's men opened fire, killed several and captured five. The colonel, making an example, word of which he knew would spread through the tribes, ordered the prisoners tomahawked.

Henry Hamilton, in no position now to buy the hair that had been brought in, watched from the ramparts of Fort Sackville. Strong walls were manned by 100 men and five cannon. Though he did not know that the enemy had only 127 men instead of the 1000 the march stratagem had made them seem, he held no thought of surrender. Odds or not, it was unlikely that a well-supplied fort would fall to assault. Meanwhile surrounding tribes might rise and cut Clark off.

But Hamilton had reckoned neither on his adversary's effective Indian councils nor on the skill of American riflemen. Clark's boat with its light cannon had not yet arrived. It was the rifles that took Sackville. Scarcely would a bastion gunport open when British artillerymen were picked off around their pieces. Defenders dared not show themselves for an instant on the palisades. One after another, men firing through loopholes dropped. An aperture big enough for a musket barrel and a glimpse of a man sighting over it was all the target the rifles needed. Before long Hamilton, his losses mounting and no relief in sight, surrendered on February 23, 1779, and was packed off under heavy guard to protect him from vengeance to Virginia where he spent the rest of the war as a prisoner. Clark, who could not afford to risk many casualties, had taken the fort at the cost of one man wounded.

He was never given the reinforcements necessary to drive through to Detroit, although he kept trying through the remainder of the Revolution. He might well have succeeded, if others had not ruined his carefully cultivated relations with the Indians. A Shawnee chief, held as a hostage, was shot in cold blood, and his tribe went raging on the warpath until Clark took the field and burned their stronghold at Chillicothe in Ohio. Earlier ninety Christian Delawares, dwelling peaceably in the Ohio Moravian settlements, had been massacred—men, women, and children—by a band of Pennsylvanians. The tribe bloodily revenged itself on the frontier and routed a punitive force of 300 under Colonel William Crawford, who was captured and tortured to death, vainly begging the white renegade, Simon Girty, to shoot him and end his agonies. Only Clark had been able to stem the tide and roll it back on Detroit.

When the war ended, and the Treaty of Paris was signed, the name of George Rogers Clark was invisibly starred above the clause that awarded the Northwest Territory to the United States. He and his soldiers would be rewarded by promised land grants of 150,000 acres, but he never received his back pay nor was he reimbursed for money he had advanced his officers and men. After further services to the Republic, he drifted into a decline and died, half-forgotten, in straitened circumstances.

The Indian tribes were not signatories to the treaty and were by no means ready to relinquish their hunting grounds, traded away by a one-time ally. Still aided and abetted by the British from Canada, they fiercely resisted the inroads of settlers. And the pioneer families pushing westward could no longer count on any protection from the United States Army, for it had all but vanished.

General Washington had urged retention of an army of 2630 men—four regiments of infantry and one of artillery—to awe the Indians, guard the Canada and Florida borders, and protect military stores. His recommendation was swept aside by powerfully backed objections: dread of the danger of a standing army to the Republic, the expense of maintaining it, and sectional rivalries. New England and New York were bickering over claims to the western lands. Granted the need of a safeguard of sorts over borders and frontier, a vague solution was finally reached. Let militia handle it, with each state furnishing a quota as required.

Meanwhile the war-weary army had melted away. Pressure forced the rapid, wholesale discharge of veteran troops, a process which would prove to be one of history's unhappier repetitions after all our wars. By mid-1784 all that remained were an artillery company of fifty-eight officers and enlisted men (Alexander Hamilton's old command) at West Point and a detachment of twenty-nine at Fort Pitt. Except for that tiny remnant the hard core of disciplined Regulars was gone. Then, as later, the price of the policy would be paid in blood.

Some of the veterans, given the opportunity, would have stayed on—men who loved the service for itself, men who knew no other way of life after years of war. There was nothing for them now, although a number would return when they were called for and serve again, on through the War of 1812. Some able ex-officers, Clark, Willett, and Proctor, were valuably but briefly employed as commissioners in Indian affairs. The Revolution's great artilleryman, Henry Knox, had as Secretary of War suggested a military academy at West Point in 1783, but that institution was not established until 1802, and it was another fifteen years before trained leadership began to emerge steadily from the portals on the Hudson.

There remained only the militia, accustomed to handling muskets or rifles in hunting—a small proportion with a semblance of military training, most with none at all. The trained citizen-soldier of the National Guard and the Reserve was far in the future.

Words of a sage rang through the centuries to prove as true for Americans as Greeks.

"There is one source, O Athenians, of all your defeats," Demosthenes had told his countrymen. "It is that your citizens have ceased to be soldiers."

V

Death of Two Armies

THE NORTHWEST was aflame again. Brant and the Iroquois, dispossessed of their old lands, went back on the warpath to defend new hunting grounds. The powerful Miamis, proud of their broad territories, were determined to hold them. Six more tribes rallied to their support. Truculent Ottawas, expert canoemen. Revengeful Shawnees, crafty and cruel. Wyandots, fierce and skillful fighters. The Potawatomi, as savage as they were filthy, a tribe so lice-ridden that the French called them *Les Poux*—the Fleas. Ojibways and Chippewas, renowned for physical strength and warlike prowess. It was the latter who would stage the last uprising in the Indian Wars when they broke out of their Minnesota reservation in 1898.

In Kentucky alone 1000 settlers had been massacred since the end of the Revolution. A boatload of troops, cruising the Tennessee River on a peaceful mission, was treacherously attacked by four canoes full of Shawnees and Cherokee, and most of the soliders shot. So it went until the killings and depredations compelled the beginning of a revival of American armed force. On through most of the nineteenth century the Indian menace would be the instrument of salvation for every dangerously depleted, postwar United States Army.

So the American 1st Infantry Regiment was organized from the militia of four states, gradually earning the name of Regulars as the men, held together by a sufficient term of enlistment, were trained. Pay for a private had been cut to $3 a month which was reduced to $2 by deductions for clothing and hospital care. Yet soldiers' pride in their profession was born again, and the 1st would prove worthy of that heritage from the Continental Line.

The making of the regiment was by other hands than its commander's. None questioned the bravery of Lieutenant Colonel Josiah Harmar, veteran of the Revolution, but he was a hard drinker and a poor disciplinarian. Furthermore, he knew nothing of Indian fighting, and he was about to face one of the red man's great chieftains, Little Turtle of the Miamis, who belongs in the brilliant line that stretched on through Tecumseh of the Shawnees, the Seminoles' Osceola, Red Eagle of the Creeks, Little Crow of the Santee Sioux, and the Apaches' Mangas Coloradas and Cochise.

On September 26, 1790, Harmar with 320 of the 1st and 1133 militia marched from Fort Washington, near present Cincinnati, against the Miami villages. The force included a company of mounted men and three light brass cannon. Not only were the militiamen of poor quality, untrained and reluctant, but they were ill-equipped. Arms were old, and there was a shortage of such essentials as axes and camp kettles. To cap the general mismanagement, a second expedition, which was to have formed a junction, fizzled out when supplies failed.

Little Turtle let Harmar come on and burn a few deserted villages. Then his Miamis and their allies swooped down on the vanguard, caught in a defile. Most of the militia ran for their lives. Some of those who were mounted excused their flight by picking up a wounded man before they spurred away. A small body of the Regulars alone made a stand and was cut to pieces.

Harmar, halting his retreat to Fort Washington, backtracked and launched a surprise attack. The Indians gave way, but as the disorderly pursuit strung out, they rallied and closed in to kill 183 and wound thirty-one of the enemy, with small loss to themselves. Long poles, festooned with scalps, were carried back to the Miami lodges that day.

The American Army, such as it was, had taken a sound licking, and there was no disguising it or the ineptitude of the whole affair by the whitewash a court of inquiry gave Harmar. Prestige and the safety of the borderlands demanded another campaign, and it had better be prompt and more effective or the tribes would overrun all the settlements and little forts of the Northwest.

Congress, now convinced that one regiment was not enough, authorized the formation of the 2nd Infantry—once more "too little and too late." Militia contingents were drafted, as unfit as before. Again President Washington made an unfortunate choice of commander. He recommissioned as major general the Governor of Northwest Territory, Arthur St. Clair, a comrade-in-arms of the Revolution.

St. Clair had fought well at Trenton and Princeton. He had extricated his army from Fort Ticonderoga when, as he had been vainly warned, British guns were hauled up onto Mount Defiance to dominate it. Behind the general's imposing façade of rough-hewn features and a big, heavy-set frame lay little real ability. Besides, he was fifty-five years old and suffering from gout. Poor planning, delays, failure to see to his troops' rations and pay, a chronic neglect of proper reconnaissance—he must be called to account for all those grave faults. The cards were stacked against an expedition with such a man in command.

On October 3, 1791, St. Clair's motley army marched from Fort Washington north through the Ohio wilderness on the road to disaster. Besides the four washerwomen per company allowed by regulations (ordinarily only for garrison duty), a throng of other women and children totaling 200 or higher, was incredibly allowed to accompany the expedition—wives or mistresses of officers and troops. Some nursed babies; others were pregnant. With their frontier upbringing, they were hardy and courageous. They could march as well as most men and in time of need were ready to snatch up a casualty's musket and fight in the ranks. But those camp followers made severe inroads on provisions, scanted from the first by the conscienceless grafting of a contractor, and otherwise hampered a force operating in hostile territory.

Militiamen, pay in arrears, ill-clothed, food running short, began to desert even before the expiration of short terms of enlistment. Floggings and hangings had little effect. The column's strength, 600 Regulars, 800 six-month levies, and 600 militia, dwindled to 1400. Morale sank lower and lower. Because of the late start, autumn frosts had killed grazing for the horses and beef cattle. Rain seeped through the sieve-like tents, chilling men and ruining powder. Surgeons, belatedly checking medical chests, found supplies short or useless.

Forts Hamilton and Jefferson had been built, and one hundred miles beyond the latter had been covered by November 3 when St. Clair, with no idea of the whereabouts of the enemy, ordered camp pitched near the headwaters of the Wabash. The site, a small, elevated meadow surrounded by dense forest, was cramping, so the militia were moved across the river, at that point fifteen or twenty yards wide and shallow. Glimpses were caught of Indians lurking in the woods, but no defensive works were built, and no security measure taken other than the posting of sentries. However, a volunteer patrol barely managed a return to camp by great stealth. The patrol leader at once warned both the militia and Major General Richard Butler, the army's second in command. That officer did not bother to pass on the alarming information to St. Clair.

Little Turtle, following his race's custom, launched no night attack which might well have proved even more calamitous to his foe than the event impending. He held concealed his 1100 Miamis and allied tribesmen, along with some British from the Detroit garrison and let the invaders manage a fitful sleep, broken by the firing of nervous sentries. He watched them turn out well before dawn and stand reveille parade. When the formation was dismissed, and the men were streaming back to camp was the moment he chose to hurl warriors whooping down on the separated militia.

Panic-stricken by the sudden, savage onset, the green troops dashed through the creek to recoil in frantic confusion on the main body. Its infantrymen and artillerymen struggled through the milling mass into a semblance of a line of defense. When at last they were able to clear a field of fire, the white smoke of musketry and cannonade wreathed the hill and drifted into the woods. Bullets, roundshot, and canister hit few targets, and the lowering battle smoke served to mask the advance of the Indians, closing in from cover of tree, log, and stump, Levies from the East, devoid of the frontiersman's skill, had not been trained to handle their muskets properly. Their frantic, random fire did no more than cut twigs from trees.

St. Clair, half crippled by his gout, was hoisted up on a horse by four men. No sooner was he in the saddle than the animal was shot through the head. A new mount and the orderly bringing it up were killed. On a third remount —he would need still another that day—the general, white hair streaming, galloped about, shouting for a rally. Eight bullets ripped through his clothing. Surely only the fact that he was wearing nondescript garb and not a uniform saved him, for Indian marksmen were steadily picking off officers distinguished by insignia.

Loudly the general bellowed for a bayonet charge. Several were gallantly led, but the red men only faded back into the forest before them. From behind trees they shot down the bayonet men. The charge ebbed, leaving a bloody wake. Another, headed by St. Clair himself, bravely hobbling on foot in its van, was equally futile.

A red cordon tightened around the hill. Indian fire, directed by Little Turtle and a white youth adopted into the tribe, continued to drop officers and concentrated on the cannoneers. The guns, all but unmanned, were spiked by surviving artillerymen when it became evident that they must soon be lost.

No reinforcements appeared. In supreme folly St. Clair had sent the veteran 1st Regiment to the rear several days before to round up sixty or seventy deserters who had sworn to take the ration-laden pack horses with them. The mission was important, but a detail from the 2nd would have served as well for it. As a result the troops most experienced in Indian fighting were absent at a time of critical need. From a distance the 1st heard the uproar of battle and marched toward the sound of the guns. En route it was met by frightened fugitives whose reports of a complete massacre caused the regimental commander, who could not have reached the field before night, to fall back to Fort Jefferson to save what he believed to be the army's sole surviving unit and protect supplies.

Remnants, stiffened by the stanch 2nd Regiment, still stood firm on the hill. The ground, Major Ebenezer Denny saw, "was literally covered with dead," including the unwary General Butler. All company officers were down but one. The living, ringing moaning wounded, fought on. By the third hour of combat they were entirely surrounded and being mowed down by fire from all quarters.

The circle narrowed under a hail of bullets and arrows. With blood-curdling yells warriors broke through. Flashing tomahawks cut down a surgeon dressing wounds and felled soldiers who, utterly demoralized, let themselves be butchered. Around the silent guns savages crouched over prone bodies, living or dead, to tear off scalps. A scalped captain, "sitting on his backside, his head smoking like a chimney," pitifully called out to ask if the battle were not almost over.

St. Clair, pistol drawn, threatened to shoot anyone who refused to fight. Remaining officers and noncoms kicked and cursed groveling cowards into redeeming their manhood. The camp women not only played a heroic part fighting in the ranks, but they, too, drove craven wretches back into combat, burning them out from their hiding places under wagons with blazing firebrands. Only three of those valiant women are said to have escaped from that fatal hill.

A little longer and all making that last stand would have been annihilated. It was near 9 o'clock when St. Clair ordered a retreat that must abandon the severely wounded and all heavy equipment. A charge smashed into massed Indians blocking the road to the rear. Two hundred whites stampeded through the gap "like a drove of bullocks." A few more managed to follow the flying wedge before red waves submerged the hill. What happened there when the bulk of the warriors returned from their pursuit of St. Clair's men is vividly described in an account based on reports that finally filtered through.

"In their frenzy of victory [the Indians] inflicted on the luckless captives every species of cruelty that savage ingenuity could devise," wrote James Ripley Jacobs in *The Beginning of the U. S. Army*. "They danced and laughed and howled at the screams of prisoners roasting at the stake; they pulled out men's intestines bit by bit; they flayed others alive and slowly hacked or wrenched their limbs away. They dashed out the brains of children against the trunks of trees and then flung their battered bodies into the brush. Some of the women were stretched naked upon the ground and run through with wooden stakes; others were cut in two after their breasts had been hacked away."

Meanwhile Little Turtle's braves scourged the flight of St. Clair's shattered remnants toward Fort Jefferson, twenty-nine miles distant. Only the general's efforts, seconded by stout-hearted subordinates, prevented the headlong retreat from degenerating into a helpless rout. The road was littered with weapons and equipment, thrown away by panicky soldiers. Here and there shone instances of courage and self-sacrifice. When mounted men refused to stop, a soldier carried on his back a comrade with a broken thigh. A few hundred yards and his strength gave out. Indians closed in. To save himself the carrier had to cut loose his burden's desperately clutching fingers with his knife, leaving him to be tomahawked. A packer caught a horse and hoisted on a wounded friend. The rider, shot through the hips, could not keep his seat; he rolled off, and a Shawnee took his scalp. The packer, tottering on cramped feet, wrenched off his shoes, and frozen ground against his soles revived him enough to be able to walk. A mother at her last gasp threw her infant son into a snowbank where Indians found the child and adopted him into their tribe. The strong spirit of a tall woman called "Red-haired Nance" lifted an exhausted squad over the last stretch to safety.

If the Indians had not ceased to harry the fugitives after four or five miles, it is probable that none would have escaped. At last, late on November 4, St. Clair, on an old pack horse able to move little faster than a walk, brought the wreckage of his army to Fort Jefferson. Its epitaph might have been pronounced in words Little Turtle once had used to gloat over the slaying of a single foe: "We met. I cut him down. And his shade as it passes on the wind shuns my walk."

St. Clair's defeat stands as the most stricken field in the history of Indian warfare. News of the heavy casualties—37 officers killed, 31 wounded; 593 enlisted men killed, 251 wounded, out of a force of 1400—shocked the nation. So appallingly high a proportion had only been suffered thereto in Braddock's defeat with its loss of 725 out of 1200. Both dwarf the toll to be taken by another Indian victory eighty-five years later: the "massacre" of Custer and 211 officers and troopers of the 7th Cavalry at the Little Big Horn, far more widely commemorated in history.

A new campaign was imperatively demanded, for triumph had elated and united all the tribes of the Northwest. The British, regardless of treaties signed or pending, clung to their forts, arming and encouraging the red men. Westward expansion was blocked. Though some Americans were content, believing gains would not be worth the cost in lives and money, the current of "manifest destiny" ran against them. Then and thereafter a famed sentence could be paraphrased to read: This nation cannot exist half Indian and half American.

St. Clair's courage remained the only bright spot on a blackened escutcheon. Yet his conscience could have been no worse than that of the government which had sent him into battle so ill-prepared in almost every respect. Allowed to resign without censure by President Washington whose first anger had cooled, St. Clair and his career were finished. So was most of the American Army.

VI

Battle Among Fallen Timbers

OUTRAGE OVER BITTER DEFEATS and growing alarm for the frontier forced a revival of the U. S. Army. Its strength was raised to more than 5000 men in the next two years. A search for a new commander ended in the appointment in 1792 of a Revolutionary general who had retired to enter politics and farming.

Handsome Anthony Wayne, of the flashing eyes and strong-chiseled nose and chin, was the *beau sabreur* type of general, reincarnated in Jeb Stuart, Phil Sheridan, and George Patton. Surprised at night by a British bayonet attack at Paoli, he had redeemed himself by storming Stony Point with the same weapon and made a fine record for himself and his Pennsylvania Line. His élan as a fighting leader seemed epitomized by his nickname of "Mad Anthony," though he came by it otherwise. A chronic deserter, having made a futile appeal to him for release from the guardhouse, had declared that the general must have lost his wits; "Anthony was mad, simply mad" to have refused his plea. Wayne, a fine organizer as well as a fighter, was the man to restore the wrecked morale of the U. S. Army.

Borrowing a name from the Romans, the Army was now designated the Legion. Each of four sub-legions, under brigadier generals, was composed of two infantry battalions, one of riflemen, one troop of dragoons, and one company of artillery. They were forerunners of our modern regimental combat teams and would become the parent units of the 1st, 2nd, 3rd, and 4th Infantry Regiments. Cockades of white, red, yellow, or green on officers' hats distinguished each sub-legion. Infantrymen's caps bore patches of cloth of the same identifying colors, along with a strip of bearskin. Dragoon headgear was a brass helmet with a horsehair crest. Marshaled ranks glittered with steel from long cavalry swords to Wayne's favorite arm, the bayonet, which he would make Indians fear as "the sharp end of guns."

Wayne wrought the Legion into a fighting force by old, tried, and essential methods. He moved it away from Pittsburgh and its dissipations and enforced discipline that was iron but not brutal. He saw to better rations and medical care and demanded that soldiers keep themselves and their camps clean. There was no lack of laundered clothing, for a washerwoman who neglected her duty was given three duckings in a river, winter or summer. With officers and rank and file required to make a military appearance and know regulations thoroughly, drills and field exercises in all weather steadily improved. At target practice the best shot won a prize of a gill of whiskey. Infantry, artillery, and cavalry learned to work together. Wayne, damned as a martinet, nevertheless hammered at the incessant training relentlessly. He sternly suppressed drunkenness, brawls, and quarrels. By the same token he curbed his own impetuous nature in his strained relations with his second in command, Brigadier General James Wilkinson, that pompous, devious man whose feet would finally stray along the dark path of treason.

Then as always it was discipline and training that weighted the prospects for victory.

Unavailing attempts to negotiate treaties with the Indians

delayed a campaign until the spring of 1793. Wayne was freed then to begin his advance. More than a thousand well-trained troops were loaded aboard flatboats and poled down the Ohio to Fort Washington. Disembarked there, they were forced to mark time again. Wayne used the delay for maneuvers, fort building, and to forward a request that Secretary of War Knox send colors and standards for the Legion. *"They shall not be lost,"* he promised.

Eight companies marched forward to the scene of St. Clair's defeat. Before they could pitch tents, the ground had to be cleared of heaps of bones of American dead, given burial. A stoutly constructed stronghold was erected and confidently named Fort Recovery. From its ramparts peered the muzzles of St. Clair's lost 6-pounder cannon, found hidden in hollow logs by scouts. The bulk of the army wintered in forts to the rear, since it was now too late in the season for a deep drive into enemy territory.

To the tribes Fort Recovery was an irresistible challenge, a gantlet flung down on the very site of their overwhelming victory. In vain they were cautioned by Little Turtle, who knew they were faced by a different sort of a general and a far tougher army. Younger, hotheaded chieftains seized control. Urged on by the British, 2000 warriors assembled, bound to storm the fort. They planned to batter down its walls with those hidden cannon, unaware that the Americans had forestalled them. With much plunder and many scalps as their prize, they would smash back this third invasion like its predecessors.

A party had just left Recovery for a march back to Fort Greenville when the Indians struck on the morning of June 30, 1794. Caught in the open, soldiers were shot down and pack horses stampeded, but most of the detachment fought its way back to the fort whose gate swung shut and was barred behind them. Cannon thundered, and a ring of flame ran around the stockade as men fired steadily through the loopholes. Indian bullets picked off some of the defenders, yet the garrison's loss was small beside that of the enemy, mowed down as they rushed forward to blaze away from behind the cover of stumps.

All day the stubborn assault continued. Though American casualties mounted toward fifty per cent, there was no thought of surrender with its certain sequel of massacre and torture. Toward dusk the Indians drew off, carrying their dead and wounded. They had violated one of their customs by attempting to storm a fortified place. Now they broke another and made a night attack. They had crept up to within a few yards of the walls when an alert sentry's musket banged. Loopholes spurted fire again. Screeches pierced the night as bullets found their mark. The baffled red men crawled back into the woods. Most of them had streamed away toward their lodges when the morning sun lit the colors flying over Fort Recovery.

Thud of hoofs on the trace through the forest. Fourteen hundred mounted militia joined the Legion at Fort Greenville, riding up jauntily with the spirit of volunteers rather than that of unwilling levies. For the first time cavalry in force was about to play a part in the Indian Wars, a part that would grow in importance when the plains gave it scope and it met the horseback tribes. For the present mounted militia and dragoons were hampered by thickly wooded country, but their value as scouts was high, and in clearings and glades cavalry would find opportunity to earn its spurs against Indians on foot.

Anthony Wayne led his army forward, its strength increased to 3000 men. Past Fort Recovery he marched, its proudly waving flag the emblem of its stanch defense. Far ahead other colors streamed brazenly over British Fort Miami (where Toledo, Ohio, now stands), a stronghold maintained on American soil, in contempt of treaty, to incite and supply the Indians. The Legion was poised like a long bayonet for a thrust toward the fort. Before it the tribes must be brought to battle.

Steadily but cautiously the Legion advanced, hewing out a road through the forest, adding to the chain of forts in its rear by building Fort Defiance. Night camps were entrenched; no surprise would be suffered this time. It was mid-August, and the Legion had reached the head of the Maumee Rapids when two small skirmishes warned that the enemy was preparing to make a stand.

Chief Blue Jacket and his warriors lay in wait at a place of their choosing, close to British Fort Miami as a comforting backstop. Nature had superbly fortified their position for them when a tornado in past years had heaped uprooted trees, splintered limbs, and jutting roots into an immensely formidable abatis that would give a name to the impending battle—Fallen Timbers.

On August 19, General Wayne issued orders for an attack at the following dawn. Lieutenant William Henry Harrison, who would carry on for him in the next Indian War, and other aides delivered them to James Wilkinson, commanding the right wing, John Francis Hamtranck, leading the left, and to the mounted contingent. They filtered down to able young officers, such as William Clark and Meriwether Lewis for whom a path to the Far West would be opened by the coming battle, as it would for the son of Captain Zebulon Pike.

The Legion was ready to follow where Mad Anthony led, though few but he fully realized the crucial quality of the combat ahead, a struggle that would put two years of preparation to the test and decide the fate of the Northwest. A third defeat by the Indians, Wayne knew, would sink the country into the depths of despair and see the frontier ravaged as never before. It would cripple the efforts of the American envoy, John Jay, now in England seeking to negotiate a treaty which would establish the rights of the United States in the Territory—rights flouted by British forts and trading posts maintained on American soil despite the pact of 1783. Destiny's moving finger would either write Fallen Timbers in history as another and greater disaster to American arms or as proud battle honor brightly blazoned on the banners of regiments that fought there.

General Wayne woke early on the day of battle, roused by pain. A Yorktown wound in his left leg had grown inflamed, bothering him throughout the campaign. He had the now badly swollen limb tightly bandaged. A barber dressed and powdered his hair, and an orderly helped him into his old blue uniform coat and buckled on his sword and pistol belt. Like St. Clair he had to be aided in mounting his horse. Then he rode forward with the Legion.

For once the Indians' scouts had failed them by reporting that the Americans were not yet likely to attack. It had been a wearing wait behind the barricade, manned by day but deserted each night when warriors hastened four miles back to the British fort, drew rations and gorged themselves on their one meal in twenty-four hours. In their defenses they went hungry, having learned that an empty man stood a better chance of surviving a belly wound. On the morning of August 20 many of the 1300 assembled braves refused to return to the timbers and another day of fasting on the off chance that the enemy might appear. Less than 800, plus sixty Canadian militiamen, were hidden in the ambuscade when hoofbeats warned that the Americans were coming after all.

Wayne's cavalry screen scarcely had given one startled glance at the upreared, tangled wreckage of the tornado when it erupted with the flame, smoke, and crash of musketry. Surviving horsemen and mounts with emptied saddles wheeled and galloped back headlong through the advancing ranks.

The Legion halted and deployed. Aides rushed orders to the commanders of the mounted troops of the right and left wings to envelop the Indians' flanks. Sight of the wide sweeps of the horsemen gave the chiefs no concern. They had coped with the like before. Let the thick woods and underbrush hamstring the cavalry, slowed to a walk as they tried to blunder their way through, to make fine targets for red marksmen, firing from cover. Meanwhile the American infantry must recoil from the timber barrier or be slaughtered in vain assault.

Forward the Legion! Wayne was attacking.

No member of the advancing Legion could have liked the look of that jagged, bristling barricade ahead. But they marched toward it steadily, ranks deployed, arms at trail—a first line with a second in close support. A spate of bullets and flight of arrows sped from the barrier. Muskets, bayonets fixed, swung to shoulders and crackled in answer. There were no volleys, no random firing. Each Legionary picked his target as he had been trained to do. "Battle is the pay-off for training."

The first line had fired, reloaded as it advanced and fired again when the second line surged through it in a charge.

British General James Abercrombie in 1758 had tried to storm a man-made abatis in front of Fort Ticonderoga, less formidable than this but stoutly defended by Montcalm's French. The British had been bloodily repulsed, with the Black Watch decimated. Here the outcome was reversed. The Indians among the fallen timber, given no time to reload, lacked the resolution to face the Legion's gleaming steel. A wave of blue flooded over the canted tree trunks. Bayonets aid officers' swords and spontoons stabbed down into copper-colored bodies. Warriors, hampered in their struggles by the very debris that had been their shelter, broke and wildly fled.

Mounted volunteers on the American left had managed to force a way through the woods, but they were too late to cut off fugitives from the shattered center. It was the cavalry of the right that found the open ground it needed, a cornfield along the river bank. A charge not only blocked off any Indian reinforcements, but the galloping horsemen, swords swinging, rode over and cut down the red rout of the Legion's bayonets.

Indians clamored around Fort Miami for refuge. Its gates were barred against them, as the commandant made his hard choice. Better forfeit the confidence of the tribes than bring on another war with the United States. For Mad Anthony and his victorious army had closed in, a chip on his shoulder, daring the British to commit an overt act. He burned a nearby trading post and corn stands. Further than this his orders would not permit him to go, but he had done enough. The Jay Treaty would be ratified, and the British compelled to quit American soil for Canada.

The Battle of Fallen Timbers had been decisively won in less than two hours. Wayne reported his casualties as 33 killed and 100 wounded. Indian losses were not heavy, but several of their bravest chiefs were dead, and utter demoralization spread through the tribes. By the Treaty of Greenville, 1795, all the tribal lands in Ohio were ceded to the United States.

The Legion paraded in review for its departing commander. These men of his, Anthony Wayne told them, had deserved well of their country. So, two centuries before, a retiring leader must have bid the valiant Roman Tenth Legion, *Ave atque vale*—Hail and farewell.

VII

The Great Reconnaissances

WITH DRAMATIC SUDDENNESS the United States was confronted in 1803 by the occasion for a new series of widespread Indian Wars whose waging would last through most of the century. President Jefferson's Louisiana Purchase from France doubled the size of the nation, adding 820,000 square miles. West of that vast stretch to the shores of the Pacific lay Oregon Territory, claimed by Great Britain, Russia, and the United States. Spanish California would be a challenge, once access to it was opened for Americans. From Louisiana south to the Rio Grande extended ground, already in dispute with Spain. Here was an immense tinder field for conflicts with foreign powers and with the tribes dwelling on it.

By right of prior tenure or seizure from each other, the Indians asserted ownership of the greater part of those lands, regardless of the claims of white nations. They had not yielded any of them, nor would they except to force of arms or now and again by treaty and sale. Yet they were destined to lose them all. Again, as throughout history, might would make right. Primitive peoples, nomadic or pastoral, must bow before the strength of a superior civilization. But they would go down fighting.

"The past being prelude," Jefferson, opening the gates to the westward march of empire, surely foresaw many of its consequences and sought to avoid the evil ones. More purchases, cessions, and peaceful settlements could and would be negotiated. His instructions to the leaders of the first deep penetration of Indian territories were pacific and conciliatory. They were to learn the tribes and their ways—to cultivate friendship and trade with them—to offer them education and the defense of vaccination against smallpox which snuffed out whole Indian villages. Such orders were faithfully obeyed as were others requiring that routes be mapped and resources noted. By them the path of conquest was paved.

In 1804 and in the following two years three epochal explorations of the West and Southwest were made. Actually they were military reconnaissances, scouting expeditions by the U. S. Army through future enemy country.

The expedition headed by Lewis and Clark and the two led by Zebulon M. Pike were far from being reconnaissances in force. Any such would have been regarded both by foreign nations and the Indian tribes as armed invasion. Nor because of the vast extent of ground to be covered and immense difficulties to be faced could the task have been achieved by larger bodies. Of necessity each expedition was a supremely daring venture manned by only some twenty soldiers and a few civilians.

In fact, no large force, had it been desirable, could have been mustered. The Navy, which had fought the undeclared war of 1798 with France and was winning glory in engagements with the Barbary pirates, was the pride of the nation. The Army had once more been allowed to slide into a dangerous decline, as the frontier became quiescent after the Battle of Fallen Timbers and the Treaty of Greenville. Now that Detroit was garrisoned by American troops, it was blandly assumed that border incidents were over and that Britain would maintain a hands-off policy. No matter that storm clouds were slowly gathering for the War of 1812. No matter either that Spain refused to relax its still extensive grip on the New World and was stirring up trouble in Kentucky and Tennessee. President Washington had died in 1799, and his counsel, that the best way to preserve peace was to be prepared for war, stood forgotten.

The Legion had been abolished in 1796, and the Army, as it was again termed, shrunken to twenty infantry companies of seventy-six men each, with cavalry eliminated and artillery reduced to one regiment without horses. Veteran officers were discharged on a pittance of retired pay. In little forts lonely bugles sounded mess call, "Peas upon a Trencher," of the "Rogue's March," as malingerers or bootleggers, with empty bottles slung around their necks, were drummed out of camp.

Yet in the Army good men remained from whom to pick the volunteers for the expeditions into the West—to give them superb leadership and a rank and file which with rare exceptions upheld the best traditions of the service.

It is the military character of the Lewis and Clark and the Pike explorations and their effect on forthcoming Indian Wars that are stressed in the following brief account. The stories in full detail are told by the reports and journals of the commanders and the diaries of their men.

The leaders were veterans. As has been mentioned, Captain Meriwether Lewis, 1st Infantry, and Lieutenant William Clark, younger brother of George Rogers Clark, had fought at Fallen Timbers. So had the father of Zebulon Montgomery Pike, who had grown up in the Army and been appointed a cadet in the senior Pike's regiment. All three were officers able to inspire and hold their commands together in the emergencies and under the tremendous hardships in store. That they brought their detachments back with the loss of only one soldier, dead of disease, rates as one of the most remarkable feats in the annals of leadership.

There were veterans, too, among their men—trusted noncoms (with the exception of one faithless sergeant) and privates, all but a very few of whom proved they deserved their honor as picked men. Worthy of that company were the supernumeraries: the Lewis and Clark interpreters and the Shoshone wife of one of them, Clark's Negro servant, Pike's civilian surgeon.

Of such were the little bands that spanned a continent to behold the Pacific Ocean or to gaze up at a towering summit of the Rockies to be named Pikes Peak. Sometimes they crossed the centuries-old trace of the Spanish Conquistadores. Elsewhere they were the first white men to set foot on far-off ground and encounter strange tribes on the trails they blazed for a nation to follow.

Two redheads bent over papers many evenings in the White House. Thomas Jefferson, President of the United States, was briefing his private secretary, Captain Lewis, who was to lead the expedition. Preparation was as thorough as for the raids and missions behind the lines of World War II. Lewis took science courses to add to his qualifications and was allowed to select personnel and equipment.

For second in command he chose his friend and fellow veteran, William Clark, of the same strong mold as his older brother, George Rogers Clark. Having left the Army, he was recommissioned as a second lieutenant of artillery. Yet he was addressed as "Captain," and his was in effect a co-command with Lewis, the leaders always working smoothly together. From various posts they hand-picked fourteen soldiers, young, unmarried and fit, who volunteered. So high were standards that the quota could not be filled from troops in the vicinity. Lewis added nine Kentucky frontiersmen, enlisting them as Army privates. The civilian component was made up of Clark's Negro servant, York (his size and strength would amaze the Indians more than his black skin), two interpreters, George Drouillard and Toussaint Charbonneau, and the latter's Indian wife, Sacajawea, who would prove to be most helpful as the expedition traversed lands and encountered tribes she knew.

Confirmation of the Louisiana Purchase was the starting gun which, on May 14, 1804, launched the expedition from St. Louis for its mighty journey. Keelboat, flatboat, and canoes carried them—the Missouri River and other waterways were used whenever possible. Thousands of miles through the wilderness were covered on foot or on horseback. They suffered heat and thirst, exhaustion and bitter cold—temperatures down to 43 degrees below zero. Game sustained them when supplies failed. Hunters brought down elk, antelope, and buffalo, but on several occasions they were reduced to eating their horses or Indian dogs. There were desperate encounters with ferocious grizzly bears, and a number of narrow escapes from those great beasts, as there would be from warriors on the verge of attacking the outnumbered little party.

Fortunately early, weak links were revealed. Two soldiers deserted. Both were caught, but one escaped again. The other was made to run a gantlet of his comrades four times and dismissed from the service. Through the many remaining months discipline was kept tight. Since only two officers were present, courts-martial were often constituted from sergeants and privates. Sentences were not light ones. Fifty lashes for a brief absence without leave and disrespectful language to superiors. Sleeping on guard—100 lashes laid on four different times. Mutinous expressions—75 lashes and discharge; the guilty soldier begged to be allowed to redeem himself but was replaced by a French voyageur. Punishments in no way lessened the loyalty of men who accepted them as just and returned to duty. "They were soldiers of the Regular Army sent upon a well-defined mission, and neither weather nor hardships nor hostile savages nor heartbreaking obstacles prevented them from accomplishing it."

Besides the desertion and dismissals, the only other loss was the sergeant's death from disease. There would be several severe injuries including the wounding of Lewis, accidentally shot by one of his men on a hunt, but recoveries in every case. The expedition came through its great ordeal nearly intact.

It was a foretaste of the future that the expedition's first critical encounter with Indians was with the Sioux. That great tribe, allied with the Cheyennes and the Arikaras, was destined to bar the way across the plains and do valiant battle with the U. S. Army.

Sioux of an encampment at the mouth of the Teton River stole a soldier's mount. The two captains summoned them to a council where at their stern demand the horse was returned. After distributing drinks of whiskey and other presents, the white men prepared to board their flatboats and shove off. Braves, yelling for more gifts, grabbed the painter, and some notched arrows and bent their bows on the heavily outnumbered little group, part embarked, others still ashore.

Lewis of the flaming hair—the tribesmen had already nicknamed him "Red-Head"—faced them calmly with Clark at his side. There was no fear on the faces of the two commanders. They knew Indians and the value of a bold front. The latter delivered himself of some strong language (he called it "positive terms" in his journal), language he might well have learned from his elder brother. A sharp command, and their men leveled rifles. For a moment it was touch and go. The Sioux could have rushed and overwhelmed them, but a look into black muzzles caused them to count the cost as too high. They lowered their weapons and were roughly shoved aside. Soldiers ashore boarded, and the boats rowed away. Thereafter the Sioux proved friendly. Then and again it was such a show of courage, no bluff but an unmistakable determination to fight, that brought the expedition through safely.

Constant vigilance was maintained. When the party wintered among the Mandans, it built a stockade and spent every night behind its walls. Indian girls in the fort overnight sometimes unbarred the gates to admit tribesmen, a practice quickly stopped. Spring of 1805, and the journey was resumed, with warnings given en route to the tribes and to British and French traders that this land now belonged to the Great White Father in Washington. In spite of many near-disasters they pushed through the mountains and launched canoes on the Columbia River. At last Clark could write: "Great joy in camp. We are in view of the Ocian." After wintering near Astoria they began their return trip in March 1806. Separating into three parties to explore more ground, they crossed the Rockies.

Lewis' group ran into trouble when they camped with Blackfeet horseherders who received them with seeming friendliness. Toward morning four rifles were stolen. Before the thieves could reach their horses, Lewis and his men were hot after them. Lewis dropped one with a quick shot, but before the wounded Indian could be disarmed, he fired from behind a rock, and a bullet whistled close past the captain's head. A soldier pursued a warrior and stabbed him to death, the only Indian killed during the entire expedition. The party recovered its rifles, but its horses were run off.

Last lap. On September 23, 1806, Lewis and Clark and their men returned to St. Louis with their invaluable reports after an absence of two and one-half years. They had covered more than six thousand miles, and the West lay open behind them.

Zebulon M. Pike, 1st Infantry, was, as it would later be termed, a career officer, still a rarity in a young army. His boyhood at Army posts and service in his father's regiment had given him a thorough military background. Now a first lieutenant, Pike, "five feet, eight inches tall, eyes blue; light hair; abstemious, temperate and unremitting in duty," possessed a knowledge of astronomy, surveying, French and Spanish, and other qualifications for heading the expedition to whose command he was named by General James Wilkinson. President Jefferson and Secretary of War Henry Dearborn fully approved the appointment. Pike's mission, complementing that of Lewis and Clark, was to explore the headwaters of the Mississippi. He was to map routes, select sites for forts and assert the authority of the United

States over territories of the Purchase, the Indian tribes occupying them, and British companies still monopolizing the fur trade.

On the first of his two expeditions Pike took off from St. Louis on August 9, 1805, his command—one sergeant, two corporals and seventeen privates—manning a keelboat for the first stage of the journey. At the confluence of the Mississippi and Minnesota rivers, he met a war party of 150 Sioux. All the power of the United States seemed embodied in the confident bearing of the twenty-six-year-old officer with his small party drawn up behind him. The Sioux did not attack. Pike not only succeeded in gaining their friendship by presents but negotiated a treaty by which he obtained from them a quit-claim to 100,000 acres of valuable land for two thousand dollars.

Pushing on into Minnesota, Pike built a strong fort where the city of Little Falls now stands and garrisoned it. Then with a small detail he dared a winter march through the forest in search of the Mississippi's source. In zero temperatures that froze noses, fingers and toes, they dragged sleds through blinding snowstorms. Every night the young lieutenant faithfully made entries in his journal until the ink congealed in his pen. British trading posts gave hospitable shelter, but Pike left them in no doubt as to their illegal status and informed the factors that they could continue to operate in the United States only if they paid customs duties at the border. When he turned back, the Union Jack, the only flag that had been displayed in that wilderness, no longer flew over American soil.

On his return to the fort Pike was shocked by a scene of drunkenness and demoralization. The trusted sergeant left in command had failed him utterly, leading his troops in swilling the whiskey stock and rations or trading them to the Indians; he had even sold some of the lieutenant's personal belongings.

Pike thought fast when he took the quick action the grave emergency demanded. The loyal men at his back were outnumbered by the guilty garrison. To have called for a court-martial with a firing squad for the sergeant and lashings for the rest might have brought on a mutiny. Instead he confined the offending noncom to the guardhouse, gave him two days to worry about his fate and then ripped off his chevrons, reducing him to the ranks and promoting a corporal in his place. The punishment, light under the circumstances, was enough to restore discipline.

In spite of short supplies, the expedition was able to manage its return journey to St. Louis. Better than 5000 miles had been covered in less than nine months, and the sway of the United States established over its new land.

Hardly more than a year later, in the summer of 1807, Pike was dispatched on a second expedition, with Lieutenant James B. Wilkinson, the general's son, as second in command. To eighteen soldiers of the first party were added two privates, a civilian surgeon, and an interpreter. This time the Arkansas and the Red rivers were to be explored, the latter as a proposed boundary between American and Spanish possessions. As before this was reconnaissance of Indian tribes, routes, and resources, with a secret mission included: Pike was to estimate Spanish strength in the Southwest.

After cruising the Missouri, they obtained horses from Osage Indian villages and rode across the Kansas prairies. Surely, Pike wrote in his journal, these vast plains, "incapable of cultivation," would stand as a barrier against "our citizens prone to rambling and extending themselves on the frontier." If arid lands failed to bar them, the fierce Pawnees, inflamed by Spain against the Americans, gave evidence that they were determined to do so.

Arrogant and angry, the Pawnees rode down on Pike and his party when they reached the Republican River, near the southern line of the present state of Nebraska. The Indians knew that a squadron of Spanish dragoons had been dispatched from Santa Fe to halt the march of the Americans. They contemptuously compared the two dozen men in worn uniforms and frontiersman's garb with the glittering cavalry of their friends, the Spaniards. These invaders of the Pawnee domain, in all likelihood forerunners of an army of occupation, had best be warned away or finished off here and now.

With furious gestures and shouts a chief ordered the Americans to retreat. Feathered lances had lowered along the heads of ponies when Pike and his interpreter strode forward to face the Pawnee leader. The interpreter translating, Pike spoke in ringing tones to the chief. "My young warriors of your great American father are not women, to be turned back by words," he said. "We will sell our lives at a dear rate to your nation. If we are conquered, we will be followed by others who will gather our bones and revenge our deaths on your people."

Again the bold front was enough. The Pawnees gave way, and the expedition forged ahead. By November they were marching up the Arkansas River on into the mountains. At length the mighty wall of the Rockies, summits already snow-covered, blocked their path to the north. From his camp, where the town of Pueblo, Colorado, would stand, Pike stared up at a lofty pinnacle rising high above the rest. He would have sought to scale it were winter not so near. Men who came later would make the ascent, but the vision in the sky the explorer beheld that day in 1806 would write his name in history and geography—Pikes Peak.

The expedition, swinging away, was close to freezing and near starvation—the killing of a lone buffalo saved it—before the Sangre de Cristo Mountains were crossed. They recuperated in the San Luis Valley near the upper water of the Rio Grande del Norte which Pike mistook for the Red River.

The Spaniards caught up with them at last by the end of February, 1807. Pike was more than willing to be overtaken; in fact, he had baited them on by sending his surgeon into Santa Fe on a pretext of private business. As one hundred dragoons surrounded Pike and five soldiers in an advance camp, their commander notified the Americans they were on Mexican soil. Pike's apology that he had been lost in the mountains was disregarded, as he hoped it would be. The Spaniards, rounding up the rest of the party, marched them all to Santa Fe as prisoners. Pike believed his reports would be confiscated—as they were and had to be reproduced from memory. Therefore he began covertly to make route notes that he hid in his soldiers' rifle barrels.

Although rightly suspected as spies, the Americans could not long be held without creating an international incident. But the Spanish governor, instead of forcing them to return the way they had come, made the error of sending them under guard on what amounted to a strategic tour of ground they were eager to learn. Escorted into old Mexico and then across Texas, the Pike expedition was put across the Louisiana line July 1, 1807. American armies would one day march where they had trod.

The plaudits of the nation and land grants rewarded those who made the great reconnaissances. Lewis did not live long to enjoy his honors. He died in a frontier inn in Tennessee, murdered or by his own hand. Clark became a brigadier general of militia, then Governor of Missouri Territory. His knowledge of Indians remained of service to the nation. He protected the frontier against them in the War of 1812 and helped put down the Sauk uprising under Black Hawk in 1832. Pike, being a protege of Wilkinson's, was questioned when the general and Aaron Burr launched their treasonable attempt to establish an empire in the Spanish Southwest, but he was cleared of any complicity and continued his Army career. Risen to the rank of brigadier general, Pike was killed in action in Canada in the War of 1812.

Lewis and Clark and Pike would still be fresh in the memories or a tradition of the Indians they met when other soldiers followed after them. Many tribes would repent friendship shown or hostility curbed when those little bands of white men daringly penetrated their lands and blazed the trail of conquest and settlement. But that time was not yet. Meanwhile a great Indian confederacy, successor of Pontiac's and that of Brant and the Iroquois, had been formed to bar the way. Its leaders were the Shawnee chieftain, Tecumseh, and his brother, the Prophet.

VIII

The Chief and The General

In all the Indian Wars the U. S. Army never faced a more formidable adversary than Tecumseh. The Shawnee chieftain was a statesman of high order, organizer of a confederacy that extended from Northwest tribes to the Creeks in the South, a combination far more powerful and threatening than Pontiac's, Brant's, or later alliances. His was the headlong valor of Roman Nose of the Cheyennes. He was a fighting leader ranking with Crazy Horse of the Sioux and Joseph of the Nez Percés and he possessed their ability to inspire and control warriors.

A meteor flashed across the sky when Tecumseh was born, a portent as dramatic as his career would prove to be. As one of the "sad stories of the death of kings," his saga would have been worthy of Shakespeare's pen. In fact, Shakespeare, and the Bible as well, had been read to him by a white girl with whom he fell in love and who would have married him if he had consented to her condition of giving up his people. Tecumseh's defiances of enemies and his eloquent exhortations of his own and other tribes glowed with poetic imagery, falling naturally into the blank verse in which they have been rendered. When General William Henry Harrison sought to overawe the chief by warning him to obey his Great White Father's wish, the Shawnee made an eloquent answer that is embodied almost verbatim in Charles Mair's poem, "Tecumseh."

My father's wish!
My father is the sun, the earth my mother—
And on her mighty bosom I shall rest.

Hatred for Americans of the frontier was early imbued in Tecumseh. His father was shot down by white hunters when he refused to act as their guide; the family lodge was burned. The murder of another Shawnee chief, Cornstalk, and his son fed his enmity as would the cruel massacre of Christian Delawares. Tecumseh when a boy of fourteen took vengeance by fighting among Britain's Indian allies in the Revolution as he would again in the War of 1812. Yet after he succeeded to the chieftainship of the Shawnees, he showed himself adamantly opposed to the slaughter or torture of prisoners, striking down his own tribesmen caught in the act. Massacres inflicted took place in his absence and against his counsel and will. Throughout the frontier he was known as a relentless foe but a fair and merciful one.

Alone or with a few followers Tecumseh made long journeys to unite all the still-unconquered tribes within reach in that confederacy he saw as the red man's only hope of survival. "Divided we fall" was his watchword, and his stirring pleas and commanding presence were extraordinarily effective. No cession of ground was valid, he insisted, without the consent of all the tribes involved. The white man's treaties never stood long unviolated, he preached. By union, by the development of agriculture and other resources, by preventing the debauchery of his race by liquor, and with the aid the British were willing to give—through these Tecumseh avowed, the Americans could be driven out of the Indian lands they had invaded and kept at bay.

Such was the "vision of glory" that burned in the hazel eyes of the Shawnee chief, tall, slim, and muscular, of proud bearing and a resonant voice which dominated councils and rang above the din of battle. His dream was fated to fade, though there were occasions when, with a different turn of fortune, it seemed that it might for a time have been realized. The man who finally shattered it, General Harrison, granted this high tribute:

"The implicit obedience and respect which the followers of Tecumseh pay him is really astonishing and more than any circumstance bespeaks him one of those uncommon geniuses, which spring up occasionally to produce revolutions and overturn the established order of things. If it were not for the vicinity of the United States, he would, perhaps, be the founder of an Empire that would rival in glory Mexico and Peru."

Assuredly it was the strength of the United States that proved as fatal to Tecumseh's confederacy as had the might of Spain to the reign of the Aztecs and Incas. The U. S. Army was charged with the duty of protecting and furthering "the established order of things," and at critical moments it was ably commanded. There would be serious reverses when others of the caliber of Harmar and St. Clair led. But William Henry Harrison was cast in the mold of Anthony Wayne as whose aide he had served at the Battle of Fallen Timbers.

Governor of Indiana Territory, brigadier and major general, Harrison would be elected ninth President of the United States on a platform of his war record. "Old Tippecanoe" became his sobriquet after he won the battle of that name—in the absence of Tecumseh—and he and John Tyler, his Vice-Presidential running mate, were swept into office on the slogan "Tippecanoe and Tyler, Too." Still more impetus was given the campaign by the memory of the Battle of the Thames, where Tecumseh fell. Indeed, Harrison was elected in 1840 by virtue of his victory over a famous Indian chief twenty-seven years earlier.

To ability as an administrator, Harrison added other qualities of a good soldier. He looked the part. Tall, spare, and erect, a forelock hung low over his high forehead. The level gaze of his eyes, and the long, firm nose over a tight-set mouth and strong jaw evidenced his character. He took care of his troops and led them fearlessly in action. His service in the War of 1812, a conflict often inglorious except for sea victories, ranks with that of other outstanding American generals who redeemed it: Jacob Brown, Winfield Scott, and Andrew Jackson.

It was Harrison's Indiana governorship that made him and Tecumseh chief antagonists on the eve of the War of 1812. Their struggle would continue until their final reckoning in 1813. Neither underrated the other.

A boast in the young United States ran: "One American can lick two Britishers, three Frenchmen, or four Spaniards." Harrison, as measure of his respect for Tecumseh and the warriors he led, made every effort to have his troops outnumber the Indians by at least two to one.

Collision was inevitable, as both Harrison and Tecumseh were well aware. For by 1807 Tecumseh had begun to make progress on his great confederation that would enlist tribes of all the Mississippi Valley from Wisconsin and Minnesota to the Gulf of Mexico. Harrison had countered with a treaty which for a time drove a splitting wedge into the promising union. Ignoring the Shawnees, he bought from other tribes three million acres of fine ground along the Wabash for a mere $10,000 in cash and annuities. Tecumseh furiously repudiated the deal. Give the lands back or fight for them was his ultimatum. Chief and general, met at a council, flung down the gantlet in angry exchanges that came close to personal combat, with the warriors and soldiers at their backs ready to pitch in. In such a fracas both leaders would probably have been killed, and the course of history changed.

When Tecumseh left on a journey south to knit his alliances, his departure was quickly reported to Harrison by settlers. They urged an attack, in the chief's absence, on the Shawnee capital beside Tippecanoe Creek, 150 miles north of Vincennes. It was called Prophet's Town after Tecumseh's brother, Elkskwatawa, known as the Prophet. On him Tecumseh depended as a keeper of the old traditions and to impart religious fervor to the red man's crusade for independence. The Prophet and his zeal foreshadowed another medicine man, Sitting Bull of the Sioux, and the Messiah craze of the final Indian uprisings.

Regardless of treaty, Harrison decided to invade the Shawnee land. Pressure from the frontier settlements for which he was responsible spurred him to overlook the ethics of the act. Moreover, he was alarmed by the growing strength of the confederacy and its increasing British support; it would be more difficult to cope with later. Obtaining a sketchy authorization from Secretary of War William Eustis, he mustered a force of 1000—Regular and militia infantry and mounted riflemen, with a train of oxdrawn supply wagons and droves of cattle—and marched from Vincennes on September 26, 1811.

Along the trail swung the 4th U. S. Infantry, good fighting men in uniforms probably the most impractical the Army ever adopted: blue, brass-buttoned tail coats, skintight pantaloons, and stovepipe hats with red, white and blue cockades. Color flashed again in the column, predominantly clad in serviceable buckskin—the yellow coatees of a stanch militia company called the Yellow Jackets. Pausing to build a fort where Terre Haute, Indiana, now stands, Harrison pushed on to within a few miles of Prophet's Town. He pitched a well-guarded camp on high ground sloping down into the marshy prairies bordering Tippecanoe Creek.

Tecumseh on his departure had ordered his brother not to fight. But the Prophet, convinced that nothing else would save the town, its store of arms and supplies, and the stands of corn ready for harvest, determined to anticipate the attack the Americans were sure to deliver. The influence of the Prophet, self-redeemed from drunkenness, was strong. Once, learning of a coming eclipse of the sun from a British trader, he had seized the occasion to overawe a great assembly with belief in his supernatural powers by commanding darkness to fall upon the earth in broad daylight. But now he risked claiming too much for his wizardry. To arouse his people to fighting frenzy he fanatically told them that the spells he had cast on the white men would turn their powder to sand and render their bullets soft as rain. Then with a baleful gleam in his one eye he chose one hundred warriors who were to charge into the enemy camp and slay General Harrison. If they failed to cut him down in his tent, and he rode mounted into battle, they would know him by his gray charger.

In the dark hours before dawn on November 7 the killers, "crawling half a mile on their bellies like snakes," reached the fringe of the camp undetected by sentries. Fires, rekindled by chilled soldiers, blazed up to outline the tents around the baggage in the camp's center. It was some time before daylight when a drummer of the 4th Infantry entered General Harrison's tent to ask if he should beat reveille. Before the general, who was pulling on his boots, could answer, a sentry's musket banged, followed by the dying shriek of an Indian. He should "have lain still and died," tribesmen condemned him; the shot might then have been attributed to the edgy nerves of the sentinel, and a more complete surprise achieved.

Shot and yell touched off the battle. Wildly whooping, the Indians rushed in. Before them pickets fell back, dropped in their tracks or wheeling to fire point-blank into red bellies. Troops sprang quickly to arms, but some of the picked killers penetrated to the tents and tomahawked and scalped several officers, struggling out of their blankets.

Harrison called for his gray charger. By a stroke of good luck the animal had broken its tie rope and wandered, and the general was brought a bay instead. An officer, following him on a light-colored horse, was bowled out of his saddle by concentrated fire. Harrison, sensing the situation, ordered his aide, riding up on the caught gray, to find another mount.

As combat surged around the triangular camp, Harrison rode around the lines to threatened points to urge Regulars and militia to stand firm. Where flanks were bending in, he braced them with reinforcements. Though a bullet thudded into his horse's neck and another sheered off the rim of his hat and grazed his head, he remained in the thick of the fiercest fighting. "His voice," a Regular remembered, "was frequently heard and easily distinguished, giving orders in the same calm, cool and collected manner which we had been used to on drill and parade."

From a knoll the Prophet watched the battle, howling incantations. In the pre-dawn darkness the still-blazing campfires silhouetted soldiers. Bullets drilled them and churned the burning logs into higher spurting flames and scattering embers. The first attack was scarcely spent before it was followed by a second and then a bloodier third one which fell on the Yellow Jackets of the right. Their captain, Spier Spencer, kept shouting, "Close up men! Steady! Hold the line!" until a fourth wound proved fatal. Gallantly the militiamen held.

Harrison, galloping to the danger point, singled out a young man in the line of Yellow Jacket rifles. Ensign John Tipton was carrying on for his father, killed in an earlier Indian War.

"Where's your captain?" the general called down to him.

"Dead, sir."

"Your first lieutenant?"

"Dead, sir."

"Your second lieutenant?"

"Dead, sir."

"Your ensign?"

"Here, sir."

The general, seeing that the Yellow Jackets were well led by their surviving officer—Tipton would be elected captain by his men that night—rode off to send in another militia company and Regulars to their support.

With fury and unusual tenacity the Indians pressed their onslaught, as if animated by the spirit of the absent Tecumseh. Obeying the signals of their chiefs, they drove for the weakest points, poured in heavy fire, retreated to reload, then advanced to fire again. Only the stubborn resistance that was displayed all along the lines was able to repulse them. Officers and enlisted men bound up wounds where they stood and fought on. A captain, who did retire to a dressing station for treatment, hastened back to his company and was killed commanding it. Even the mortally wounded fired on until they bled to death. Ranks wavered but rallied.

A little before dawn General Harrison noted some diminution of the Indian onset. He massed troops on both flanks for a simultaneous charge. Regulars fixed bayonets, and dragoons mounted up. At first light the general sent them in under cover of a fusillade from militia rifles. Bayonets flashed and cavalry bugles blared, as the two-pronged assault struck the Prophet's massed warriors. The roar of battle rose to a crescendo. Before thrusting bayonets and swords, the Indians broke and fled, ridden down by the horsemen till they found safety in the marshes or flooded past the doomed town into the forest. Retreating braves swept the discredited Prophet from his knoll, trussed him up and lugged him away in disgrace. His spells had proved powerless to avert their heavy losses.

On the battlefield exhausted troops thronged around General Harrison to cheer him. He had won his victory, but by a perilously narrow margin and at a cost high. Casualties ran to 37 killed and 151 wounded, of whom 29 later died, and 2 missing. The general led his army on to Prophet's Town, which was looted of supplies and weapons, including British muskets. The torch was put to the lodges and the grain fields. Soldiers took all the scalps of Indian dead they could carry on their ramrods. Then many of the army's own provisions were burned to give space in the wagons for the numerous wounded, and a cold, hungry march was made back to Vincennes.

Tecumseh returned to find that a severe blow had been dealt the prestige of his confederacy. Yet it was not one beyond the resources of so indomitable a man to repair, especially since the time was close when he could ally his tribes with the British in a fullfledged war against the United States.

At the outbreak of the War of 1812 the U. S. Army listed seventeen regiments of infantry, four of artillery, and two of dragoons, with the beginnings of the engineer, ordnance, and quartermaster corps. It was largely paper strength. Until ranks were filled, soldiers were trained, and competent leaders emerged, it remained for the Navy to fend off defeat. And defense of the Northwest frontier was not the Navy's province, though it would finally open the way for victory through Lake Erie.

Meanwhile American arms in that quarter met a succession of disasters, most of them at the hands of Tecumseh. Despite the shock of Tippecanoe, tribes rallied under his magnetic leadership. From northern Illinois and Wisconsin Chief Black Hawk, with whom the United States would have to deal in a later war also, brought a band of Sauk, Foxes, and Winnebagos. Wyandots and Chippewas joined from Canada, and Sioux from far-off Minnesota. Elsewhere tribes of his confederacy, from the upper Mississippi down into the Deep South, prepared to take the warpath. The United States was beset on all its land flanks and by the British at sea.

Fortune favored the chief through the miserable incompetence of his first opponent. Brigadier General William Hull was a veteran of the Revolution, but "the tooth of time, whiskey, and tobacco had unnerved him." From Detroit he invaded Canada with an army of 3000. Tecumseh ambushed his scouting parties, captured his dispatches, cut of his communications and supplies and drove him back in panicky retreat to his base.

Major General Isaac Brock, a first-rate soldier, arrived to take command of the gathering British forces, and again Tecumseh was fortunate. The two able leaders quickly realized each other's worth. Brock, though all but one of his own officers were opposed, took his red ally's advice to attack Detroit immediately. While British cannon in Fort Malden opened fire across the river, the Indians crossed and swerved in between a relief column and troops Hull had sent out to meet it. Staving off the former while the latter beat a hasty retreat, Tecumseh closed in around the Detroit fortifications. Then the chief employed the old ruse George Rogers Clark had successfully used at Vincennes. Three times he marched his warriors in single file out of the woods and across a clearing in full view of the fort.

Fainthearted General Hull was certain that the Indians had been heavily reinforced and must now number a full 5000 braves. Against the raging protests of his officers, he ordered the white flag hoisted over Detroit. When Brock and Tecumseh rode past the loaded, never fired guns on the ramparts into the surrendered town, and the Indians pitched camp around it, no harm was done inhabitants or the 2500 prisoners of war marched to Canada.

The fall of Detroit on August 16, 1812, was followed by the storming or siege of other frontier forts. Doubtful tribes embraced Tecumseh's cause. His hopes high, he left for the South on an embassy which brought the Creeks into the war, and returned with reinforcements picked up along the route. By the spring of 1813 he headed a formidable Indian army of 3000, one of the largest ever assembled.

But during his absence General Brock had been killed in battle, and leadership of the British Army assumed by Colonel Henry Proctor, "a fat, haughty man, disdainful of

Indians." Together, Brock and Tecumseh had been winning the war in the Northwest. The advent of the contemptible Proctor, whom the chief would soon call "a squaw" to his face and brand as unfit to command, was the beginning of the setting of Tecumseh's star.

A bloody event that took place while Tecumseh was away had given him an extremely low estimate of Proctor before they met. A force of 850 Kentuckians was overwhelmingly defeated on the River Raisin by British troops and Indians under Proctor. Some 500 survivors surrendered on Proctor's promise to treat them as prisoners of war and give them protection from the Indians. Those able to walk were herded toward Canada, numbers being robbed and stripped of clothing by their Indian guards before being turned over to the British in exchange for liquor.

Near the battlefield, heaped with unburied dead, from sixty to eighty seriously wounded Americans had been left in huts under the care of two surgeons and one British officer, all Proctor would allow despite pleas. Transportation, he pledged, would be furnished them. Had it been sent, it would have come too late. The Indians came whooping back. Guzzling more of the whiskey, forbidden by Tecumseh, they set fire to the huts. One Kentuckian, Elias Darnell, lived to tell of the fate of the other helpless wounded men.

"My feeble powers cannot describe the dismal scenes exhibited. I saw my fellow soldiers, naked and wounded, crawling out of the houses to avoid being consumed in the flames. Some that had not been able to turn themselves on their beds for four days, through fear of being burned to death arose and walked about. Some cried for help, but there was none to help them . . . A number unable to get out miserably perished in the unrelenting flames.

"Now the scenes of cruelty and murder we had been anticipating with dread commenced. The savages rushed on the wounded, shot, tomahawked and scalped them and cruelly mangled their naked bodies while they lay agonizing and weltering in their blood. A number were taken toward Malden, but being unable to march with speed were inhumanly massacred. The road was strewed with the mangled bodies, and all of them were left for birds and beasts to tear in pieces and devour."

Laden with scalps and severed heads, the savages rejoined the British, not only unreproved by Proctor but even congratulated by him for their "bravery." Spiked on the palisades of Detroit by the Indians, those heads confronted the horrified American inhabitants and soldiers of the British garrison who did not dare remove them. One who beheld them could never forget the grisly spectacle. He wrote of "their matted locks deeply stained with gore—their eyes wide open, staring out . . . Some with pleasant smiles, others, who had probably lingered long in agony, [with] a scowl of defiance, despair or revenge; others wore the appearance of deep distress and sorrow—they may have died thinking of their far-off wives and children, and friends and pleasant homes which they should visit no more. The winter's frost had fixed their features as they died."

Tecumseh, when he returned from his southern journey, would have scanned with equal horror those relics of savage slaughter he must surely have curbed had he been present. But the deed was done, and there was no time for more than angry indignation before he took the field. All the frontier was seething with fury, resistance to the enemy in red coats and red skins stiffening and mounting. And an American army under Tecumseh's old antagonist, General Harrison, was assembling to march on Detroit, redeem its disgraceful loss and avenge the massacre on the River Raisin.

Near the scene of the Battle of Fallen Timbers, Harrison prudently built Fort Meigs on the Maumee River, flowing southwest from Lake Erie which was controlled by a British flotilla. It was well he did so, for on April 25, 1813, he was suddenly besieged by Tecumseh and Proctor. Eight hundred Kentucky reinforcements, advancing to break the enemy's grip, crossed the river and stormed the British batteries. Elated by triumph, they swept on in a disorderly pursuit which all Harrison's recall signals could not halt. Tecumseh's braves surrounded them, drawing a deadly cordon which the British helped close to only a narrow outlet. Only 150 Americans escaped to the fort; 500 were killed and the rest captured. While Tecumseh remained in the siege lines, the prisoners were driven to the rear and made to run the gantlet. A mild protest by a British officer failed to deter the blows of clubs, musket butts, and tomahawks rained down on captives dashing desperately between two long red lines. Twenty or thirty had been killed, and a general massacre was imminent when Tecumseh galloped up, summoned by another British officer. Men remembered his terrible aspect, his eyes flashing fire, as he felled one warrior, about to slaughter a prisoner, by a stroke of the flat of his sword. Jumping from his horse, he grasped another brave by the throat, almost throttling him, and flung a third to the ground. Before his furious shout, "Are there no men here?" the Indians slunk away. Then followed his scathing denunciation of Proctor for failure to protect prisoners. When the Briton lamely answered that Indians could not be controlled, the chief's withering words blasted him: "You are unfit to command. Go and put on petticoats. I conquer to save, and you to murder!"

Tecumseh's co-command with General Brock had worked perfectly. If he had been given the King's commission, British troops might well have fought better for him than their present worthless leader. But the chief was not able to cope with his evil genius, Proctor, who would not take his advice to press the siege of Fort Meigs but forthwith abandoned it. When the Shawnee persuaded him to renew it two months later, Proctor pusillanimously again gave up after a halfhearted effort. Meanwhile Harrison had been allowed opportunity to train his army and had received reinforcements Tecumseh had earlier blocked off. He was ready at a strategic location when the hour struck, and the campaign began moving swiftly to a climax.

Through the spring and summer months of 1813 Commander Oliver Hazard Perry had been building an American fleet on Lake Erie, long dominated by the British. By autumn, with a superior number of vessels, though lighter gunned, he was ready to give battle except that his ships were undermanned. From Fort Meigs General Harrison sent two contingents of volunteers to fill out crews. On September 10, Perry won his great victory at Put in Bay, and a naval officer brought Harrison the Commander's historic message: "We have met the enemy and they are ours."

Not only was the British supply line across the lake cut, but it was open for the transportation of American troops to invade Canada. Perry ferried a large part of Harrison's army to take Fort Malden and then volunteered to serve as an aide on the general's staff. Along the shore rode Colonel Robert M. Johnson's regiment of Kentucky mounted riflemen. After recapturing Detroit, they joined the main body.

Before the American advance Proctor retreated deeper into Canada, with Tecumseh begging, then demanding that he stand and fight. The best the chief could exact was a promise that the British withdrawal would halt at the Thames River, about eighty-five miles northeast of Fort Malden. As Proctor fell back, the Indians spiritedly served as his rearguard, delaying American pursuit. Not many warriors drifted away or went over to what now appeared to be the winning side. Tecumseh held his men together as have few other chiefs in the history of the Indian Wars.

Harrison, with an army of 3500, composed of Regular and volunteer infantry, the 1500 mounted riflemen, and some Indian allies, faced 700 British troops and an Indian array estimated as high as 2900, though probably considerably less. Behind the Americans was the impetus of recent success. In their enemy's favor was the choice of the battleground, and Tecumseh chose well for the reluctant Proctor. The main body of the Indians was posted in a large swamp on the right flank. They linked up with the British, covering an interval of open ground between that swamp and a smaller one in the center of the position. The left, wooded land between the small swamp and river, was held by redcoat Regulars in open order, unusual for them, to take advantage of tree cover. At last Proctor was making a stand. Tecumseh saw a chance of victory, though the premonition grew in him that he was about to enter his last battle.

October 5, 1813. A bugle call sounded on the road from Detroit. Hoofs thudded as Colonel Johnson's mounted riflemen trotted into view and halted to reconnoiter. General Harrison was too old a soldier to blunder into an ambush. On the word of the enemy's dispositions he swung one division to the left to face the Indians in the big swamp, while a second was deployed across his front. Before he could deliver the infantry frontal attack he had decided on, information reached him that the British in the woods on his right were aligned in open order. At once he changed his plans. "American backwoodsmen ride better in the woods than any other people," he declared, summoning Colonel Johnson from the left where his regiment was to have charged the Indians in the swamp when the infantry broke the lines.

Harrison pointed to the right, as he gave an order to the cavalry commander. "You will now form your regiment and charge the enemy by the heads of columns."

The stocky ex-Congressman, who never bothered about wearing a uniform, may have managed a sketchy salute but more likely grinned with pleasure. His regiment, trained during the march from Fort Meigs to deliver smashing charges while hundreds of rounds were fired to accustom the horses to the din of battle, formed up smoothly. Picked squads took their places in the van of each column. They were volunteers for the perilous duty of drawing the first volley so that the ranks behind them could overrun the enemy before muskets could be reloaded.

Johnson, like other hell-for-leather cavalrymen before and after, took liberties with his orders. He swung one of his battalions, headed by himself, off to the left on what he considered the more dangerous and important mission of cutting across the small swamp and striking the Indians in the big one. As a trumpet blared, the second battalion, commanded by his brother, Lieutenant Colonel James Johnson, flung itself on the British lines with wild yells of "Remember the River Raisin!"

Now for a time the open order and tree shelter of the red-coated Regulars paid off. The first whooping charge was beaten off. The younger Johnson dismounted his men as his brother was also being forced to do in the hampering brush of the swamps. Battle roaring along the Thames saw a revival of the cavalry tactic of dismounted fighting, tellingly used by Americans at King's Mountain in the Revolution and to be reintroduced by Buford, Forrest, and Sheridan in the Civil War. With accurate fire James Johnson's riflemen whittled down the British defense, remounted and galloped forward. In ten minutes the field and scores of prisoners were theirs. Only Proctor and forty dragoons escaped. The fat general, his traveling carriages captured, hoisted his bulk on a horse and fled to safety.

There was no flight in the woods where Tecumseh held command. His great voice, shouting orders, soared over the rackets of conflict. Indian bullets emptied the saddles of fifteen of Robert Johnson's vanguard troopers. The colonel, wounded five times, his mount entangled in the brush, pistoled an Indian chief attacking him. He may have shot Tecumseh, who had already been many times wounded. Yet the chief's voice still rang out, as Harrison's sturdy infantry closed in to the support of the dismounted cavalrymen.

Men remembered how the muskets flamed as crimson in the woods as the autumn foliage. It was Fallen Timbers again, with the mire of morasses clutching at legs instead of the interlaced branches of tornado-torn trees. Once more bayonets, legacy of Anthony Wayne and the Legion, lunged at painted warriors. Slowly the Indians, ammunition exhausted but tomahawks still hacking, faded back through the swamp. They must have carried the body of Tecumseh with them, for it was never found among the thirty-three dead tribesmen left on the field.

The American Army remained on the alert against its mighty adversary until the melting away of the confederacy he had inspired gave evidence that the chief no longer lived. Even the generation that fought him came to acknowledge his greatness. The capital of the new state of Indiana was almost named after him. An Ohio man, recalling the chief's humanity as a warrior, did bestow his name on his third son, destined also to become a famous leader: William Tecumseh Sherman.

Harrison's losses in the battle were reported as 25 killed and 50 wounded, 601 enemy prisoners taken; British casualties, 35. Lake Erie, the Thames, and the death of Tecumseh paved the way for following American victories in the North—Chippewa and Lundy's Lane. But in the South Tecumseh's dream still lived where he had kindled its hope in the Creek Indians. In August of 1813 they had perpetrated one of the bloodiest of massacres, and the war carried on into the next year, spreading to the Creek's allies, the Seminoles of Florida. Against the grave threat Andrew Jackson, a tough soldier who would well earn his nickname of Old Hickory, led the U. S. Army.

Again the Indian Wars, along with a post-peace victory over the British at New Orleans, were to make a President of the United States.

IX

Red Clubs

"THEY ARE," a Creek chieftain declared, "like a river, so very full that its banks cannot contain it, so that it overflows the neighboring ground."

He spoke of the swelling stream of American emigration for which the Louisiana Purchase had opened the floodgates. The Spaniards, the French, and the English had never penetrated far beyond the coast into the lands of the Creek nation, covering most of Alabama, south Georgia, and part of Florida. With their kinsmen and allies, the Seminoles, the Creeks, as estimated in 1789, numbered some 24,000 people, dwelling in a hundred communities. Yet strong though they were, they were failing to stem the American advance. By treaty and cession or outright encroachment the Creeks steadily lost more and more of their territory. Only efforts toward fair play and just administration by Colonel Benjamin Hawkins, an understanding and capable Indian agent, kept smoldering embers of hostility from flaring up.

Gradually the Red or War towns of the Creeks began to predominate over the White or Peace towns. In the former red clubs were brandished and runners were readied to carry from one town to another bundles of red sticks tallying the days before delivery of a general attack.

That color symbolism curiously manifested itself in another respect. There had been frequent alliances between Creek women and white men. Some of the offspring of mixed blood cast their lot with the whites, others with the red men. Of the first group was Alexander McGillivray, son of a Scots trader and a beautiful half-breed Creek girl. Educated in Scotland, McGillivray served as a British officer in the Revolution, intrigued with Spain, styled himself "Emperor of the Creeks and Seminoles," and finally became a brigadier general in the U. S. Army. From every contact he made money and died a wealthy man in 1793. Most noted of the breeds who chose the Indian side, though he was seven-eighths white, was William Weatherford, son of McGillivray's half-sister. Adopting his name of Red Eagle, he became the foremost chief of the Creeks in the war about to erupt and in its bloody outset at Fort Mims he was opposed by an American militia officer who was also part Indian.

It was, as aforementioned, Tecumseh who inspired the Creek uprising with the matchless eloquence by which he induced a number of their tribes to join his confederacy. But for the great Shawnee the Creeks might have continued to sell their lands and to succumb further to the dissension that was the red man's downfall. Despite Tecumseh's crusade, many Creek towns still clung to the white of peace, yet after his second embassy the red sticks summoned 1000 braves of the Upper Creeks to take the warpath under Red Eagle.

The chief struck with that frightful savagery which many Indians believed was the only means that could succeed in damming the American tide. That Tecumseh would never have urged or condoned so merciless an act was no deterrent; the Shawnee was far away then in his own country. The massacre inflicted by the nearly white Red Eagle and his followers was one of the most appalling in all the Indian Wars, and its horror was heightened by the fact that it was permitted by the folly of utter unwariness on the part of the commander and garrison of Fort Mims.

Red Eagle, like Tecumseh, saw his opportunity in the War of 1812. With the United States contending with Britain, the chief could discount the fact that he must fight without the aid of the Lower Creeks, persuaded to remain friendly by Colonel Hawkins. The agent would succeed in enlisting many of those tribesmen on the American side.

On August 29, 1813, Red Eagle and his warriors crept close to Fort Mims. The stronghold, forty miles northeast of Mobile, was no more than a stockade built around the fortified house of Samuel Mims, a Creek half-breed. Yet it was defensible and was garrisoned by seventy Louisiana militiamen, led by another breed, Major Daniel Beasley.

Rumors of an Indian revolt had packed Fort Mims with 480 refugees from the surrounding countryside: planters and farmers, their families, and their Negro slaves. Numbers of the plantation owners were breeds who had prospered in white settlements, but their mixed blood, however marked by features and swarthier skin, was not to save their lives. Regardless of the threat of danger, Major Beasley had neither sent out scouting parties nor posted pickets. He was worse than heedless of the warning of Negroes in the crowded fort who spotted Indians in the surrounding tall grass and promptly reported them. His angry answer was to brand them liars and order them roped to posts for a whipping next day. There the black men, bound and helpless, were soon to perish.

All night and through the sweltering morning of August 30, Red Eagle held his warriors concealed in their grassy ambush as near as 400 yards to the stockade. When a drum beat for noon mess, the Creeks rose up and rushed forward with blood-curdling yells. Through criminal negligence the gate stood open to them. Major Beasley died trying to swing it shut. Red clubs battered in his skull and those of the poor slaves, trussed to posts. Another half-breed officer tried to rally the soldiers. It was muskets against bows and arrows, clubs and tomahawks, for the Creeks had been unable to obtain firearms, but the surprise had been too shattering, the odds too heavy.

Surviving troops fell back from the first enclosure into a second where the refugees were huddled. A stand there beat back the assault for a time. Furiously Red Eagle renewed it, ordering fire arrows loosed. The roof and walls of the Mims house burst into flame. All within who were not paralyzed by terror or trapped by falling beams and burned alive dashed out to fight or kneel and beg for mercy. They found none. Red Eagle, some say, sought then to stay his warriors' hands, but they were beyond control. Men, women, and children were slaughtered and scalped. Only thirty-six managed to make their escape.

The results of the atrocity were the same as for massacres before and after it. Settlers were not discouraged from running such risks as Fort Mims had bloodily demonstrated. They were still willing, as always, to dare such a fate. Meanwhile outraged demands for crushing retribution echoed through the alarmed South.

A tall, spare man, in bed recovering from severe wounds in his left shoulder and arm suffered in a Tennessee quarrel, was called on to lead troops mustered to punish the Creeks and protect the settlements.

"By the Eternal, these people must be saved!" swore Andrew Jackson, accepting the command.

"He's tough—tough as hickory," soldiers had said of General Jackson.

Until the Creek campaign they did not realize how apt was the nickname of Old Hickory they had bestowed—that it might even be rated an understatement. Strict as he was in disciplining troops, he was more severe on himself. He rode to the Creek war with his left arm, wounds unhealed, in a sling. His hand was seamed by an old scar. Fighting as a boy of thirteen in the Revolution, Jackson had been captured and dealt a vicious saber stroke by a British officer whose boots he refused to polish. His chest near the heart showed a bullet puncture, inflicted by an opponent in a duel just before Jackson's pistol killed him. As always the spirit of the truculent and indestructible Tennessean flamed unquenched. During the forthcoming campaign, he would stoically endure the painful attacks of dysentery that frequently wracked him. Near starvation with his army, he would share his last food, a handful of acorns, with a famished private.

Such was the soldier who led one of the columns converging on the hostile Creeks in the fall and winter of 1813. Georgia volunteers were dispatched from the east and a force of Regulars from the south. Choctaw and Cherokee allies took the field along with friendly Creeks. But the great bulk of the fighting would fall to Jackson's army from Tennessee.

Starting out in October, Jackson with 3000 infantry and cavalry moved fast—marches of twenty or thirty miles a day. Only pauses to build supply depots delayed him. A road was cut over Raccoon and Lookout Mountains for a train of impressed wagons. The general intended to thrust through to Mobile and then, if the government did not halt him, to invade Florida and end Spanish aid to the British and the Creeks.

On the Coosa River, Jackson erected Fort Strother as a base for his operations. Thence on November 3 he mounted an attack on a war party of 200 Red Sticks at the town of Tallushatchee, also on the Coosa. Using his favorite crescent formation, he enfolded the town in it, closing the tips. As the cordon drew tighter, the Creeks fell back, fighting around and from within the houses. The frontiersman, Davy

Crockett, death in the Alamo still years ahead, was among a group of volunteers who surrounded a building into which some forty warriors had run. He saw a squaw, sitting in the doorway, bend a bow with her feet, notch an arrow and let it fly. It killed a lieutenant by Crockett's side. Bullets riddled the squaw and the thin walls. "We now shot them like dogs," Crockett recorded, "and then set the house on fire and burned it up with the forty-six warriors in it. I recollect seeing a boy who was shot down near the house. His arm and thigh was broken, and he was so near the burning house that the grease was stewing out of him. In this situation he was still trying to crawl along; but not a murmur escaped him, though he was only about twelve years old. So sullen is the Indian, when his dander is up, that he had sooner die than make a noise, or ask for quarter."

First blood for Mims—186 Creeks shot down, with American losses light—was soon followed by more. Word that Red Eagle was besieging a band of friendly Indians in the village of Talledega, thirty miles south, speeded Jackson to the rescue. He crossed the Coosa at 1 A.M. and force-marched his army through trackless forests the rest of the night and all next day. While exhausted and hungry troops slept, Jackson, in agony from dysentery, propped himself against a tree trunk and took reports from scouts. A courier rode in with the gravely alarming news that the army's base with all the wounded and sick and reserve supplies lay virtually unprotected because of the refusal by the commander of another column to send a force to guard it. Jackson could not retreat and leave his Indian allies in the lurch. Risking his base, he must win the battle ahead.

At 4 in the morning of November 9 the sleepless general led his army forward. Again the crescent formed, and three companies of cavalry trotted out to decoy the hostiles into it. Friendly Indians behind the village barricades shouted a warning, pointing to a tree-fringed creek. A fusillade roared from it, as the Red Sticks dashed out in pursuit of the horsemen who wheeled and galloped back. Heavy volleys from the American lines mowed down the forefront of the red charge. Still it surged on. With warriors and soldiers locked in hand-to-hand combat, the crescent tips folded in. Under fire from all quarters the Creeks fell by scores and hundreds. But this time a gap in the encirclement was left when a detachment of volunteers fell back. Seven hundred

Red Sticks escaped through the opening before cavalry could close it. When firing ceased, 300 warriors lay dead within the circle. Andrew Jackson had won his battle at a cost of fifteen killed and eighty-five wounded.

Red Eagle had been badly beaten twice, but he and the strong remnant of his warriors, vigorous men who waged war as fiercely as they played lacrosse in peacetime, were far from giving up. And now the army of the victorious general began to dissolve before he could strike a final blow.

It was the same, old, dispiriting story of expiring enlistments. Militiamen and volunteers, who had fought well, considered they had done their part. Their time was up, and the were going home. Let others finish the job. That there were no other troops at hand did not matter. The army was tired, hungry, and homesick and it was pulling out for Tennessee.

For a few days Jackson staved them off, halting departing militia with volunteers and vice versa. Only the cavalry commanded by General John Coffee voted to stay. Then rations dwindled so low that Jackson could no longer withhold the order to abandon the fort and march homeward. Twelve miles had been covered when they met a herd of beeves and a wagon train of flour. But satisfied hunger did not save the situation. When a command to countermarch to the fort was given, only a single company moved out and it headed for Tennessee.

Jackson spurred in front, his aide at one side, Coffee on the other, and a loyal troop of horse backing them up. As the deserters, threatened by the general with a volley, gave ground, a whole brigade prepared to support them and resume the retreat. Old Hickory rode straight into the glaring ranks. He snatched a musket, cradled it in his one good arm and leveled it across his horse's neck. The first man who disobeyed his order to return to the fort would be shot, he shouted. Sullenly the army retraced its steps. The musket was later discovered to be in disrepair and unfireable.

Again Old Hickory blocked the brigade's desertion by confronting it with two small cannon. He let it go only when 1450 reinforcing troops arrived. But the time of the reinforcements would expire in ten days, and they showed no disposition to stay beyond it. The general promptly packed them off back home, "declining to waste rations and breath on such men." Even the cavalry now failed him and rode away, though Coffee and a company made up of officers stood by him. The crowning blow was a letter from the Governor of Tennessee advising that all troops be withdrawn and the entire campaign abandoned.

Sternly Jackson refused to listen and held the fort. For a time its garrison was reduced to 130 men. With these and a contingent of 800 recruits from Tennessee he beat off renewed attacks by the Red Sticks in desperate little battles that were barely won.

At last Jackson's demands brought help from home, 5000 troops, but they were green and poorly equipped. He placed little confidence in them or their commanders. Having already put two colonels under arrest, he dismissed a major general and a brigadier. A seventeen-year-old recruit, who threatened to shoot the officer of the day, was tried and executed. It was the arrival of the 39th U. S. Infantry from the south that gave his army the hard, disciplined core it needed for the war to be pushed to a conclusion.

When Jackson advanced, Red Eagle was absent on a mission, but he had stationed his warriors in a strong position at Horseshoe Bend of the Tallapoosa River. To its natural advantages for defense—gullies and thick brush—strong log breastworks had been added. Canoes moored to the bank provided for retreat. Eight hundred braves in the Bend faced odds in the American field army of 2000; however, the latter must take the offensive. And the mettle of the Creeks had been well tested on earlier occasions and was about to be proven again to the last man.

The Americans closed in, sealing off the land end of the Horseshoe. Jackson held his attack until the Creek women and children could be ferried over the river to refuge in a swamp. Then Coffee's scouts swam across, with enemy bullets, splashing around them, and cut loose the canoe moorings. Now the Creeks were caught in a trap—if it could be sprung.

"Any officer or soldier who flies before the enemy without being compelled to do so by superior force shall suffer death," ran the order of the day. Andy Jackson was given to such resounding pronouncements, but it was known he meant them. At 10:30 A.M., March 27, 1814, American 6-pounders slammed, opening the battle. Balls only embedded themselves in the log breastworks, failing to breach them. Peppered by the fire of Creek sharpshooters, artillerymen were unable to move their pieces forward and close the range.

Drums of the 39th Infantry beat the charge. In a gallant storm of the flaming breastworks, a major, the first man to scale them, toppled back, shot through the head. Close behind him, a young officer, sword drawn, pistol flashing, led the rush onward. Ensign Sam Houston was displaying the fighting spirit that would win Texan independence from Mexico at San Jacinto twenty-two years later. A barbed arrow drove deep into one thigh. When he was unable to tug free the jutting missile, he called on a brother officer to help. Twice the other tried, failed and, sickened, gave up the attempt. Houston raised his sword and forced the man to wrench the arrow out through torn flesh in a gush of blood. His wound bound by a surgeon, the ensign limped back into the thick of the fight. Not even a direct order from Jackson could make him leave it.

"The action now became general, and more than two thousand men were struggling hand to hand," a biographer of Houston wrote. "Arrows and spears and balls were flying; swords and tomahawks were gleaming in the sun; and the whole Peninsula rang with the yell of the savage and the groans of the dying."

On through the afternoon the battle raged. The Creeks fought with utmost valor in disdain of General Jackson's offer to spare their lives if they surrendered. Priests moved among the warriors, promising that the Great Spirit would give them victory when a small cloud appeared in the heavens. The cloud formed but signified no more than a brief rain shower. Still the Red Sticks fought on. A remnant manned a small roofed fort and beat off every attempt to take it. It only fell when Jackson brought the war to full circle by ordering a flight of the fire arrows the Creeks had used at Fort Mims. In the burning fort the last of the warriors died. The bodies of 757 were counted on the field and in the river. The American loss was forty-nine killed, 157 wounded.

With the Creek power broken, it only remained now to hunt down Red Eagle. Jackson was saved the trouble, for the chief came into camp and gave himself up. Magnanimously the general released him. Some years later the onetime Indian leader, William Weatherford again, returned to become a prosperous planter. Most of his nation did not fare so well. The hostile Creeks lost a large area of their territory but were permitted to retain some. Counterbalancing the latter, lands of the friendly Creeks were taken despite their indignant protests that they had helped the Americans. A certain amount of compensation for the ground could not justify a discreditable treaty. No more could Jackson's explanation that the strip was appropriated for white settlements to become a barrier to the Spaniards and the Seminoles.

A brilliant campaign, though tarnished by its aftermath, stood on the record of General Jackson. As had Harrison in the north, he had played his part in a two-front war, and Old Hickory, like Old Tippecanoe, had fought largely with troops mustered from the frontier. Until time-expired volunteers and militia, except for such stanch men as John Coffee, deserted the colors, most of them had endured hard marches and short rations, close to the point of starvation, and served gallantly against a courageous and unyielding foe. Andrew Jackson made heavy demands on citizen-soldiers and, inspired or overawed, they won victories for him. Well deserved was the promotion to major general in the Regular Army that was his reward.

Soon he left the prostrate Red Sticks and faced the redcoats. Fortunes of the War of 1812 had swayed back and forth from American victories in the North to the British capture and burning of Washington. But with the successful defense of Fort McHenry and Baltimore and Macdonough's naval triumph on Lake Champlain, the war was won. The Treaty of Ghent had been signed but news of it had not yet crossed the Atlantic when Jackson shattered the British invasion at New Orleans. Over the smoke of battle floated The Star-Spangled Banner hymned by Francis Scott Key when he beheld it still flying on McHenry's ramparts to give us a national anthem.

Three years later General Jackson carried the flag into Florida and the swamp fastnesses of the Seminoles.

X

The Swamps and The Seminoles

"After all, Florida is certainly the poorest country that ever two people quarrelled for," an Army surgeon declared in his journal. He wrote of " 'torrid realms of more than burning day' "—"sad haunts of death and putrid air"—"a most hideous region to live in; a perfect paradise for Indians, alligators, serpents, frogs, and every other kind of loathsome reptile . . . Then why not in the name of common sense let the Indians have kept it?"

Spain and England had been willing to let the Indians keep part of it, but the Americans were not, even though the most sanguine could not foresee in 1817 what Florida would become. So then and nineteen years later bitter wars were waged to oust the Seminoles from their good lands and finally from the swamps which were their last refuge.

The name, Seminoles, given by the Creeks from whom they had separated, signified runaways. However, the true runaways of Florida were fugitive Negro slaves from South Carolina and Georgia, escaped to settle in free communities, sometimes interbreed with the Indians, or sometimes know servitude again under the Seminoles and Creeks. Both tribes were still slave holders in 1842 after their deportation to Indian Territory when Negroes they had owned in Florida were shipped to them.

Recovery of American slaves, who for years had been fleeing from plantations to the north, brought on the conflict in Florida, with demands for action increasingly insistent when slave values soared after the outlawing of further importation to the United States. The First Seminole War, called "the first slave-catching expedition undertaken by the Federal Government," not only led to the cession of Florida by Spain and the ultimate conquest of the Indians but formed a link in the chain of events ending in the Civil War.

It was a new role for the Army, aided by the Navy—a task accepted as in line of duty—part of the service a man could expect when he went for a soldier. Campaigning in subtropical heat, or winter station in a lonely fort in the Northwest, was a matter of orders for one who followed the profession of arms. Frostbite and monotony may well have been preferred to Florida's buzzing clouds of mosquitoes, midges, and other stinging insects—the deadly rattlesnakes, moccasins, and copperheads—the red-eyed, mighty-jawed alligators lurking in rivers—the fevers and chills that sapped strength. The soldier was paid his meager money, but he didn't take his choice.

As surely as malaria, postwar reaction had weakened the Regular Army after the War of 1812. Numbers sank from 33,000 toward a low of 7500, then still lower. Rosters listed an organization of eight infantry regiments, one of light artillery, eight artillery battalions serving ordinarily as infantry, and skeleton staff corps; no cavalry. The eight new infantry regiments were mergers from the wanton wreckage of fifty old ones, regardless of the preservation of battle honors and other traditions. Five out of every six officers were discharged; numbers of others were "deranged," as it was then termed—that is, reduced in rank. Such treatment was almost enough literally to derange one who had given long and faithful service. There was only one ray of encouragement beyond the fact that retained troops contained a good proportion of veterans: the appointment of a strong Secretary of War, John C. Calhoun.

The Army was as improperly equipped as it was undermanned. Leather shakos, decorated with black cockades and brass eagles, made a handsome show and lent height but were no better adapted to campaigning under a blazing sun that the officers' chapeaux. No more suitable were woollen uniforms of blue or gray (General Winfield Scott had clad his men in the latter color before the Battle of Chippewa because of a blue cloth shortage, the gray being carried on by the Corps of Cadets, U.S.M.A.). White crossbelts were targets for enemy marksmen. Collars jutted up uncomfortably—"not too high in front to prevent the chin being turned," regulations considerably provided. However, that overcoats were issued for Florida was no mistake, for some winter days could be cold. Despite handicaps, the spirit of the American fighting man survived undimmed.

The Seminole wars must be fought with such Regular troops as could be spared from guarding seacoast and frontiers, a force that had to be pieced out with militia and Indian allies. Before the two conflicts were over, they would have exacted a disproportionate cost in American lives and treasure and would have come close to breaking the careers of a succession of generals. They would witness the emergence of a great Indian chief, Osceola, and would pave the beginning of the path to the White House for an American commander in the line of Jackson and Harrison —Zachary Taylor. As for other Indian Wars, valor and treachery and massacre wove the fabric of their story with golden, black, and scarlet threads.

One of the Negro settlements in Florida, long existing under Spanish or English rule, was a strong fort on the Apalachicola River. It contained 300 men, women, and children, ex-slaves—recent fugitives or descendants of those who had been escaping from American masters since Colonial times. A number of Indians helped garrison the stronghold and man its cannon, amply supplied with ammunition in two large powder magazines. This "Negro Fort" was the objective of U.S. land and naval forces which, joined by a band of Creek Indians eager for plunder, advanced against it in the summer of 1816. Refusing to surrender, the garrison opened a furious but ineffective bombardment on surrounding troops and on the two gunboats that sailed in close and returned the fire. A furnace-heated roundshot from the battery of one of the vessels plunged into a powder magazine. It blew up with a tremendous blast. The explosion killed all but fifty of those in the now helpless fort. Of the survivors two leaders were executed, and the rest were restored as slaves to owners claiming them. The victors, who had suffered only two casualties, took possession of the considerable store of powder in the intact magazine and other valuable loot.

A war party of Seminoles, marching to the fort's relief, quickly withdrew on the news of its fall. But the tribesmen did not long remain quiet. Even without the warning incitements of British agents, they were aware they would be the next target for attack, and they struck first. In 1817 a Seminole ambush trapped a lieutenant and forty men escorting a number of women and children. All the whites were slaughtered except for six soldiers who got away and one woman who was spared and taken prisoner.

The Seminoles now raided into Georgia, killing and scalping, and retreated to their Florida fastnesses. Countermeasures by the ineffective General Edmund P. Gaines achieved nothing. It was time to call on Old Hickory again.

That tough soldier, crowned with the laurels of New Orleans, was ready as always. His instructions from the Administration appear purposely indefinite and elastic; it may well have been expected that the headlong General Jackson would stretch them to the limit and beyond. He was convinced that punishment of the Seminoles should become the entering wedge of a blow battering foreign powers out of Florida. Scots and Englishmen, enjoying a profitable trade, were active in arming the Indians and were reported to be following the old British custom of buying American scalps. As a domain of Spain, Florida served as sanctuary for the Seminoles. The peninsula geographically was part of the United States and, in the opinion of Andrew Jackson and others, ought to be so politically. He proceeded to see to it.

Jackson marched in the spring of 1818 with the 4th and 7th Infantry, a battery of artillery, a thousand militiamen, and a band of friendly Creeks. He overran and burned Seminole villages, his powerful force meeting virtually no opposition. The American Army had penetrated as deep into the interior as the Suwanee River when two British subjects were captured. Jackson tried them on charges of arming and rousing the Indians and, on conviction by a court-martial, ordered them executed. Two hostile chieftains were decoyed aboard a vessel and hanged. Though Jackson was widely condemned for both deeds, they were passed over. By the end of May the relentless, hard-driving general had pushed through to Pensacola. After a three-day siege he took that Spanish stronghold and added other forts to his trophies. Confronted by Spain's irate protests, the United States Government disavowed the acts of the high-handed Jackson and directed the forts be returned. Yet the end result of the military *coup d'état* was the cession in 1819 of Florida by Spain in return for five million dollars.

Florida was American, but the Seminoles were still there and must be reckoned with in a longer and fiercer conflict.

The Second Seminole War, prolonged through more than

seven years of bitter fighting, displayed some startlingly modern aspects. Collapsible rubber pontooon boats were employed at times instead of heavy wooden ones; it was a valuable innovation that would be allowed to fall into disuse for many years. The war rockets devised by British General Congreve were fired—those missiles which had helped rout Americans at Bladensburg in the War of 1812 and found at Fort McHenry a place in our national anthem. Although they struck more terror than they did execution, they proved effective then and more so in the Mexican War. Thereafter rockets, except for signaling, lay discarded for nearly a century. And this struggle presented an example of guerrilla warfare as fought today. So in fact did other Indian Wars but none so outstandingly as that in the Florida swamps. Only after the Army adopted counter-guerrilla tactics did it prevail.

On into the third decade of the nineteenth century the Seminoles, their backs to the swamps, had clung to their homeland. With the American force mustered to evict them came that young surgeon who would prove willing to let the Indians keep Florida. Jacob Rhett Motte, Charleston born and Harvard-educated, having failed to receive an appointment to the U. S. Military Academy, had then taken his medical degree and entered the service as a doctor. Love of Army life was strong in him. Whether Seminole banishment was wrong or right, it was directed by government orders the Army must obey, and Motte would not question them.

He knew pride in the uniform and the stirring sight of the flag he followed. He heard the notes of bugles that echo in a soldier's dreams as long as he lives. When drums beat "The General," he admiringly watched every tent in camp struck simultaneously at the third roll. The cadenced tread of marching feet and the thud of hoofs—those too he would never forget, nor the feel of a good horse under him and its flowing mane in the wind of a gallop. He rode with the artillery or dragoons through battle and skirmish, bandaging wound under fire, performing amputations, stoically endured without anesthetic. The pang of a last look at a dead comrade; that also he knew.

Besides the danger, the blood, and the grief, his journal recorded distractions and gay moments. Fishing and hunting the abundant game. Strummed guitars and songs around a campfire. A voice raised in *"Quoi Liset, Ect-ce Vous?"* and a rollicking chorus of "Cigars and Cognac" that frightened the owls into flapping flight. A dance in a frontier settlement—the double-shuffle to the strains of a cracked fiddle with two strings missing, and the whiskey jugs making frequent rounds. A ball in St. Augustine, graceful waltzes, and the dark beauty of belles of Spanish or Minorcan descent. An Army career in wartime, for all its perils and hardships, held compensations and mitigations.

The Treaty of Payne's Landing, 1832, provided for migrations of the Seminoles from Florida to lands west of the Mississippi, the tribe to be recompensed by a sum of money and supplies. However, a clause excluded Negroes and those of Negro blood. All such must be returned or sold into slavery. In consequence only a few chiefs signed the treaty. It was denounced by others, notably the fiery Osceola who, when an Indian commissioner laid the document on a table before him, furiously plunged his knife through it deep into the board. Not only did he adamantly refuse to consider terms but he struck mercilessly at those accepting them, killing or kidnaping chiefs who collaborated with the white men.

Osceola, who had fought against Jackson, was ready to fight again. Tall and muscular, his handsome features resolute, crowned by a feathered turban, the Indian leader confronted an American general with the classic defiance that began the Second Seminole War.

"You have guns, and so have we. You have powder and lead, and so have we. You have men, and so have we. Your men will fight, and so will ours, till the last drop of the Seminole's blood has moistened the dust of his hunting ground."

First Osceola took vengeance on the Indian agent, Wiley Thompson, who had attempted to force the treaty on him and upon refusal had ironed him and confined him to the guardhouse for four days. When Thompson, a former general, and a lieutenant strolled away from their headquarters, a little fort, toward the sutler's store, Osceola and twenty warriors were lying in wait for them. The two white men, riddled with bullets, were scalped and mutilated, along with those in the store.

It was all the declaration of war needed, for the Seminoles, inflamed by Osceola, were displaying increasing resistance to deportation. Troops began to converge on Florida to reinforce those stationed there. On the same day as the Thompson slaying, December 28, 1835, an Army detachment commanded by Major Francis L. Dade had been crushed in a bloody battle which insured that the United States would fight the Second Seminole War to a finish.

The Dade "Massacre" (so called) was not one in the sense that the slaughters at Wyoming and Cherry Valley and Fort Mims had been. It was an overwhelming defeat at the hands of the Indians, comparable on a smaller scale to that of the armies of Harmar and St. Clair and another to come, Custer's at the Little Big Horn. Rashness, neglect of elementary military precautions, and underestimation of the red man as a warrior led to all four disasters.

One hundred and twelve men in blue swung along a road of sorts through open pine country that December morning: Major Dade, his officers and a surgeon; a company of the 4th Infantry and one each of the 2nd and 3rd Artillery with an oxdrawn 6-pounder and its ammunition cart; a creaking ration wagon. Most of their long march from Tampa Bay to reinforce the garrison of Fort King, 130 miles to the northeast, lay behind them. The end of their journey was not far now, they were told by their Negro guide named Luis. Indeed it was closer than they thought, for Luis had sent word to the Seminoles of the column and its route. Up ahead in a palmetto grove west of the road 180 warriors were waiting in ambush.

Major Dade, assured he was on the last lap, relaxed the march discipline thereto maintained. A small advance guard still preceded the column, but there were no flankers out, and no insistence on vigilance. Most culpable of all was the order given that cold morning when camp was broken. Overcoats would be worn—which was sensible—but the men were allowed to button them on *over* their cartridge pouches. Adjusting belts to fit around the bulkier garments would have caused a little delay, but that time-saving was the difference between life and death.

On into the ambush they marched with no regard to the crafty Seminole. The Army would learn better after today from a lesson which was about to cost a high price in blood. Suddenly a rattling volley burst from the palmetto clump and the tall grass along the roadside. It wiped out the advance guard and Dade and his staff close behind. Following ranks were scythed by fire that could not miss at a range of thirty-five yards. Half the command went down, dead or wounded. Survivors fired the one round in their muskets, then desperately tugged at their overcoat flaps while more died helpless before they could reach cartridges.

Only the artillerymen had their ammunition handy. They unlimbered their piece, loaded with canister and blasted back the oncoming enemy with bursts of lethal, spraying balls. That gave the remnant a respite. While the Seminoles pulled back under cover, small pines were hastily hewn to build a low barricade. From behind it the blue troops fought to meet a second attack. Muskets flamed, and the fire of the 6-pounder raked the red men closing in. Second Lieutenant R. Henderson, his left arm shattered, helped man the little cannon until he was killed. Seminole bullets whittled down its crew and their replacements. Second Lieutenant W. E. Basinger kept the piece in action as long as a single gunner remained. Then he himself was wounded, and it fell silent. Whooping warriors, tomahawks hacking, swept over the barricade and finished off all within it who still lived. Only three soldiers, all severely wounded, managed to creep off through the tall grass. One was shot during the escape. The other two won clear to bring back word of the disaster.

A vivid account of the fight from the Indian standpoint, rarely recorded at that period, was obtained some time later from Chief Alligator.

"So soon as *all* the soldiers were opposite, between us and the pond, Jumper gave the whoop. Micanopy fired the first rifle, the signal agreed upon, when every Indian rose up and fired, which laid upon the ground, dead, more than half of the white men. The cannon was discharged several times, but the men who loaded it were shot down as soon as the smoke cleared away; the balls passed far over our heads. The soldiers shouted and whooped, and the officers shook their swords and swore.

"There was a little man, a great brave, who shook his sword at the soldiers and said, 'God-dam!' No rifle ball could hit him. As we were retiring to the swamp, supposing all were dead, an Indian came up and said the white men were building a fort of logs. Jumper and myself and ten warriors returned. As we approached, we saw six men behind two logs placed one above the other, with the cannon a short distance off. This they discharged at us several times, but we avoided it by dodging behind trees just as they applied the fire. We soon were nearer it, and the balls went over us.

"They had guns but no powder. We looked in the boxes afterward and found them empty. When I got inside the logpen, there were three men alive, whom the Negroes put to death, after a conversation in English. There was a brave man in the pen; he would not give up; he seized an Indian, Jumper's cousin, took his rifle, and with one blow with it beat out his brains, then ran some distance up the road. But two Indians on horseback overtook him, who afraid to approach, stood at a distance and shot him down.

"The firing had ceased, and all was quiet when we returned to the swamp about noon. We left many Negroes upon the ground looking at the dead men. Three warriors were killed and five wounded."

Two months later another expedition reached the scene. Among the soldiers' bodies lay the gun team oxen, dead in their traces, and charred bits of the gun carriage. The tube, thrown into a swamp by the Indians, was salvaged to mark the graves as a fitting memorial.

The Dade defeat had aroused the nation. Only then were the resolution and the fighting qualities of the Seminoles fully realized. More troops poured into Florida.

Osceola, Alligator, and other Seminole chiefs marshaled their warriors and the free Negroes against the U. S. Army. Its superior numbers were discounted by its uncoordinated campaigns, the toughness of the terrain, and the tactics of the Indians who seldom risked a pitched battle but depended upon raids and harassments. Duncan L. Clinch was the first of the procession of generals broken on the rock of Seminole resistance. In a hot little fight in the scrub early in 1836 he drove Osceola from the field after three charges. But casualties were about equal, and Clinch, with bullets through his cap and a sleeve, had almost paid for the inconclusive victory with his life.

General Gaines, bringing an expeditionary force of 1100 from New Orleans, fared no better. Next month he barely held off the Indians in a second engagement. The two American commanders proved unable to combine and co-operate. Little hindered, the hostiles ravaged the countryside, killing settlers and destroying plantations.

The next vain attempt to subdue the Seminoles was made by no less a commander than General Winfield Scott. In Florida glory took leave of absence from a hero of 1812 and the future captor of Mexico City. Ill feeling between him and President Jackson hampered the efforts of Scott, hamstrung from the start by inefficiency in the supply system that left him short of necessary arms and equipment. Camp epidemics of mumps and measles cut down his manpower, as did the departure of local short-term volunteers. Scott's railing at that old American practice made him as unpopular in Florida as he was in the White House. His campaign a fizzle, he was recalled and faced a court of inquiry. Although exonerated, his record would need the redemption a later President almost deprived him of in the Mexican War for political reasons.

Still another general had come, seen and failed to conquer when General Thomas S. Jesup was handed the mission to round up the Seminoles in their swamps. Given the needed troops and supplies, Jesup was also fortunate in such able subordinates as Colonels Persifor F. Smith, Zachary Taylor, and William S. Harney and Major Ethan Allen Hitchcock. The last, an able young officer who would go far in the service, belonged to the line of Marinus Willett in the earlier wars and Hugh L. Scott in the later ones —Army men who fought the Indians hard but strove for understanding of and fair play toward the red man at the risk of being branded devil's advocates.

The new general, brave and vigorous, thrice in the late spring and summer of 1837 brought the hostiles to battle and drove them back. In one engagement when he tried to lead reluctant volunteers forward, and none followed, he advanced alone and was struck in the face by a bullet that broke his spectacles and ripped a cheek. He picked up the shattered glasses and organized a rally. Many Seminoles, despairing of further resistance, gave themselves up. Three thousand men, women, and children assembled, drew Army rations and supplies and made ready to be herded to Tampa Bay where transports waited to ship them west.

But Osceola refused to acknowledge defeat and allow his people to suffer exile. By eloquent persuasions, threats, and force against chiefs who had yielded, he swept the entire encampment back into the swamp refuges of the tribe.

General Jesup, believing he had won the war, had let his guard down. Now with the frustration of one who sees all his work undone he stooped to conquer. He called a council which Osceola and seventy-five of his warriors were induced to attend under a flag of truce. Jesup ordered them made prisoners. The blot he left on the Army's honor could not be erased by attempted justification that the Seminoles had earlier broken their own pledge to surrender. Punishment by force of arms had been foregone for treachery.

Osceola did not long survive imprisonment. His grave was marked by a stone with the inscription, *Patriot and Warrior*. Jesup, recalled from Florida, was castigated at a Congressional investigation, but his successful defense by Senator Thomas Hart Benton saved his commission.

The war dragged on bitterly as ever. Command was now taken over by a seasoned Indian fighter, Colonel Zachary Taylor, soon to win his generalcy and his nickname of Old Rough and Ready. From the Second Seminole War dated the military accolades, carried on through the conflict with Mexico, that elected him President of the United States with such reminiscent verses as:

> "I knew him first," the soldier said,
> "Among the Everglades,
> When we gave the savage redskins
> Our bayonets and our blades.
> I think I hear his cheerful voice,
> 'On column! Steady! Steady!'
> So handy and so prompt was he,
> We called him Rough and Ready."

Rugged, rather handsome features; a tall, lean frame; brusque, profane, and ungrammatical in speech—that was Zach Taylor. The longer he stayed in the Army the less he cared about wearing a uniform; by the Mexican War he had shed blue and gilded epaulets for rough civilian clothes. Fearless to the point of rashly exposing himself to enemy fire, he was the sort of a leader soldiers readily follow into battle. While major tactics and logistics were beyond him, he provided himself with first-rate staff officers to take care of such problems. When he went to Florida, considerable frontier service stood on his record, including a gallant defense of a fort against Tecumseh's braves, and the Black Hawk War.

From the outset Taylor had his hands full, even before he took over from the departing Jesup. Seminole chiefs and tribesmen were burning to avenge Osceola. They would not surrender again nor obey orders to leave for the West until they were routed out of the maze-like morasses of middle Florida where they were making their stand. Toward the end of November 1837 Taylor disembarked his troops, his baggage train of eighty wagons, and his pack mules at Tampa Bay.

He marched inland at the head of one thousand men: 727 Regulars of the 1st, 4th, and 6th Infantry and the 4th Artillery, with the balance Missouri volunteers, all mounted.

Two small forts were built along the route, and in the second the artillery and baggage were left. Pontoons had bridged the rivers, but now the army was moving onto swampy ground surrounding that great inland sea, Lake Okeechobee, north of the Everglades. The going, impossible for wheeled vehicles, grew increasingly difficult for ridden horses. Foot troops slogged through the mud, immemorial enemy of armies, along a trail marked by abandoned Seminole camps.

On rising ground called a hammock, not far from the northeastern lake shore, the Seminoles waited under the redoubtable Chief Alligator, he who had laid the ambush for the near-annihilation of Major Dade's command. For his outnumbered warriors he had chosen a position that seemed to defy assault like a strong medieval castle. Thick groves of cypress and palmetto were its battlements. Its moat, the swamp, oozing with black slime waist-deep or worse, was bordered by *chevaux-de-frise* of saw grass, sharp-pointed, keen-bladed, growing as high as five feet. Sheltered by trunks of trees or up in their branches, masked by Spanish moss, the Seminoles peered over their musket sights.

Taylor attacked a little after noon on Christmas Day which before and since has failed to forbid battle. He sent out a detachment of mounted volunteers to flank the Indians' left, but it was protected by a deep creek, and they could not circle it. The bulk of the cavalry was ordered to dismount—horses would quickly sink to their bellies in the swamp—and lead the assault with Regulars in support.

That decision to send in less trained troops to bear the first brunt, to sacrifice them if need be to open the way for victory, was one of the hard choices a commander must make. Old Rough and Ready no more hesitated over it than the question of whether it was wise to attack at all, considering the obstacles confronting him. The offensive was his forte, and his duty was to beat the Seminoles wherever they could be brought to battle.

Neither was any hesitation shown by Colonel Richard Gentry and his Missourians, though there may have been bitter glances cast at a Regular officer who was sparing Regular troops at the expense of volunteers. Gentry led his men forward gallantly, rifles held clear of the muck through which they waded or crawled. Saw grass clawed at their legs. Blood reddened the mire even before the whole length of the hammock ahead flashed crimson with spurts of musket fire. The colonel, mortally wounded, was one of the first to fall. An instant later his sergeant major son was severely hit. Ranks wavered as men reeled and toppled face down in the suffocating slime. It would be an army predominantly of volunteers that won Buena Vista for Taylor in the war with Mexico, but this first wave of his at Okeechobee had all it could take soon after Gentry dropped. It broke and ebbed. Survivors floundered back to the rear.

Past still or struggling bodies the Regulars came on steadily, as steadily as men could over such a battleground, taking their losses. Seminoles in the sniper posts in the trees were crack shots and they picked their targets, concentrating on officers and noncoms. Two bullets drilled Lieutenant Colonel Alexander R. Thompson of the 6th Infantry. As he reeled with a mortal wound from a third ball, he called to the ranks behind him: "Keep steady, men. Charge the hammock! Remember the regiment to which you belong." Twenty-one-year-old Second Lieutenant W. H. T. Walker, a West Point graduate of the previous June, thrice severely wounded, would be brevetted a first lieutenant for gallantry in action and live to fight through both the Mexican and Civil Wars.

In the 6th all the officers but one, most of the noncoms, and sixty privates were down. The regiment staggered back but not far. It closed ranks and held its ground, maintaining a heavy fire. On the left the 4th Infantry made better headway. Faced by a less resolute sub-chief, it drove him and his warriors in flight from the hammock. Taylor then threw in his reserves, the fresh 1st Infantry. Before its charge the rest of the line of defenders gave way and ran. By 3 o'clock the field was won.

Okeechobee was the bloodiest battle of the Seminole War. The bodies of twelve Indian and one Negro dead and of nine wounded were found; other casualties had been carried away. The American loss was heavy: twenty-six killed and 112 wounded. At formation that evening there were frequent grim silences when the roll was called.

But the victory no more ended hostilities than had others before it. The Seminoles faded back into their swamps and fought on, and no way to rout them out was found. At the initiative of the Florida legislature thirty-three bloodhounds were bought in Cuba at $151.52 each and imported with five Spanish trainers. While the dogs were said to be wanted more to track down fugitive slaves than Indians, they were successful at neither. The Seminoles made friends with them and taught them to attack white men. Taylor had approved that early predecessor of the K-9 Corps of World War II; though he had not originated it, he took much of the blame in the outcry it caused as a cruel and uncivilized measure.

Old Rough and Ready, brevetted a general for Okeechobee, planned to divide the country into squares and systematically blot them out as Seminole refuges. Given little backing, he asked for relief from the command.

Cavalry was back in the U. S. Army—the first since 1815—and the 2nd Dragoons, frequently fighting dismounted, had been seeing the same hard service in Florida as the foot regiments. Captain Ben Beall and his company rode on a fresh trail of the Seminoles that led into Okefinokee Swamp of the Everglades. The officer tried to push on, but the horses were deeply mired at the first step. They were turned over to horse-holders, and the command plunged on. "The heat soon became so oppressive as almost to impede respiration. It seemed like a spot where the breath of heaven was forbidden to enter, while the rays of the sun poured down, as through a convex glass, upon the aching heads of the party. After following the trail about four miles, on a surface that continually trembled under foot and at last became entirely obliterated, the ground began to give way, the soldiers frequently sinking to the waist in black mud, the stench from which soon became so intolerable as to induce vomiting."

The dragoons were compelled to countermarch, abandoning the pursuit, like many before them. It is not surprising that under such conditions the Army paid an enormous toll in illness. Out of 5000 present for duty during the period from June 1841 through February 1842 sick reports listed 16,000 cases.

As often as the Seminoles fled to the safety of their swamps, they issued from them in sudden, deadly raids on detachments of troops. Even that veteran Indian fighter Colonel Harney had been caught unawares when a large band swept down on his encampment of twenty-five men of the 2nd Dragoons. Sentries were overrun in the first rush. Stripped to his underclothes to sleep that humid night, Harney ran for his life, dove into the nearby river and swam to a fishing boat. A few troopers escaped with him. The rest were slaughted by the Seminoles.

The recessional of generals resumed until General William J. Worth was handed the task. Through the spring and summer of 1841 he methodically eliminated centers of resistance. Although he was able to kill or round up few hostiles, he could and did destroy huts and crops. Facing winter starvation, threatened with the hanging of several captured chiefs, the tribe at last surrendered and submitted to exile and resettlement in the West. By the signing of a final treaty in 1842 a total of about 4000 Seminoles had been deported. Some 150 more were gathered in between 1850 and '59. An unyielding group remained hidden in the Everglades and the Big Cypress where their descendants now live.

For six years Seminole warriors had defied the might of a nation, which sent 30,000 troops in all against them, by virtue of their own stubborn valor and the nature of the ground, along with failures in command by their adversaries. Arrayed against them had been a large part of the U. S. Army, more than half the Marine Corps, and Navy warships and transports. Of the toll they had taken, Regular Army casualties ran to 1466 killed, 215 of them officers. The national war chest was drained of nineteen million dollars.

Florida had been won from the Seminoles at a price almost quadrupling that paid the Spaniards for its cession. As the frontier was pushed westward, the cost would mount on, and the U. S. Army continue to pay a share of it in lives.

XI

Circling Hawk

THE BLACK HAWK WAR, which intervened between the two with the Seminoles, sounded a bugle call that blared on into after years summoning soldiers to greater conflicts. So likewise had other Indian and foreign wars from 1812 onward. Yet none marshaled such a galaxy of leaders for the struggles in Mexico and of 1861-65 as this campaign in the Middle West against the Sac (Sauk) and Fox tribes. Winfield Scott and Zachary Taylor. Joseph E. and Albert Sidney Johnston. That top staff officer, W. H. H. "Perfect" Bliss, W. S. Harney, and Robert Anderson of Sumter. And the future Civil War Presidents of the United States and of the Confederate States of America, Abraham Lincoln and Jefferson Davis.

Of them all only Taylor bore more than a minor part in these brief but bloody combats of the early 1830s in Illinois and Wisconsin. But so strongly would they prove the past prelude that the mantle of the prophet once descended on the then Colonel Taylor. It is recorded that Old Rough and Ready roared at a column of near-mutinous militia, which may have included Captain Abe Lincoln's company: "You are citizen-soldiers and some of you may fill high offices, or even be President some day, but never unless you do your duty. Forward, march!"

The bracketing by the Black Hawk War of Lincoln and Davis (though without personal contact) is one of history's curious footnotes. Davis, the Regular, the West Point graduate who would continue in the Army through gallant action in the war with Mexico and yet in the Civil War fall far short of matching the military leadership of his opposing

Commander-in-Chief, the twenty-three-year-old Illinois lawyer and volunteer of 1832. Lincoln would deprecate his martial career. "In the days of the Black Hawk War," he drawled, "I fought, bled [the blood being drawn by mosquitoes] and came away." The fact remained that he ably handled the headstrong company that had elected him captain, once disciplining a defiant private by offering to fight or wrestle him. When as time-expired militia his men went home. Lincoln stayed on as a scout. His honorable though undistinguished service gave him more than a war record for a political asset—an understanding of soldiers in the field, their wearing marches, hunger, and other hardships, that would stand him in good stead.

Although Black Hawk, war chieftain of the Sacs and the Foxes, would meet defeat, he could have boasted that he had conducted a good training school for American Army commanders.

Black Hawk—gleaming eyes, a great beak of a nose, the crest of his roached scalp lock jutting along his shaven skull—resembled the bird of prey for which he was named. In 1812 he and his fellow tribesmen had fought for Britain and were still known as "The British Band." Those veterans formed the warlike faction whose hostility to Americans Black Hawk rekindled.

The majority of the tribes abided by a treaty of 1804 in which they had ceded vast acreage to the United States in return for annuities aggregating twenty-seven million dollars by the 1830s. They had agreed to move from western Illinois into the prairies west of the Mississippi River and most of them had done so. Black Hawk and his band, however, clung to ancestral domains until settlers with Army support forced them across the river.

Repudiating the treaty, Black Hawk attempted to organize a confederacy on the order of Pontiac's and Tecumseh's and sent an envoy to Canada to ask British help. But even the friendly Winnebagoes, overawed by the Army, fell away as allies, and the day was past when Indians could count upon aid from across the border. Black Hawk, undaunted, went ahead, longing for the hunting grounds and more fertile fields of his old home. Besides, in the case of the Sacs and Foxes, as with other peoples pushed across the Mississippi, their backs were to the wall, and the wall was the formidable Sioux, nemesis of lesser tribes and destined to be the Army's greatest antagonist until the end of the Indian Wars.

So, early in 1832, Black Hawk and several hundred followers recrossed the river and pre-empted former tribal land to raise corn. It was a declaration of war as clear as the defiance he flung at General Gaines in a conference in which he branded that officer a liar and was barely restrained from trying to kill him.

"I am a Sac. I am a warrior and so was my father," the fiery chief proclaimed. "Ask those young men who have followed me to battle, and they will tell you who Black Hawk is. Provoke our people to war, and you will learn who Black Hawk is!"

War Department orders mustered Regular regiments for another Indian campaign. Along the threatened frontier the militia was called out and readily responded. Ranks contained a proportion of seasoned Indian fighters, veterans pensioned with land tracts, as well as other frontiersmen, "whose bodies carried lead placed there by Indian muskets"; settlers "tired of tilling the soil with rifles lashed to the plowbeam and of being constantly called away from the field to awful scenes of carnage, where perhaps neighbors . . . had just been burned at the stake." But there were too many fair-weather soldiers who looked forward to this campaign as a short frolic spiced by a bit of danger, an excursion to be abandoned as soon as their time expired, with some of it allowed for the march home. Most of their commanders were as green as they. Nor could they be prevented from rushing into battle before undergoing the training Wayne, Harrison, and Jackson had insisted upon, and that fatal shortcoming would be the death of scores of them.

A large contingent of Illinois militia, estimated at 1800 and many of them mounted, turned out. Some 600 of them joined the force of 400 Regulars of the 6th and 1st Infantry that Brigadier General Henry Atkinson, with Colonel Taylor as second in command, led toward Black Hawk's village on the Rock River in May 1832. Atkinson, rated an able officer though slow and overcautious, failed to keep the militiamen under control. They galloped ahead, riding their horses into the ground. When three warriors appeared under a flag of truce, the Illinois men, ignoring such a nicety in the case of Indians, fired on them and killed one. Then under Major Isaiah Stillman they charged whooping and blundered straight into an ambush. Black Hawk and his braves, though outnumbered five to one, swooped down on the milling rabble. A panic-stricken flight, leaving dead and wounded behind—it was dubbed "Stillman's Run"—gave Atkinson no choice but retreat. Victorious tribesmen ravaged the frontier settlements.

Furious indignation erupted in the newspapers, and the government mustered the might of the U. S. Army to wing Black Hawk, his few hundred warriors, and such allies from the trans-Mississippi and other tribes as his success might bring. Troops converged from the East, the South, and the Great Lakes forts to form a force under the over-all command of General Winfield Scott. The swift and efficient transportation of the 4th Artillery from Virginia—1800 miles by water, rail, and marches in eighteen days—set a long-standing record for troop movements.

But a more powerful ally of Black Hawk's than all the red men he might have assembled was the Asiatic cholera. Stricken en route, the artillery regiment lost 30 per cent of its strength. The 2nd Infantry at Detroit also suffered severely. Two hundred dead and many ill was the toll taken of the 1500 troops of the several expeditions. The remnant with which Scott reached the field was too small to be a factor. Worse still, men of Scott's infected command were allowed to mingle, unquarantined, with troops already in the field. Twenty-four-year-old Lieutenant Philip St. George Cooke, a West Point graduate, made grim notes in his journal:

"They came; and soon after their arrival, the terrible disease broke out with new virulence; it was uncontrolled; there was no shield from the danger; . . . to be seriously attacked was certain death; the first forty died to a man. Fort Armstrong was converted into an hospital, whence all that entered were soon borne in carts, and thrown confusedly—just as they died, with or without the usual dress—into trenches, where a working party was in constant attendance; and it is a fact that an officer in charge of it, making an inquiry as to some delay on one occasion, was answered that there was a man who was moving, and they were waiting for him to die. Your messmate at breakfast—

you heard with little concern for *him*—was buried at the going down of the sun."

Pestilence had proved to be the deadliest of the Four Horsemen, as it would until the Second World War.

It was up to Atkinson now, and the knowledge spurred him on. In June, reinforced by another contingent of Regulars and 1000-plus volunteers, he pressed after Black Hawk in forced marches. Some of the militia, terms up, decamped, and others again rode their horses to exhaustion. Enough remained, mounted and dismounted, to pin the Indians against the Wisconsin River near the present city of Madison. At the Battle of Wisconsin Heights, Black Hawk, taking and inflicting losses, fought them off and skillfully managed to extricate most of his warriors with the women and children, escaping across the river.

Atkinson caught up with him at the confluence of the Mississippi and Bad Axe Rivers. This time, the chief realized, he was cornered, retreat over the water all but cut off. For the little steamboat, *Warrior*, ready for action, the muzzle of a 6-pounder peering over her bow, came chugging down on the Indian encampment. Black Hawk showed a flag of truce and asked for a conference ashore. Send a boat out if you want to talk, canny Captain Throckmorton called back. When the chief refused, the skipper gave him time to remove some women and children out of range. Then the cannon belched canister, and muskets spat over the bulwarks. The *Warrior* steamed in closer and anchored, peppered by return fire but suffering only one man wounded. Except when she was compelled to leave for more fuel wood, she fought steadily through the Battle of the Bad Axe, August 1 and 2.

Now Atkinson's army closed in against savage, last-ditch resistance. The Indians, assailed front and rear by musketry from the oncoming ranks and the steamboat's fusillade battled for three hours. Slowly they were forced into the river. On a willow island in the shallows a group made a final, desperate stand. Taylor, Bliss, and Harney led their men wading across in a valiant charge that cleared the island. All the shore flamed with fire, as soldiers picked off swimming Indians, a number of women and children being unwittingly killed. It was Armageddon for the Sacs and the Foxes, with from 150 to 300 slain or drowned, 50 taken prisoner, and not a few of the escapees falling victim to war parties of Sioux. The American loss was 30 dead.

Black Hawk won free for a short time; some say that the Winnebagoes turned him in, some that he surrendered himself. He died on an Iowa reservation in 1838.

Midway in the Second Seminole War occurred other Indian troubles. They involved no fighting but were no less tragic for being almost bloodless. The Cherokee episode brought part of the U. S. Army into the field on a war basis.

From 1721 the Cherokee had been losing ground to the white man, fighting him off when they could, ceding tracts and falling back when they must. By the third decade of the nineteenth century they still held broad lands which covered parts of North Carolina, Tennessee, Georgia, and Alabama. They had developed a remarkable civilization, comparable to that of the Iroquois and in some respects superior. Not only were they capable farmers and house-builders but many, both men and women, had been educated in mission schools and become Christians. By 1827 they were publishing a newspaper.

But gold was discovered within their boundaries and that or lead mines and, later, oil was tantamount to a warrant of death and exile for an Indian tribe. Gold discoveries increased the inroads of settlers, particularly Georgians, into long-craved, fertile acres. The Cherokee, more numerous than the already defeated Creeks, might have taken the warpath and made a fight for their homesteads. They chose instead peaceful protest and appeal for legal rights, carried to Washington by their chiefs. Strongly supported by white friends, they obtained a favorable Supreme Court decision, ignored by Georgia on the ground that Indians were not citizens of the United States nor a foreign nation. President Andrew Jackson intended to settle the question by conquest, if need be as he had with the Creeks and the Seminoles. In vain the cause of the Cherokee was pleaded by Old Hickory's one-time ensign, Sam Houston, adopted son of the tribe. General Worth and other Army sympathizers made equally futile representations. In 1838 the order for the deportation of the Cherokee to Indian Territory (Oklahoma) was given.

General Scott drew the disagreeable mission. He performed it as humanely as possible with Regular troops, and

1. The Death of Jane McCrea
JOHN VANDERLYN
(Courtesy of Wadsworth Atheneum, Hartford)

2. Joseph Brant GEORGE ROMNEY
(From the Collection of the National Gallery of Canada, Ottawa)

3. The Stars and Stripes Flies over Fort Stanwix, Its First Raising against an Enemy EDWARD BUYCK
(Courtesy of the Rome Historical Society)

4. General Herkimer at the Battle of Oriskany FRED C. YOHN
(Courtesy of the Utica Public Library)

7. Battle of Tippecanoe KURZ AND ALLISON PRINT
(From the Collections of the Library of Congress)

The Battle of Pea Ridge KURZ AND ALLISON PRINT
(From the Collections of the Library of Congress)

9. Massacre at Fort Mims ALONZO CHAPPEL
(Courtesy of the Chicago Historical Society)

10. Scenes from the Seminole War
(From the Collections of the Library of Congress)

11. Marines Battle the Seminole Indians in the Florida War, 1835-1842
SERGEANT JOHN CLYMER
(Courtesy of the Marine Corps Museum)

12. The Battle of Bad Axe, Sac and Fox War
(From the Collections of the Library of Congress)

13. A Sutler's Tent
(From the Collections of the Library of Congress)

14. Execution of the Minnesota Sioux
(From the Collections of the Library of Congress)

15. Sand Creek Battle
ROBERT LINDNEUX
(Courtesy of the State Historical Society of Colorado)

there were few instances of brutality or other undisciplined action. In one instance a soldier was killed; several Indians involved were tried and executed. For the most part the Cherokee yielded to the inevitable, selling what property they could and suffering the hardships of concentration camps. Then they took the "Trail of Tears," herded emigration through the dry season westward. Like groups of the Seminoles, some slipped out of the roundups and fled to refuge in the high reaches of the Great Smokies. This eastern band of the Cherokee was later enabled to buy land which was consolidated into a reservation of 56,000 acres. There their descendants, numbering some 3200 people, live today, farming and conducting a thriving tourist business in handicrafts and motels and each year staging a historical drama of the tribe in an amphitheater. As for the tribesmen resettled in the West, they were not destined long to enjoy peace bought by exile. Along with the Creeks, Seminoles, and other deported tribes, they would be drawn into the Civil War, some fighting for the Union, others for the Confederacy.

The frontier had leaped the Mississippi and was being thrust steadily westward. One by one the tribes had given way. Others beyond would stand and fight when their lands were invaded. After the defeat and banishment of the Seminoles half a century of Indian Wars still lay ahead. As Charles Wesley points out in *Guarding the Frontier:*

"The United States, through its instrument, the Army, was in the paradoxical position of opposing and protecting the Indians, of taking their land from them and of guaranteeing their possession of the land. The military alone could not solve so complex a problem."

Nor was solution the province of soldiers of the U. S. Army. "Theirs not to reason why" but to obey orders.

XII

Frontier Army

ALONG THE FRONTIER guarded against the Indians in the 1830s and '40s the Army wrought a chain of forts, as it always had done since its westward march began. Behind lay the rusted links of lines of old strongholds, ruins or relics, landmarks in history. Forts Pitt, Stanwix, Defiance, Deliverance, Necessity, and the rest. More of the forts of this chain would survive into the twentieth century as Army posts, but most of them would be swallowed by the cities and towns of Iowa, Nebraska, and Kansas they founded.

The forts thrust like spearheads into the lands of the Comanches, Kiowas, and Pawnees. They pierced the prairies between the Arkansas and Platte Rivers where rode the Cheyennes and the Arapahoes and lanced into the country north of the Platte where the fiercely warlike Sioux held sway. Warily the tribes watched them rise, knowing them for what they were: bastions standing sentinel over the path of conquest.

Safeguards of peace—so the forts were called. Yet the chain was long and tenuous, extending across a frontier of more than 6000 miles. And the peace could not be kept—not with emigrant wagon trains streaming through, deep into the red man's hunting grounds, and the violations of treaties by fur trappers, gold and lead miners, lawless traders, whiskey sellers, and squatters.

It was a little Army that guarded the frontier, a few thousand troops spread over the vast borderlands, usually in small, scattered units. All manner of men filled its thin ranks. Seasoned soldiers who knew and desired no other career. Adventurous youths. Increasingly in succeeding years, European immigrants mostly Irish and German. Men who had failed in business or farming. Derelicts and drunkards.

Recruits signed up, lured by the payment of a bounty with which some of them decamped at the first opportunity.

"Enlist today, desert tomorrow" was the slogan of the bounty jumpers who in an eight-year period bilked the government of half a million dollars. Hard times with widespread unemployment, such as occurred in 1837, proved far superior as recruiting agents. They opened a steady flow of men into the Army, sought as a last resort, as salvation from destitution and skid row. Better the perils and rigors of frontier soldiering at pay that made the words of a later bugle march, "You Can't Get Rich," ring all too true. Privates were paid $5 a month, brought up to $15 by the value of allowances.

Such was the Army that fought the Indian Wars and built the frontier forts—Leavenworth, Snelling, Laramie and others, named often for officers now half forgotten. Faded, too, in the national memory is the record of the extraordinary contribution of those Army outposts to the development of the civilization of the West.

Garrisons raised crops of wheat which settlers had believed would not grow on the prairies. To construct the forts the Army built and operated sawmills, originating the western lumbering industry. It laid out military roads, foundations of the great network of highways to come, and launched the first steamboats on western waterways. For its beef ration the Army brought cattle herds to the plains, pioneering another great industry. The Army made possible the chronicling of the West by writers and artists such as Francis Parkman, George Catlin, and Frederic Remington, and its own personnel, from Lewis and Clark onward, added notably to those annals. Under its aegis both military and civilian scientists, ranging from geologists to ornithologists, recorded invaluable data.

There was no civilian help, or, had it been available, any money appropriated to hire it. No wonder that Fatigue Call sounded often. Garrisons were able to put a remarkable variety of skills into manifold tasks. A draft of 203 recruits, reporting to Fort Gibson, Arkansas, in 1837, included blacksmiths, carpenters, clerks, mill hands, farmers, hatters, machinists, harness makers, masons, tailors, wheelwrights, bookbinders, bakers, druggists, gardeners, jewelers, printers, and teachers, along with four re-enlisting soldiers and five sailors.

Troops, called upon to perform all manner of labor "in addition to their other duties," sometimes bitterly complained. Though it was not peacetime, their swords were being beaten into plowshares. The second line of the previously mentioned bugle march would have then been a travesty.

You're in the Army now.
You're not behind the plow.

A member of the interminable fatigue details delivered himself in his diary of a hearty soldier's gripe.

"I am deceived; I enlisted for a soldier; I enlisted because I preferred military duty to hard work; I never was given to understand that the implements of agriculture and the mechanic's tools were to be placed in my hands before I had ever received a musket or drawn a uniform coat. I never was told that I would be called on to make roads, build bridges, quarry stone, burn brick and lime, carry the hod, cut wood, hew lumber, construct it into rafts and float it to the garrisons to make shingles, saw plank, build mills, maul rails, drive teams, make hay, herd cattle, build stables, construct barracks, hospitals, etc., etc., which take more time for their completion than the period of my enlistment."

Reveille at sunrise commenced the soldier's day, never fuller in after years. Followed policing of quarters for inspection and stables if there were cavalry or artillery on the post. Sick Call at 7:30, morning mess at 8. Cleaning of arms and equipment. Dress parade at 9—raising the colors to field or band music—passing in review. Guard mount and hours of drill and fatigue. Retreat and lowering the colors at sunset. An interlude of the only leisure the soldier knew, except at mess calls, until 9 o'clock roll call and Tattoo. "Lights Out," predecessor of "Taps" (composed in the Civil War), was blown half an hour later, and the troops were free to enjoy "bunk fatigue" unless Fire Call or the Long Roll or the Call to Arms turned them out.

As inexorable as duty were penalties for its neglect or for commission of the military crimes of desertion, cowardice, mutiny, habitual drunkenness, or stealing. Milder sentences were such as walking post all day for a week, shouldering a heavy bag of roundshot or log. As many as a dozen culprits were sometimes to be seen wearily standing long hours in stocks beside a post's parade ground, heads and hands locked in the apertures. A water cure was given one bibulous soldier: fifteen-minute immersions in a winter-icy river before morning mess for ten days. One cavalryman who lost his carbine was made to dismount and trudge twenty-three miles, leading his horse.

Punishments rising from severe to brutal prevailed in the Army of the time. On one expedition three dragoons had soaked themselves so thoroughly in rotgut liquor that they rolled out of their saddles. They were doused in cold water and tied to the backs of wagons by ropes around their chests. When they fell and were dragged, they were helped back to their feet and hauled on. One, inert, was heaved on to the feedbox at a wagon's rear. He and the others were dead in twelve hours as a result, a court of inquiry determined, of the poisonous whiskey they had drunk. On occasion deserters were branded by a hot iron with a "D" on one cheek. Floggings, with salt rubbed into the bloody welts afterward, were fairly frequent. A drummer or a bugler was detailed to wield the whip, as musicians customarily were. One drummer recalled in his journal the lashing of a drunken soldier who had struck an officer. When the culprit, stripped to the waist, had been bound to stacked muskets, "the signal was given, and with an instrument called familiarly a cat-o'-nine-tails, fifty successive lashes were laid upon the back of the wretched victim. The first six or eight, although applied with force enough to make the blood flow copiously from the lacerated wounds, brought no sign of flinching, but as the subsequent successive strokes fell upon the wounded flesh, groans, and at length piercing shrieks rent the air, and before the last blow had fallen, the unhappy man had sunk into a swoon."

In extenuation of the brutality of punishment it was maintained that an iron hand was needed to control hard men. And undeniably in the Indian country discipline was the difference between life and death.

Soldiers who got drunk and riotous with such consequences, soldiers who could hold their liquor, some who were teetotalers—the frontier army contained them all. Not only were the Indian Wars fought with the aid, comfort, and detriment of *spiritus frumenti*, like all wars in history, but for part of their duration it was GI—Government Issue. A daily ration of one gill of whiskey per man amounted for the year 1830 to 72,537 gallons at a cost of

$22,132. No soldier could manage intoxication on that allowance unless he saved it up, but it was readily augmented by purchases from sutlers and peddlers.

General Winfield Scott had issued an order "that every soldier or ranger who shall be found drunk or sensibly intoxicated . . . be compelled, as soon as his strength will permit, to dig a grave at a suitable burying place large enough for his own reception, as such graves cannot fail soon to be wanted for the drunken man himself or some drunken companion. This order is given as well to serve as a punishment for drunkenness, as to spare good and temperate men the labor of digging graves for worthless companions." Often enough the order failed as an object lesson and became just another pick-and-shovel fatigue. As firewater had proved the ruination of Indian tribes since the white man first proffered it, so over-indulgence caused the downfall of many a good soldier. Whiskey sellers camped close to the posts until their huts were burned and they were beaten and driven off by provost guards. Such control measures helped save the soldier from himself, as did the establishment at a later period of the army canteen or soldiers' club, where only beer was sold.

Monotony and the need of some sort of relaxation, despondency or a craving, made an institution of the monthly pay-day spree. A provident commander put every teetotaler in the garrison on the guard roster for that day to make certain of enough sober men for the post's security and to handle the situation. The sodden were thrown in the guardhouse to sleep it off which most of them did to return shakily to duty next morning; others, if they had any money left, bought and swilled more liquor to drown "the horrors."

Gradually came some amelioration of the Spartan conditions of garrison life. Bunks were built into barracks where soldiers had slept on the floor, wrapped in their blankets. Base pay rose to $8 a month. Medical care and sanitation improved, hospitals were built. The high mortality record of malarious Fort Gibson on the Arkansas River was lowered. Deaths from disease of six officers and 293 enlisted men in two years had branded it "The Graveyard of the Army." Jolting wagons, endured by the wounded and sick on a campaign, were finally replaced by ambulances.

Fort Leavenworth, on the west bank of the Missouri

River in the future state of Kansas, rose from the primitive to become a frontier post showplace, "the acknowledged Eden of the beautiful West." Even in its earlier days it was praised as an attractive cantonment by George Catlin, the artist and writer, when he made it a base for his investigations of North American Indians. The fort was then garrisoned "by six or seven companies of infantry, and ten or fifteen officers; several of whom have their wives and daughters with them, forming a very pleasant little community, who are almost continually together in social enjoyment of the peculiar amusements and pleasures of this wild country. Of these pastimes they have many, such as riding on horseback or in carriages over the beautiful green fields of the prairie, picking strawberries and wild plums—deer chasing—grouse shooting—horse-racing." Later shade trees towered higher around its parade ground, flanked by officers' quarters and colonnaded barracks with porches. On another side stood twelve whitewashed stables, ample for the mounts of six companies of dragoons. However, rations sometimes failed to live up to the fort's appearance. Christmas dinner there in 1849 marked the occasion with no more sumptuous fare than boiled pork, bread, and coffee. Considerably better had been done for the garrison of Fort Towson on the Red River at a celebration of the Fourth of July, 1838. A veritable banquet was served, replete with cheers for patriotic toasts, each followed by suitable music; "The Washington Grand March," "Yankee Doodle," "Blue Bonnets Over the Border," and "Towson's Grand March." Other selections were "Soldiers Gratitude," surely welcomed as highly appropriate, and "Home, Sweet Home," which must have caused many a gulp and moisture in corners of eyes.

The number of churches and chapels increased from the very few of early days where officers, traveling preachers, or missionaries to the Indians had conducted services. The Corps of Chaplains, abolished after the War of 1812, was not revived until 1838.

Schools were established and libraries whose shelves slowly filled with such titles as *Robinson Crusoe* and a biography of General Francis Marion, "the Swamp Fox" of the Revolution. There was card-playing and finally garrison theaters. Fort Towson's theater, built in 1839 to relieve the tedium of garrison life, staged a soldier-author's original play, *The Warrior*, "including fine songs." Soldiers also wrote and produced there a blackface minstrel show, *Gumbo Chaff*.

Music enlivened many an evening, from scratch sessions of fiddles, banjos, and clarinets, punctuated by bugle blasts, to band concerts. By the 1840s the 6th Infantry boasted a good band of fifteen musicians. Dances were staged, ranging from hops and cotillions for officers to the lively jigs, reels, and quadrilles enlisted men enjoyed whenever the washer-women of Soapsuds Row or the girls of a nearby settlement were available as partners.

Women were rated fifth among the good things of life by the Indian, according to Lieutenant G. P. Kingsbury's journal. They were preceded in the order named by whiskey, tobacco, guns, and horses, with the law of scarcity and abundance apparent. For the frontier Army, affairs with Indian women often meant trouble, though there were occasional romances like that of the Fort Snelling lieutenant who fought a duel with a brother officer over his Sioux sweetheart whom he later married. At Fort Gibson there were frequent marriages of the military and of settlers with attractive maidens of the nearby Cherokee reservation. Many present families in that vicinity, now part of Oklahoma, are descended from those unions.

The white women of a post were officers' families or the laundresses of Soapsuds Row, some of them wives of non-coms. While their influence could greatly soften the roughness of garrison life, though they nursed the sick and wounded and helped arrange entertainments, their presence was not always regarded as a blessing by the rank and file. In a change of station by a detachment of the 2nd Dragoons, the party included an officer's lady and her maids whose care moved Chief Bugler William Drown to caustic comments in his reminiscences.

"Ask a soldier," he wrote, "which he would rather have to wait upon, one woman or five horses, and he will tell you *horses* by all odds. I don't believe the ladies know the trouble they are on the march, to a body of troops, or they would stay home, where they ought to be, in time of war at least. They do not consider that a soldier has his own tent to pitch, his horse to care for, and his supper to cook after coming into camp, but think he has nothing to do but wait upon them, bring them wood and water, spreading down carpets in their tents, etc., and it will probably be 10 or 11 o'clock at night before he can lie down to sleep, knowing at the same time that he might be up by 3 in the morning, in order to get breakfast in time to strike tents, shake carpets for the ladies, roll up feather beds (pretty things for the prairie), pack wagons, etc., in order to be in readiness for a start at 5. 'God bless the ladies!' I say, and keep them out of the way of hostile savages; but as long as they travel with troops, they must necessarily be attended to, as they cannot attend to themselves."

The sergeant's sentiments were shared by others of the opinion that "The Girl I Left Behind Me" of the fife tune had not been left behind far enough—she should have stayed back East. Complained one commander, irritated by the late start of march which was the fault of an officer's wife: "Hang all women in camp! If Love (female) wants to mount the warrior's steed, let her wait until the steed is brought home from the war again."

Causes of extra duty indeed, the Army women, but they would not stay home—no more than the womenfolk of the settlers, daring perils of Indian country with their men. When troops marched out of a fort on patrol or campaign, and fifes shrilled that ditty, "The Girl I Left Behind Me," usually the only girl it applied to was the wife of the officer commanding, yet for all the marching ranks she lent chivalry to the lists. The women of Officers Row and their children brightened the isolated little posts and lightened their loneliness.

Passing years saw the establishment of more families on the posts. Young West Pointers married the daughters of senior officers or wed visiting girls. While the former appeared a wiser choice—they had already proved they could take frontier life—maidens from the effete East often devotedly adapted themselves. In 1846 Fort Gibson was graced by a double wedding. The brides, arrayed in muslin gowns and veils, were seated in the post's only carriage, a victoria built for two. Beside it marched the bridegrooms in full dress uniform, making a circuit of the parade ground. The band played them into the chapel with "Haste to the Wedding."

A rough, often unlettered man, the frontier soldier; occasionally a gentleman and a scholar who could match the knowledge and culture of any West Pointer or other educated wearer of shoulderstraps. Serving his country for a pittance of pay, hazard, it has been well said, is all he had in plenty. The fierce elation of battle stirred him, and the thrill of the drums and the trumpets and the flag fluttering at the garrison staff. Often enough they led him to the end of "the path of glory," an unmarked grave on the prairie or burial beneath a wooden slab in the post cemetery. His requiem was the mournful strains of "Roslin Castle," shrilled by the fifes, beaten by muffled drums, or the solemn notes of the "Dead March," sounded by the band. Three farewell volleys, fired by his comrades wrote his epitaph. If he survived and served out his term of enlistment he might retire on a small pension and find a Western homestead or a billet in a soldiers' home. On discharge he frequently re-enlisted on the spot or after a disillusioning interval of civilian life where the old soldier often went unwelcomed. He turned back to "re-up" and form again, to paraphrase Kipling's "Tommy," the thin blue line of heroes.

Hazard and duty—to lead or to follow where they called. These the frontier soldier—officer, noncom, or private—knew. His was the creed so eloquently expressed by Paul Horgan in *A Distant Trumpet* when a young officer declared all his Army career had given him.

"Well, I reckon, nothing but war, sir. Battle. Working to get men to do what they're told, I guess that's pretty much of life. And death. Know death, for I've seen enough of it. And then duty. I know that too. And I suppose that's all I know, sir."

The epilogue is spoken in the same book by a general when he discovers the body of a sergeant. Chased by Apaches, the sergeant had fallen into a deep, inescapable desert pit and before he died written a warning of the place of ambush for comrades who might find him. "Yes, duty" —the general muses—"there's this about it. It never ends."

For the frontier soldier it never did, as long as he served.

XIII

Horse, Foot, and Dragoons

AGAIN THE HORSE SOLDIER rode onto the stage of the Indian Wars. Prairie and desert gave him scope, freedom of operation he had not known in the wooded country to the east. And he was imperatively needed to confront the Plains tribes, superb horsemen mounted on descendants of steeds the Spanish Conquistadores had brought to the New World more than three centuries before.

Officers and troopers, Riding master and master of the sword. Trumpeter, blacksmith, farrier, and saddler. They emerged from a limbo into which the very name of dragoon had vanished not long after muster-out of the dashing regiments of the Revolution. The cavalry arm had only been kept in existence by units of irregular horse with a battle record ranging from fair to miserable. Not until 1833 did Congress, convinced of the necessity of regular mounted troops in the West, authorize the establishment of the 1st U. S. Dragoons, to be followed by the 2nd and 3rd. "The need had become obvious enough to overcome the demands of economy." Even so, Congressional penny-pinching dismounted the 2nd Dragoons for a time in 1842 and relegated them to riflemen.

Heard again was the old term: horse, foot, and dragoons, signifying a force of cavalry, infantry, and soldiers trained to fight both on horseback and afoot, tactics practiced by dragoons in the West and their successors in the Civil War when they were designated cavalry. So close to oblivion had the mounted service come that it had to be reconstituted from infantrymen. Before becoming a dragoon, Lieutenant Philip St. George Cooke, 6th Infantry, had only once fought on horseback; his commanding officer gave him permission to ride because an upset tin of scalding coffee had injured one foot so painfully he could not walk. The ex-infantrymen stood to horse willingly. Soon some of them were maintaining that they had long considered it beneath their dignity to go into battle on foot.

Troopers were enlisted on the assurance that dragoons were the elite of the Army and must count it a disgrace even to speak to a mere infantryman. Overzealous recruiting officers (who should have been court-martialed) promised them the status of West Pointers, with no such annoying inconvenience as fatigue duty. In consequence, when a new draft was ordered to build stables, more than a hundred of the disillusioned deserted. Horse shortages forced some of the cavaliers into unwelcome footslogging after all. On one change of station, two out of five companies of dragoons were compelled to resort to shanks' mare. However, their hard lot was lightened somewhat by rearward glances at the guardhouse prisoners also trudging along in the dust and each dragging a ball and chain. As for the infantry, they took in their stride both the lofty attitude of the dragoons and of the Indians, who called them "walk-a-heaps" and scorned them for plodding on foot like squaws. The fact remained that red horsemen dreaded steady infantry volleys more than a cavalry charge.

Smart in his uniform, the dragoon quickly acquired the cavalryman's swagger. He twirled the sweeping mustache which for a period only his arm of the service was allowed to cultivate. He wore a blue jacket, pantaloons of lighter blue or white, and a flared forage cap with an orange band, a hue that would eventually change to cavalry yellow. Full dress called for a tall cap topped by a horsehair plume and sometimes for white gloves instead of gantlets, a refinement that drew snorts from old-timers. As a colonel observed, "Something soldierly and colorful was needed to impress the Indians," and the dragoon filled the bill. Horses were matched in color to heighten a regiment's or battalion's appearance; one company rode blacks, others grays, bays, chestnuts, and roans. By tradition and in order to be quickly spotted in the field by a commander, trumpeters were mounted on grays or creams, as were bands.

"Boots and Saddles" brought the dragoon companies hurrying from barracks, carbines slung, Harpers Ferry pistols holstered, heavy spurs clanking on the steps. They made a handsome spectacle when they mounted and marched. The long column of twos wound across the prairie, followed by mule-drawn wagons laden with ammunition, rations, and equipment, and perhaps by one or a pair of brass howitzers. "Wagons that shoot," the Indians called the cannon and kept as clear of them as they could. The mobile dragoon column with its own artillery and supply train was the ancestor of the modern armored force. Where water, grazing, and wood were available, camp was made, sentries posted, animals herded, and vehicles parked in an orderly manner. Tents were pitched in straight lines, and even the cook fires were dressed to the right.

They ranged far and wide, the U. S. Dragoons and Infantry, on explorations, expeditions against hostile bands of Indians, or as escort for emigrant wagon trains. That last detail provided trials and troubles but offered some compensation. At evening camps the dragoons could strut under the admiring gaze of settlers' pretty daughters. One of them donned her finery for the occasion and paraded in the latest fashion with a bustle, in the military phrase that may well have been voiced by some troopers, bringing up the rear.

One of the most remarkable reconnaissances since Lewis and Clark was made as a private though semiofficial venture by Captain Benjamin L. E. Bonneville with 107 volunteers from the 7th Infantry. The letter in which Major General Alexander Macomb granted him permission and leave of absence is well worth quotation as illustrating the Army's thorough method of accumulating information of military and other value. Bonneville was directed to explore the country to the Rocky Mountains and beyond "with a view to ascertaining the nature and character of the several tribes of Indians inhabiting those regions and also the quality of the soil, the productions, the minerals, the natural history, the climate, the geography and topography . . .

"It is desirable," the general continued, "that you note particularly the number of warriors that may be in each tribe or nation that you meet with; their alliances with other tribes and their relative position as to a state of peace or war . . . their manner of making war; their mode of subsisting themselves during a state of war, and a state of peace; their arms, and the effect of them; whether they act on foot or on horseback; detailing the discipline and manoeuvers of the war parties; the power of their horses, size and general description; in short, every information which you may conceive would be useful to the government."

Bonneville's private objective was to develop the fur trade, and he and his party dressed and acted as trappers, not soldiers. Setting out in May 1832, he was absent for three years, overstaying his leave and finally being dropped from Army rolls as dead. He returned with his mission fully accomplished. He had visited the Blackfoot, Crow, Nez Percé, Bannock, and Shoshone tribes and made friends with leaders of the mountain men. Thomas Fitzpatrick, William L. and Milton Sublette, and Jim Bridger, who would serve the Army well as scouts. Washington Irving based a book on his journals, *The Adventures of Captain Bonneville, U.S.A., in the Rocky Mountains and Far West.*

Ten years later Second Lieutenant John C. Frémont, of the Topographical Engineers, won his name as "the Pathfinder" by exploring and mapping the Platte River territory for the benefit of emigrants moving over the Oregon Trail. Next year, in search of an easier route to the Pacific Coast, he crossed the Rockies to the mouth of the Columbia River and thence south to Sacramento; on his return after two years he had traversed more than 10,000 miles.

Most of the senior officers were veterans of 1812 and of subsequent Indian campaigns who would carry on through the war with Mexico; their juniors would fight in the Civil War. Among the latter, besides Frémont, were Edwin V. ("Bull") Sumner and Philip St. George Cooke. Frémont's genius was for exploration and not military; his Civil War record was undistinguished. Sumner and Cooke, far better soldiers, won corps and division command, respectively, on the strength of their long Western service, but neither met with marked success. Years of Indian campaigning had robbed them of the flexibility to adapt themselves to the differing tactics and large-scale operations of the great conflict of the 1860s, as younger officers were able to do. "The Graveyard of Old Army reputations"—so the Civil War has been termed—and in it rested unpeacefully the erstwhile fame of commanders who "knew everything about handling fifty dragoons and nothing about handling fifty thousand men."

A still older group, colonels when Cooke and Sumner were subalterns, included such stalwarts as Henry Dodge and Stephen Watts Kearny. Colonel Dodge, highly respected both by his own troops and the Indians, led his mounted riflemen on an expedition to the Pawnee villages on the upper waters of the Red River in 1834 and on another into the Colorado Rockies the following year. A real frontier soldier, Dodge, his men conceded—"very fond of talking over his own exploits," but they were all he said they were. Stern Colonel Kearny, strictest of disciplinarians, belonged to that line of hard-bitten commanders, alernately hated and admired by all ranks, a leader who asked the seemingly impossible of troops— and got it. At the head of five companies of cavalry, assigned to protect overland routes, he rode out of Fort Leavenworth in May 1845, and returned ninety-nine days later with 2200 miles behind him. As a general in the Mexican War, Kearny would lead the Army of the West on a grueling, 900 mile march to capture Santa Fe without a shot and on to the conquest of California.

The remarkable record of mileage covered is underscored by the perils and hardships encountered. More than a few times buffalo and other game staved off starvation, but the great shaggy herds threatened as well as gave salvation. Repeated platoon volleys were needed to turn aside a stampede about to overrun a column. On one campaign troops might run a gantlet of treacherous weather ranging from stifling heat and dust to cloudbursts and mud that bogged down the pack mules until the struggling beasts died from exhaustion. In the mountains bitter cold and late snowfalls caught them traveling light without tents. Pairs of bunkies slept as close as they could to the campfires, pooling blankets and taking the cavalryman's precaution of putting horse blankets innermost to keep them dry. In the morning they heaved out from under a foot or more of snow, thawed themselves and their half-frozen mounts at the fires, saddled up and rode on.

A patrol, escort, or punitive expedition, could at any moment sight a cloud of warriors galloping down on it. Sometimes a bold front was enough to fend them off. When the odds heavily favored the red men, brisk and desperate fighting ensued. Recruits quickly learned, as veterans had, that they were facing savage cavalry as fine as any in history. Cooke paid tribute to their expert horsemanship.

"The Indians who dashed by the rear—their left flank exposed to a sharp fire-extended themselves along the right side of their horses, hanging by the left foot and arm; this last with a bull's-hide shield attached, passed around the horse's neck, from beneath which they rapidly discharged their arrows—the shield covering the arm, horse's neck, the head, and the right arm below! Excited as they were, they seemed the best of horsemen; and rushed up and down places which few persons in cold blood would think of attempting . . . the fiercest and most formidable pursuing enemy in the world."

It was horsemen against horsemen, with the dragoons often outridden. Saber versus lance. Bullet against arrow more frequently than at a later period, for firearms odds still lay with the soldier. Yet carbine and pistol were somewhat countered by flights of feathered shafts launched at the gallop by red riders, as splendid mounted archers as the ancient Parthians. The outcome of many an encounter hinged on a tactic taken from American history: the action of the riflemen of the Revolution who rode to King's Mountain, tied their horses to trees and, fighting on foot, shattered and routed a British attack.

Dismount. Call up horse-holders, every fourth man, to link and quiet restive animals. Forward as skirmishers. Those orders won more battles with Indians than the ringing command, beloved of cavalry: Draw sabers. Charge! Gradually, the latter echoed less often across the plains as galloping lines swept over ground emptied by elusive foemen. The shock of a charge on an unwary village was effective, or on other rare occasions when the red man could be caught by surprise. Elsewhere the U.S. Dragoons learned that their horses chiefly meant the mobility that brought them around the rear of the enemy, blocking his retreat, while the main body, infantry or cavalry, struck his front.

Young cavalry officers, reporting for frontier duty in the 1850s, were schooled in such tactics, though Jeb Stuart, for one, was seldom able to resist the opportunity of a hell-for-leather charge when he commanded Confederate cavalry. None more thoroughly learned the lesson than Lieutenant John Buford. Eight years later it would pay off when his Union horsemen, fighting on foot—remounting to retreat and form a new line—dismounting to open up again with their Spencer repeaters—held for vital hours on the first day of Gettysburg against the Gray division of Harry Heth, a comrade of Buford's in Indian campaigns.

Kiowas, Comanches, Pawnees, and Apaches harried the

Sante Fe Trail, for wagon trains of the traders carried rich booty: arms, goods, and money. Besides there were horses, oxen, and beeves to be stolen and white men for the warriors to cut off, count coup on them and take their scalps. In 1828 alone the amount of the Indians' plunder was reckoned at from thirty to forty thousand dollars.

Mexican troops afforded protection at the Trail's terminus but at no great radius from it. Traders' protests at rising losses prompted the U.S. Government to provide military escorts, the first of which, a battalion of the 6th Infantry under Major Bennet Riley, marched from Fort Leavenworth and made rendezvous with the homeward-bound caravan of 1829. There were signs of Indians in the vicinity when the escort and train camped in the sand hills near the Arkansas River but, regardless, four time-expired soldiers demanded their discharges on the spot. Since they could not be dissuaded, they were given their muskets and some rations and departed. The three who soon rejoined the column, leaving the arrow-riddled body of their comrade, were lucky to be alive. Only the timely arrival of a hunting party had saved them.

Having drawn blood, the Indians closed in. Some four hundred yelping braves swooped down on the cattle herd, jumped and drove back its small guard. Riley's men rushed to rescue the animals, both the train's transportation and its sustenance; all had been on half-rations for some time. Counterattack for the moment beat off the band, which quickly split and drew a whirling circle of racing riders around the camp. In this combat of horse against foot, the infantrymen were unable to come to close quarters. Bullets of long-range volleys rattled off the bull's-hide shields of the enemy, darting in to run off groups of cattle. It was chiefly the column's 6-pounder that saved the bulk of the herd. Manned by Second Lieutenant Joseph D. Searight and a smart crew, the cannon dropped a roundshot into a mass of Indians a mile away. Then Searight loaded with grapeshot and shifted aim to break a gathering charge from another direction. He even made use of ricochet shots, skipping balls along the river surface to scatter warriors on the banks. At length the Indians, carrying their dead and wounded, disappeared over the southern hills.

The battalion, resuming the escort that brought the train safely back, had suffered only one casualty in the sand hills fight. Private Samuel Arrison died from his thirteen wounds and was buried with the honors of war.

Such prairie graves as his marked the path of the Army in the west. Every campaign added to their number, as soldiers met death that came with merciful swiftness or cruelly slow, enduring ordeals of which a fight of the 2nd Dragoons with the Mescalero Apaches gives instance.

In the freezing temperature of the mountains the dragoons had shed overcoats and gantlets for freer action as they rode into battle. After the first shots their hands grew too stiff from cold to reload carbines. They drew sabers and charged, blows by heavy blades killing and routing the enemy. When the fight was over, Trooper Rooney was found to have been wounded by a barbed arrow which had struck him over the right ear and pierced to the skull bone. Since there was no surgeon with the expedition, amateurs did what they could for him. A Mexican vainly tried to pull the arrow out with his teeth. Also futile were efforts of a trader, using a bowie knife to pry the missile loose. Finally a saddler managed with a pair of pliers. Rooney, raving from the torture he had suffered, could not be kept on a horse litter. The column could not halt but must carry on its mission. At last resort the Mexican was paid $50 to take the wounded man to the nearest settlement, ninety-five miles distant. The trooper was slung across his mount's saddle while the Mexican rode beside him and held him on. He was still alive at the end of the dreadful journey but died soon afterward.

Dragoon recruits had discovered they were not to enjoy the promised status of West Pointers, yet many lived and died by the proud motto on the crest of the United States Military Academy: "Duty, Honor, Country."

XIV

The Army Storms A Castle

It was the year 1847 when Lieutenant Colonel Sterling Price with infantry, cavalry, and artillery laid siege to the pueblo of Taos in the province of New Mexico, yet combat seemed to have shifted back to the Middle Ages. The ping of bullets echoed the thud of crossbow bolts, and the impact of shells the crash of stones hurled by catapults or ballistas.

The pueblos, fortress-like dwellings giving their name to the tribe of Indians who inhabited them, rose from three to eight stories in receding tiers above the plains. Though they were built of adobe and not of quarried stone like the towers of the earlier Mayas, now swallowed by the jungles to the south, their walls were thick and stout as those of medieval castles. Their drawbridges were ladders, hoisted to upper story doors at night or on the threat of attack, and there was no other access to these citadels. The two lofty pueblos of Taos jutted upward like bastions at corners of a close, a walled rectangle 250 by 200 yards, into which a stream flowed. The inclosure's walls incorporated storerooms, corrals, and a church dating from the time of the Franciscan missionaries. Projecting angles afforded opportunity for flanking fire on assault that might otherwise have sheltered at their base. Narrow, crennelated windows for bowmen and musketeers pierced the masonry. Such were the strongholds, well guarded and provisioned, which the Pueblo Indians had held for centuries against the inroads of nomadic tribes.

Several times the Pueblos had risen against the Spanish invaders of their land, notably in the bloodily crushed revolt of 1680. The rule of Spain, to be succeeded by that of Mexico, was not riveted on them until 1692, and then Taos was not crushed but submitted. Thereafter the fort-homes had given their people security from raiding Utes and Comanches. It remained for the war between the United

States and Mexico to cause the downfall of Taos and bring the Pueblos under a new yoke.

From the outbreak of the conflict in 1846 Mexicans had made strenuous efforts to stir up the Pueblos against Americans. Instigators made headway when General Stephen W. Kearny and his Army of the West had captured Santa Fe in the first year of the war and marched on to conquer California. Meanwhile detached forces under Colonel Alexander W. Doniphan and others fought to bring all of New Mexico and Arizona under American control. Then the planned Pueblo uprising flared up. Though its plot was betrayed, the warning came too late to save the lives of a number of victims.

Charles Bent, first American Governor of New Mexico, and several other officials were caught in the town of San Fernando de Taos, not far from the pueblo, by the bloody flare-up of the revolt. The Christianized Indians, reverting to savagery, scalped and hacked them to pieces, though Bent's family was spared and rescued by a Mexican friend. Rampaging Pueblos raided a mill and killed five of its defenders, three managing to escape. Prompt retribution was demanded lest other restive tribes of the Southwest take the warpath, as the Navajos already had done, imperil American gains and divert strength from a deep thrust into Mexico without which the war could not be won.

Three days after the massacres Colonel Price mustered a force of some 400 men at Santa Fe: foot, horse, and four 12-pounder mountain howitzers, later augmented by a 6-pounder. He would have to fight his way to Taos, seventy miles up the Rio Grande, through Mexican irregulars and Indians, reported to outnumber him by three to one.

Price found the enemy, some 800 strong—Indians and Mexicans—waiting for him along the rims of a canyon containing a little town called Canada. They commanded his route and must be dislodged. He ordered the howitzers into action under Lieutenant Alexander B. Dyer, a future Union Chief of Ordnance.

"When the fight opened by a discharge from the artillery," a letter to a Virginia friend written by that young officer relates, "our ammunition and provision wagons were more than a mile in the rear, and this being discovered by the enemy a considerable force went to cut them off, and it became necessary for us to detach largely for their protection.

For an hour and a half my battery was exposed to a heavy fire of small arms from two houses and surrounding walls at 180 to 200 yards distance and during that time I had six men wounded out of a command of twenty and several others shot through the clothes. After the wagons were brought up, a charge was ordered, and in a few minutes we had possession of the houses and three of my guns were established on a neighboring hill; the fourth had been disabled in firing. The enemy were in rapid retreat to the more distant heights.

"By night we had full possession of the town where we took up quarters for the night. The following morning some of the enemy were seen on the distant hills, but they were so shy that it was impossible to get near them, and thus ended the fight. Our loss was two killed and 8 wounded; that of the enemy not less than 36 killed and 50 wounded. We remained two days in the town where we took everything our troops wanted, and from what I saw I should think that the races of chickens and pigs have there become extinct.

"Before leaving Canada we sent to Santa Fe for a 6 Pdr Gun, and an additional supply of ammunition which was brought up by Captain [J. H. K.] Burgwin, 1st Dragoons, who joined up on the 28th. We then destroyed the grain, wood, and residences of the richest and most influential of the leaders [of the revolt]. On the 29th our march was resumed, and when near the approaches of a very strong mountain we learned that the enemy was in wait for us. A halt was called and Capt. Burgwin immediately ordered to march with 180 men and attack. In a short time we distinctly heard rapid volley firing. We were immediately all anxiety and expectation. We soon learned that the enemy was routed with a loss of 15 or 20 killed and more than 50 wounded. Our loss was 1 killed and 1 wounded.

"The next day's march was a fatiguing one, the road being covered with 8 inches of unbroken snow. We camped without tents, water, or forage for the animals."

They pushed forward into the Taos mountains, still breaking road for the wagons and suffering from the intense cold. Lacking tents, men slept wrapped in blankets and finally without even those since they had left them with the outdistanced supply train. There were several deaths from exposure and numerous cases of frostbite. At length they reached the town of San Fernando de Taos, scene of the massacre. Yet the weary column did not delay but marched straight on to the Pueblo.

On February 3, 1847, Pueblo de Taos and its garrison stood beleagured by the Army. "They were face to face: the oldest civilization of the United States and its newest; the one confident in its numbers and its massy walls, the other in its engines of war, its discipline, and its valor."

The actions of the besieged, as well as their defenses, harked back to the medieval times. They yelled jeering defiance from the walls, daring the foe to assault. Barbed tips of arrows, notched on taut bowstrings, protruded from the embrasures. Indeed long-past sieges lived again except that no caldrons of boiling oil and Greek fire stood ready on the ramparts to be poured down on the heads of stormers.

At once the mountain howitzers were unlimbered and bombarded the church walls futilely for two and one-half hours. Only heavy artillery, siege guns, would have served. Thick, spongy adobe absorbed the projectiles of the light pieces like sand bags. Not a single breach was opened. To the taunts of the garrison, Price retreated to the town to thaw out his half-frozen troops and replenish ammunition.

Next morning siege lines were closely drawn around the pueblo, dragoons and mounted riflemen stationed to cut off the escape of fugitives to the mountains. Again artillery fire proved incapable of penetration. Dyer's guns turned to spraying the battlements to cover a charge.

"Our troops reached the church and adjacent walls without losing a man," Dyer wrote, "but immediately a deadly fire was opened on them from the church and neighboring houses. All that our troops could do was to shelter themselves as well as they could beneath the walls. Capt. Burgwin (a noble fellow) and a Lt. of Volunteers [they had climbed over the corral in front of the church and vainly tried to batter in the door] were soon carried off mortally wounded. Five dragoons were dead, and a number of the troops wounded.

"An attempt was made to cut through the walls of the church with axes, but they were so thick and the fire so deadly that it was found to be impracticable. During all this time I kept up a warm fire on the town, running the guns up within good rifle range. The 6 Pdr was soon afterwards ordered up to that part of the church where our troops had charged, and we scattered our grape shot over all the ground fom which we were fired on . . .

"In a short time I was ordered to run the 6 Pdr up within 60 yards of the church and breech the wall. I found that a solid shot would not go through the wall which was more than 3 feet thick, but a part of it having been reduced in thickness with axes, I soon made a breech large enough for five or six men to enter abreast. The roof of the church (a flat one with a heavy covering of earth) was then fired, and I ran the 6 Pdr up within 30 feet of the breech and poured grape shot into the church. Lighted shells were also thrown in which bursted handsomely.

"The order to storm the church was then given. The bursting of a shell within was immediately succeeded by a discharge of grape, and the storming party marched in. We found the smoke and dust so dense that it was impossible to exist in it unless near the opening, and that the enemy had all retired except from the gallery. As we entered, they fled and were shot down by our troops from the neighboring walls."

A gallant assault had carried the castle. Some of its defenders lived to seek temporary safety in the Pueblo itself. Others raced toward the hills where waiting cavalry cut most of them down.

In the morning those who had taken refuge in the pueblos issued forth carrying white flags and crucifixes and begging for mercy. Colonel Price granted it except to leaders of the Bent massacre who were tried and executed. Their last stand at Taos cost the Pueblos 150 killed and many wounded out of the garrison of 650. Army casualties were fifteen killed, forty-seven wounded. For the Pueblo Indians insurrection was forever ended.

The Navajos, too, possessed their stronghold, a natural one—the great chasm called the Canyon de Chelly; situated in the northeast corner of Arizona, just west of the New Mexico line, it is today a national monument. Rivers anciently had hewn it deep and tortuously. Along its sandstone ledges long-vanished tribes, forerunners of the Pueblos, had built cliff dwellings, their wooden beams and whitewashed walls still perfectly preserved in the dry air. Few white men had ventured to approach that awesome defile, and none had explored it. Not until the war with Mexico did troops march against it in the first of a series of campaigns that extended into the Civil War. A U. S. Army officer, who penetrated part of its length in 1858 and emerged with his men unattacked from that place ideal for ambush, breathed a sigh of relief and reported, "No command should ever again enter it."

Yet for all the canyon's formidability the Navajos chose chiefly to use its thirty-mile length for last resort retreat and refuge or a strategical threat to draw enemy scouting parties who usually found it empty. The Navajos, sheep raisers, cattlemen, and farmers, could not live in Chelly's partly barren depths. It was their fields and ranges they must defend.

Warriors wore plumed leather caps, ornamented tunics, blanket mantles, buckskin breeches, and greave-like leggings. Thus accoutered and armed with shield and spear (until they obtained firearms), they strikingly resembled Roman legionnaires. However, their women were no vestal virgins. They were known for their lack of chastity, free love being one of the Navajo women's rights, and venereal disease was prevalent in the tribe. A betrayed husband's only recourse under the law was to strip his erring wife naked before the lodge, a punishment that bothered her little except in cold weather. Great thieves, the Navajos swelled their own extensive herds and flocks by raiding neighbors', red or white. From 1847, when territorial records began to be kept, to 1867 they stood accused of wholesale robberies totaling 3559 horses, 13,473 cattle, and 294,740 sheep. They must assuredly be dealt with in the course of the American conquest of New Mexico and Arizona. Now in a mountain campaign through the snowy Cordilleras and onward the U. S. Army was about to play the role of Hannibal and his Carthaginians opposite the Roman-like Navajos.

Colonel Doniphan of the Army of the West put three columns in the field against them at the approach of the winter of 1846. Heavy clothing was short or not available at all, and forage for animals and fuel for campfires would soon be hard to find, then vanish altogether. Wagons, which could never manage the rough going ahead, must be left behind at depots and with them tents, for pack horses and mules could carry only rations and ammunition. In severity of hardship this minor, laregly forgotten campaign ranks high among those the Army met in the Indian Wars.

Doniphan had to move fast or be blocked by winter. The two columns under his command converged on a rendezvous, there to be joined by the third, led by Major William Gilpin—two companies, 180 men, with sixty-five Mexican and Pueblo Indian allies.

On the first stage of his march, begun in late November, Gilpin covered one hundred miles in six days. Then he thrust into the Cordilleras, eternally snowcapped and now cloaked heavily in drifts that avalanched down from the peaks to fill the passes to a depth of feet and even fathoms. Skirting yawning crevices and huge boulders, soldiers and pack train struggled ahead. Somehow they mustered the strength to pursue Indians, watching from eminences, but those scouts faded away before them. As they descended onto an arid plain, progress eased though only a trifle; the ground was jagged gypsum, devoid of wood or grass, the only water bitter and nauseating. Now they climbed the snowy Tunicha Ridge where slabs of granite and basalt all but barred their steep ascent. Pack animals perished from exhaustion or lost their footing and tumbled headlong over the precipices to crash in abysses hundreds of feet below.

The weather turned freezing cold, fierce winds wrenching at the winding column among the peaks. Hair and beards bristled with icicles. After a night encampment on the desolate summit blanketed men emerged from under mounds of new-fallen snow, "as though they were rising from their graves," and tackled the descent, even more terrible than the climb had proved. Packs slipped forward on the mules and flung them downward, head over heels. Soldiers and animals, plunging into snow-hidden crevasses, were hauled out. At last they reached a sheltered cleft at the mountain's base where water, forage, and fuel for fires revived them. More miles over snow to the rendezvous at Bear Spring lay before them, but they had achieved the perilous passage. The shade of Hannibal must have looked down approvingly on Gilpin's march, made without benefit of elephants.

The other two columns also had accomplished heroic crossings of heights, forging through snow, thirteen inches deep in the valleys and thirty-six in the mountains. When assembled, troops numbered 180, soon reinforced by 150 more, and they were in position to threaten the Navajos' livelihood, their great herds and flocks. At Doniphan's summons the chiefs came in, prepared to make a treaty. "If New Mexico be really in your possession," they said, "and it is the intention of your government to hold it, we will cease our depredations and refrain from future wars upon that people. We have no quarrel with you and do not desire to have any war with so powerful a nation. Let there be peace between us."

The treaty was concluded, but the Navajos broke it and others that followed faster than white men generally did. Further expeditions against them accomplished little. A final reckoning must wait for Colonel Kit Carson's bold campaign in 1864.

The victorious conclusion of the war with Mexico confronted the United States with numerous other tribes, half or wholly hostile and only in a few cases friendly. And the duty to protect a vast area of 1,200,000 square miles of territory, gained by the nation through conquest and purchase, fell to the Army.

In spite of the huge size of the task, inevitable postwar reaction reduced the Army to slightly more than 8000 men. Its ranks were further depleted when wholesale desertions were caused by the California gold rush, a temptation to riches which ill-paid soldiers found hard to resist. Disease took heavy toll—cholera caught while guarding emigrant trains—yellow fever contracted in crossing the Isthmus of Panama where 107 men of the 4th Infantry alone died in 1852. A voyage around the Horn, while freer from sickness, did not lack perils. The near-wreck of a transport cost the 3rd Artillery 300 deaths from drowning and exposure—rank and file and members of their families. Part of the survivors of the regiment's original strength of 600 re-embarked and this time safely covered the sea route. Another detachment marched all the way across the continent to California.

In tardy and meager recognition of the need of troops, Congress raised Army pay by a re-enlistment bonus and allowance for foreign service. Oregon and California counting as such, but the enlistment period was extended to five years.

It was a more than decimated Army (less troops retained to garrison forts and posts in the East) that remained to fight the Indian Wars. Gradually it was recruited back up to strength or somewhat short of it, great care being taken never to exceed the authorized limit. Spread thin, in the Southwest it faced the Navajos, Yumas, Mojaves, and, increasingly, the deadly Apaches. On the Great Plains and in the Rockies the path of westward expansion was blocked by some 250,000 Indians, among them the Comanches, Kiowas, Cheyennes, Arapahoes, and, most formidable of all, the Sioux. Lesser but still dangerous tribes of the remote Northwest and the Pacific coast took the warpath. The Army, its hands more than full with the red men, must also mount guard over the Mormons, harried out of the East by persecution and seeking to establish an independent state in Utah.

As inadequately armed as it was undermanned, the Army was belatedly provided with better equipment. Smoothbore muskets (the old long rifle with its slow rate of fire had never been standard) had been adapted for percussion caps instead of flints. Now their barrels, caliber .69, were relined and rifled. They fired a hollow base, conical bullet perfected by the French officer, Captain Claude Minié. Adopted by the Army in 1855, it had begun to count in the Indian Wars before it became famous as the "minnie ball" of the Civil War. In the nine steps of loading and firing, a soldier bit open the paper cartridge, poured the powder down the barrel, rammed in the paper to seat the charge, and then rammed the bullet home. He next put the cap on its nipple, full-cocked the piece and pressed the trigger. Sparks from the cap fired the powder. The force of the explosion expanded the hollow base of the bullet to fit the rifling, and the bullet left the barrel with considerable accuracy. The rifle's maximum range ran to more than 1000 yards; its effective range from 400 to 600. An expert rifleman could fire three rounds per minute. At last the frontier soldier had a weapon long deserved. With a mounted warrior galloping down on him, he could shoot straight and fast for the first time.

While the breechloading carbine had been invented, the Army was slow in its adoption, and even later, during the Civil War, it was used mainly by mounted troops.

While the Army was better armed—although usually outnumbered—by no means was combat with the Indians always a matter of rifle versus bow and arrow, of saber versus lance or tomahawk. The red men had long managed to supplement primitive weapons with firearms and they supplied themselves increasingly by capture and purchase. As allies they were armed by the Mexicans and subsequently by the Confederates as well as the Federals. Illicit traders had always been as ready to sell them guns as liquor. Emigrants, reduced to sore straits, exchanged for food rifles that might be used to raid their trains a few days later. Another source was sympathetic Mormons, as eager for independence as the tribes. Finally the Indian agents of the United States Government furnished their charges with modern arms "for hunting," though the quarry was as apt to be a trooper as buffalo, elk, or antelope. The post-Civil War soldier with his single-shot breechloader would often be forced to face red enemies armed with Winchester and other repeaters. On the conscience of a hidebound, economizing bureaucracy should have lain the death of many a brave man in blue, sent to fight its wars without the best available arms.

Among the veterans of the Mexican War who stayed on in the service was a New York volunteer, Lieutenant Thomas W. Sweeny, born in County Cork, Ireland. "Fighting Tom" fought Indians with one arm, his left. He had lost his right when infection of the second of two wounds suffered at the Battle of Churubusco, forced its amputation. Nor was he altogether atypical in the Indian Wars where a surprising number of maimed and partly crippled soldiers did full duty—others like him with one arm, with one eye, fingers and toes missing, lamed by rheumatism.

Assigned to the 2nd Infantry, Sweeny pinned his empty sleeve to his tunic and worked his left hand into a kid glove whose story is told by Arthur Woodward as editor of the lieutenant's journal.

"Captain Philip Kearny of the First Dragoons also lost an arm while leading a charge toward the gate of San Antonio Abad, near the end of the fighting at Churubusco. Kearny's loss was the left arm and one day after the fight he was given a parcel of kid gloves as a present.

"'Hang it,' said Kearny, 'my left flipper is gone, and what can I do with a pair of gloves?'

"Remarked a friend, 'Tom Sweeny has lost his right arm. Why not send him the left glove? He could use it.' Accordingly this was done, and when Sweeny returned from the reception and ball, Kearny's gift awaited him."

Sweeny learned to overcome his handicap as did Kearny who rode with reins in teeth, leaving his remaining arm and hand free for pistol or saber. In November 1848, Lieutenant Sweeny's regiment shipped around Cape Horn and took station in southern California at Fort Yuma where the Colorado and Gila rivers meet. The fort was an inferno of heat in an arid land of rattlesnakes, scorpions, and burning thirst, which might catch a command on an extended scout with empty canteens despite care to husband every drop. Once a parched detachment under Sweeny saved itself by scooping out an eight-foot well between rock clefts with the only digging implement on hand—a tin cup.

Subjugation of raiding Yuma tribesmen was one of those inglorious, little campaigns that were often the lot of the Army, an affair of many vicious, minor fights. The Yumas, though somewhat short of firearms, were accomplished archers, using six-foot willow bows, and wielding spears, two-foot war clubs, and long knives. Troops to cope with them, too few in the first place, were depleted by the Gold Rush stampede which dangerously drained every regiment. So many troopers of the 1st Dragoons went "over the hill" that replacements had to be called for from the 2nd Dragoons, short also to the point where it could furnish only a number of privates, farriers, and musicians. Deserters decamped with arms, horses, and all their equipment; most of them got away. Two, overtaken, were desperate enough to kill a lieutenant colonel and wound a sergeant who tried to persuade them to return with a promise of intercession. Eventually they were caught and turned in by the Indians to face a court-martial death penalty for desertion and mutiny.

The Army, taking its losses in dead and wounded, finally fulfilled its mission by such exploits as one of Lieutenant Sweeny's. With twenty-five men he made a swift foray into Lower California, burned villages and wheat fields and forced the surrender of 150 armed warriors, herded back to Fort Yuma.

Sweeny fought in the Sioux campaign of 1855-65. In the Civil War he would lead a Union brigade in the West, to be severely wounded at Wilson's Creek and again at Shiloh but not to leave the service he loved until his retirement in 1869. For him the Mexican and Indian Wars had been training grounds for the great conflict that followed, as they had for soldiers with far more famous names, but none who served more gallantly than "Fighting Tom" Sweeny.

In the Northwest, Phil Kearny, who had shared a pair of gloves with Sweeny, was about to campaign against the Pacific Coast tribes. So were other officers whose names were to loom large in the Civil War: Grant, Hood, Sheridan, Crook, and more.

XV

Reverse of The Medal

A SERVICE MEDAL for the Indian campaigns was finally awarded, though not until most of the veterans entitled to it were long dead. Pendant from a ribbon with alternate stripes of red and black, its obverse shows a mounted warrior above a buffalo skull and arrowheads and the legend, "*Indian Wars.*" On its reverse is a trophy composed of an eagle perched on a cannon, supported by crossed flags, rifles, an Indian shield and lance. (A machete and a kris incongruously were added to allow it also to represent the Philippine campaign.)

Had such a military token been issued during the full length of the Indian Wars, its obverse would have reflected the glamour of combat, often so brightly that it seemed transformed into a decoration for valor. In contrast its dull and tarnished reverse, without devices, could have commemorated the phases of service soldiers have known far better than the thrill of battle: privation and loneliness, frustration and monotony. Never could that side of the medal have been more appropriately worn outward than for the operations against the tribes of the Far Northwest. Most of those campaigns of the 1840s were as remote from glory as they were necessary to conquest.

To the prelude of the Lewis and Clark reconnaissance the

wars along the Pacific Coast were an inevitable sequel in the westward course of empire. The conflict with Mexico had opened the way into northern California. Oregon was organized as a Territory in 1848. Tribes once peaceable—the Nez Percés still remained so for years—turned hostile under the aggressions of settlers. "As the Indians saw their lands being taken without compensation, their treaties unfulfilled, and the men who 'spoke with authority' to them being constantly changed, and unable to carry out their agreements, they lost all confidence in their white friends." Raids and reprisals by red men and white, bloodshed and burnings, completed their span of the continent. Massacres of emigrated families prompted retribution sometimes as blackly treacherous as that to which a captain of volunteers stooped. He invited a group of Modocs to a poisoned feast; when the poison failed to work, he and his men shot down all but a few of their guests.

Again the Army was given the thankless task of subjugating a troubled frontier, and history repeated the result. When the smoke cleared away, the Northwestern Indians had been confined to reservations after being forced to sell the bulk of their lands. While the price looked large in aggregate, it amounted to as low as three cents an acre which for sixteen years afforded each tribesman an annual income of $2.75.

Before the Indians gave in, they made a fight for it, taking toll in deaths and wounds. And among the Army casualties from other causes—from those invisibly inscribed on the reverse of the medal—was the future commander of the armies of the Union, Ulysses S. Grant.

Newly promoted Captain "Sam" Grant was ordered to California's Fort Humboldt, a bleak little post on a hill overlooking the bay of that name. Built to protect settlers, the fort had long outlived its usefulness except as a possible base for expeditions against hostiles. Indians in the vicinity were cowed and beggarly. Grant could find no distraction in fighting. In the Mexican War he had sought it out, though an infantry quartermaster—at Monterrey galloping across a blazing front of musketry, clinging to the far side of his horse Indian-fashion, to carry an urgent call for artillery ammunition—in the storming of Mexico City when he and the crew of a mountain howitzer manhandled the piece up into a belfry and blasted breaches in street barricades. There were no such opportunities at Humboldt. It was one of many small, isolated Army posts, too often, as in this case, under the command of an aging officer who had developed into a martinet.

Grant did all he could to lighten boredom and discouragement by riding, hunting, and planting crops, managing everything himself from plowing to harvesting and at his own expense. The ducks he bagged and his pumpkins, tomatoes, and buckwheat often supplemented tasteless Army rations. For the benefit of officers and enlisted men he stocked the larder of a nearby tavern blessed by an excellent cook, with game and vegetables. But good food could not match liquor as nepenthe. Whiskey was readily available, bottled or a mighty slug of a dipperful for ten cents. Sam Grant was one of its victims, numbered among all ranks. Despairing of action and advancement—infinitely slow promotion bid fair to keep him a captain for most of his days—he too frequently drank more than he could handle. Threatened with a court-martial by his overbearing commanding officer, he resigned his commission and went home to Illinois.

Major Phil Kearny, in spite of having seen some action against the Klamath Indians, also resigned in boredom. Like Grant he returned to the Army in the Civil War, but his brilliant career was cut short by a mortal wound at Chantilly. Another future general, one who stuck it out in the Northwest, was George Crook, fresh from West Point, a friend of Grant's. Lieutenant Crook possessed more resources: not only an interest in hunting but in fauna and flora generally, as well as a developing understanding of and compassion for the Indians he faced as enemies. Those qualities would splendidly manifest themselves in his resettlement of the Apaches after victories over them in campaigns in the 1870s and '80s. Now at Humboldt he was too young and eager to succumb to disillusionment with Army life. Also some Indian outbreaks relieved inaction, and Lieutenant Crook, 4th Infantry, took the field.

His first fight came near being his last. On horseback he pursued an Indian, wounded him with his rifle and finished the savage off with his pistol. Then, well separated from his command and both guns empty, he was suddenly jumped by a big warrior whose arrows flew close past him "with such velocity that they did not appear over a couple of inches long." Crook rode for his life and rejoined his men. He was not so lucky in the next skirmish. An arrow, fortunately not poisoned, pierced his right hip. He jerked out the shaft, but the head remained embedded in his body all his life. Of the fine archery of the Rogue River Indians, Crook wrote in his journal: "These arrows in their hands were no insignificant weapons to contend against. At a distance of sixty yards and even further, they could send an arrow through one's body so that the arrow head would project on the other side, and at this distance they could keep an arrow in the air all the time, whereas we had the old muzzle loading rifle that took so long to reload.

"An arrow wound was worse than a gunshot wound, for the latter as a rule would go through the body, whereas the arrow was so constructed that it had one or more short joints together with the head that were fastened together with a little moistened sinew. When it came in contact with the warm blood of your body, it came apart, so that when the arrow was pulled out, these other parts remained in your body. Then, in addition, these Indians had the reputation of poisoning their arrows . . . The advent of the muzzle loading gun in the hands of the Indians made them less formidable at close range than they were before, but it was the breach loader that has entirely changed the Indian problem, and has made the Indians of today so formidable."

The young lieutenant led daring charges, throwing the enemy off balance and, careful of his dispositions of his men suffered few casualties. A crack shot, Crook's marksmanship often began the breaking of resistance. Such was the early service of an officer whose final record stands unexcelled in all the Indian Wars.

The Spokane, Coeur d'Alene, and Pelouse tribes in eastern Washington Territory were growing restless after having been long at peace with the whites whom they called "Bostons" from that city's trading ships, carriers of West Coast hides for shoes. The Pelouses killed two miners, and an expedition was mounted at Fort Walla Walla to punish them.

Colonel E. J. Steptoe, commanding, marched May 6, 1858, with 157 infantry and dragoons, and a few Nez Percé scouts. That force might have been adequate to cope with one tribe in a short campaign. Even considering that limitation, it was dangerously short of ammunition, only forty rounds per man being provided. Until more was issued, with a larger pack train to carry it, Steptoe should have refused to march, regardless of orders from higher authority. Also most of the troops were armed with the short musketoon, its range little better than a thrown stone. Ten Sharps carbines, revolvers, and the howitzers were the only really effective weapons. The colonel assumed an ill-calculated risk, and it very nearly proved to be a fatal one.

For the approach of a body larger than a scouting party aroused such apprehensions in the Indians that the Pelouses were joined by warriors from the other two tribes, the Spokanes and Coeur d'Alenes, along with a number of Yakimas. Twelve hundred of them closed in on the rear of the blue column and opened fire. Dragoons galloped to hold a hill, beating back the enemy with repeated charges, until the infantry could reach that vantage point. There the howitzers kept the Indians at bay until the cavalry detachments could fight their way back through the horde. No water was available, and canteens were emptying. Steptoe was forced to fight his way through the enemy to the nearest stream. It took him half an hour to cover one bloody mile, so closely beset that his men must battle with swung guns and sabers, and the howitzers constantly unlimber to blast back red waves. Three officers were dead, and numbers reeling and limping from wounds before the troops reached water and formed up, completely surrounded, on a second hill where panicky pack animals were barely restrained from breaking loose and stamping on the fifteen wounded. At nightfall their assailants drew off. No more than three rounds of ammunition remained to each man.

Although to stand and die at first seemed their only choice, it was finally decided to attempt a retreat with a chance of survival for some of them. The dead were buried along with the howitzers, now without teams, and horses were led over the graves to trample and conceal them. With white and gray animals blanketed lest their light color betray, and horseless dragoons mounted on mules, the column moved quietly out through the darkness. By rare good luck the almost defenseless expedition managed to regain Fort Walla Walla, but it had been a near thing.

Failure to avenge so disastrous a defeat would have wrecked the Army's prestige and fed the flames of hostility in all the coastal tribes. In September 1858, Colonel George Wright, an officer not given to taking unnecessary risks, organized an expedition against the Northern Indians. He marched from Fort Walla Walla in August 1858 with two squadrons, 1st Dragoons, an artillery company manning two 12-pound mountain howitzers and two 6-pounders, a battalion of the 3rd Artillery serving an infantry, a battalion of the 9th Infantry, a pack train, and Nez Percé scouts. Not only was the ammunition carried ample but it was extraordinarily effective, since it consisted of the newly issued Minié cartridges for rifled muskets. The forthcoming engagements were early instances of their use in the Indian Wars, and the more accurate and rapid rate of fire they enabled would count heavily. Colonel Wright, proceeding "prudently and cautiously" as he had reported he would, crossed the Snake and Pelouse rivers and found his battleground at the Four Lakes where hills bordered the arena of a broad plain.

Some 500 mounted warriors, mustered in barbaric splendor on a hilltop, whooped and shook plumed lances in defiance. Wright charged them with horse, foot, and guns—swept them from the height. They rallied undaunted on the level ground. From the summit Lieutenant Lawrence Kip, adjutant of the artillery battalion, surveyed the vivid scene spread out before him.

"On the plain below us we saw the enemy. Every spot seemed alive with the wild warriors we had come so far to meet. They were in the pines on the edge of the lakes, in the ravines and the gullies, on the opposite hillsides, and swarming over the plain. They seemed to cover the country for some two miles. Mounted on their fleet, hardy horses, the crowd swayed back and forth, brandishing their weapons, shouting their war cries, and keeping up a song of defiance. Most of them were armed with Hudson Bay muskets, while others had bows and arrows and long lances. They were in all the bravery of their war array, gaudily painted and decorated with their wild trappings. Their plumes fluttered above them while below skins and trinkets of all kinds flaunted in the sunshine. Their horses, too, were arrayed in the most glaring finery. Some were even painted, and with colors to form the greatest contrast, the white being smeared with crimson in fantastic figures, and the dark colored streaked with white clay. Beads and fringes of gaudy colors were hanging from their bridles, while the mane and tail, fluttered as the breeze swept over them, and completed their wild and fantastic appearance.

> " 'By heavens! it was a glorious sight to see
> The gay array of their wild chivalry.' "

As troops advanced to the attack, Kip saw braves, toppled from their ponies by the infantry's fire, caught up and carried off by mounted comrades, and the sun flash on dragoon sabers, rising and falling to cleave skulls. A lieutenant, galloping beside a warrior in a running fight, leveled his pistol for a point-blank shot. It misfired, and there was no time to draw his saber. He leaned over, grappled his adversary and flung him from his mount to the ground where a trooper finished him off. Through the smoke of a grass fire dragoons rode down the rearmost of the fleeing red horsemen. When recall was sounded the roll called, it was found that Colonel Wright had quickly and handily won the battle with not a single man of his command killed or wounded.

Allowing the enemy no surcease, he followed up and struck again at the Battle of Spokane Plain, another rout of the tribes where the bulk of their pony herd was captured. After troopers needing remounts had taken their pick, many more remained than could be handled. "I could not hazard the experiment of moving with such a number of animals (many of them very wild) along with my large train," the colonel declared in his report. "Should a stampede take place, we might not only lose our captured animals, but many of our own. Under those circumstances I determined to kill them . . . I deeply regretted killing these poor creatures."

In all wars—until the day of merciful salvation by the development of motor transport—the hearts of soldiers have been wrenched by the death of horses that so loyally served them. Those hours of deliberate slaughter on the Spokane Plain seemed even harder to bear than destruction in battle. Six hundred and ninety animals were penned in a corral built for the purpose. "Then they were lassoed, one by one, and dragged out and dispatched by a single shot, without waste of ammunition, the colts being knocked on the head. During the night following the camp was continually disturbed by the distressing cries of mares whose young had been thus slain."

Captain E. D. Keyes, 3rd Artillery, watching with the mounted service's affection for horses, set down his sad memory.

"It was a cruel sight to see so many noble beasts shot down. They were all sleek, glossy, and fat, and as I love a horse, I fancied I saw in their beautiful faces an appeal for mercy."

The burning of lodges and storehouses, along with the capture, trial, and hanging of Indians convicted of the killings that brought on the war, broke the power of the Northwestern tribes.

Theaters of warfare opened again to the south. All the formidable tribes of the Sioux, though still disposed to keep peace, were growing restless under the onsweeping, relentless white tide. The spark that kindled a flare of hostility was struck by the action of a single lieutenant, U. S. Army.

Now and again, fortunately seldom, a death-or-glory officer swaggers into the arena of the Indian Wars. The same characteristics mark them all. Audacity that degenerates into rashness. Supreme self-confidence, unshattered till their last moment. Contempt for the foe, based on a victor's laurels or a braggart's ignorance—contempt never deserved by the red warriors they faced. Almost always they met the death they courted. The tragedy lay not in their own frustrated finish but in its penalty: that good soldiers they led died with them.

Such an officer was Second Lieutenant John L. Grattan who in 1854, fresh from West Point, reported for duty at Fort Laramie. All Indians were cowards, he loudly proclaimed. He shook his fist in the faces of those who visited the post and threatened what he would do to them. With ten men, he boasted, he could thrash the whole Cheyenne Nation and with twenty put all of the rest of the Plains tribes to flight.

A minor disturbance that could have been easily settled gave him an opportunity to attempt to clinch his arrogant claims. After a sick cow, abandoned by an emigrant, had been slaughtered by a Sioux for its hide, the owner, who had callously left the animal to die, came to the fort and demanded reimbursement. Promptly a Siouan chief promised to bring in his tribesman and make payment through the Indian agent. But Grattan insisted that he could handle the matter, and the lieutenant commanding Laramie, though well aware of his junior's bombast, incautiously allowed him to take over. Grattan called for volunteers "for dangerous service" and got thirty men with two howitzers. Blustering that he would "conquer or die," he marched on the camps of three bands of Sioux and unlimbered his howitzers.

Chiefs, again pledging payment, vainly parleyed with him for an hour. Then a trigger-happy soldier loosed off a shot. The howitzers boomed. One of the chiefs fell mortally wounded, and the Sioux opened fire. Grattan's forced retreat toward the fort was blocked off by yelling braves. A fierce melee of a few minutes, and every man in blue was killed.

"Massacre," headlined the Eastern newspapers, and the War Department believed them, not the true circumstances as reported by Laramie. In the late summer of 1855 a punitive expedition took the field under Colonel William S. Harney. The benign-looking, graying full beard and mustache, lending that veteran dragoon the aspect of a kindly, military Santa Claus, were belied by his reputation as a grim, implacable fighter. He had never forgotten the humiliation of his flight in underclothes and narrow escape from the Seminoles who jumped his camp in Florida.

From Fort Leavenworth marched Harney's command—six companies of the 6th and 10th Infantry, one of the 4th Artillery acting as infantry, and four companies of dragoons—to Ash Hollow on the North Platte River. There he found a large encampment of Brulé Sioux and demanded the surrender of those guilty of "the Grattan murders." That formality concluded, Harney sent his cavalry widely circling to ambush an Indian retreat, while his infantry advanced to drive the enemy into the trap. The Sioux, scattering in flight, ran into a long blue line of horsemen. Sabers flashed out—an officer shouted, "As foragers, charge!"—the line thundered down. A number of warriors got away through one outlet left open. They left behind them eighty-six dead and five wounded and seventy squaws and children and a large pony herd captured. The troops' loss was five killed, seven wounded. Scalps of two white women found in the camp were reported as added justification for retribution.

Far from conquered, the Sioux continued to be harried

through their hunting grounds. Campaigns against them in the 1850s were too often featured by such galloping, hell-for-leather cavalry charges as Remington later loved to paint. Dismounted tactics in conjunction with infantry and artillery were always more effective. Yet the Army proved its mettle in hard service. In those years it fought twenty-two little wars with the Indians—from Florida to Arizona, from the Missouri River to Oregon. In 1857 alone it engaged in thirty-seven combats and accomplished many other missions, without a fight. The following year every regiment in the West marched an average distance of 1234 miles.

Rash and careless officers and enlisted men, who threw away their lives and those of their comrades, were, as has been emphasized, rarities. So were outright poltroons and malingerers with shoulderstraps or of the rank and file. The Army that fought the Indian war deserved the gallant memory of it. That shining sense of duty which marched with the columns from commander to trooper riding point is eloquently expressed by James Warner Bellah in *A Thunder of Drums.*

"When you are out in front on an approach march, with nothing between you and the enemy, there is an excitation that beggars description. It takes a man's heart in hand and lifts it up mightily. At the same time it puts the somber weight of full responsibility upon him. It makes him the sole custodian of the sovereign dignity of the United States—its farthest western march of empire. All that has gone before him since the first shot at Concord Bridge is now in *his* hands and he must not fail."

XVI

The Blue, The Gray, and The Red

WARS BETWEEN THE UNITED STATES and foreign countries had presented the American Indian with opportunities to win back some of his lost hunting grounds or, at least, for a time, to hold their dwindling remnant. Yet never was so splendid a chance offered as when the nation was divided against itself in a conflict threatening its existence. Hope revived in thousand lodges and mountain refuges. "Perhaps the Great Spirit had brought on the Civil War that his red children might make a successful stand against the white invaders." The spring of 1861 saw the renewal of savage attacks on settlements and mail stations. Uprising tribes raided on their own account or took sides with the Blue or the Gray.

In all the wars in which American Indians have fought, as enemy, ally, or soldier in Army ranks, never were the circumstances as strange as when war whoop mingled with the Rebel yell, and red men in Yankee blue marched singing chants with the martial swing of "John Brown's Body."

The Civil War saw a major battle, Pea Ridge, in which Indian regiments served with the Confederate Army and, "civilized warfare" regardless, scalping knives were unsheathed. Divided tribes, loyal to the Union or in alliance with the seceded states, met in bloody encounters in the Middle West. Two outstanding chiefs emerge to become regularly commissioned brigadier generals, one C.S.A., one U.S.A. In the Far West the Indian turned the Civil War into a two-front one, as he had the Revolution, 1812, and Mexico. On the broad prairies beyond the borders of embattled Kansas and Missouri, Federal forces were faced with an Indian menace whose seriousness has been scanted by historians of the grand panorama of the war. So formidable was the threat to communications, emigrant trains, towns, settlements, and ranches that considerable Union strength had to be diverted from main sectors. Still more reinforcements were demanded and furnished by an extraordinary expedient. Confederate prisoners of war, called "Galvanized Yankees," were released from Northern stockades, uniformed in blue and sent, with the proviso that they would never serve against the South, to fight Indians on the frontier.

From the moment when Fort Sumter was fired on, it was inevitable that tribes settled on lands in Indian Territory and Arkansas be drawn into the conflict. All the Indian's tragic destiny offers no more cruel an example than the fate of the Five Civilized Tribes: the Cherokee, Creeks, Seminoles, Choctaws, and Chickasaws. Conquered and uprooted from their homes in the East, they had made the best of their exile and were living in peace. Now they were compelled to choose sides in this white man's war because they were caught between the contending armies. They were sources of fighting men and of supplies—grain from their fields and half a million head of cattle pastured on their grasslands—and their only option lay in a choice to their best advantage. In the end, notwithstanding the side picked, they would pay a high price for involvement in the war. It amounted for the first three tribes to a heavier loss in percentage of population than that of any state, North or South.

The United States and the Confederate Governments bid for the Indians' support, the latter, odds in manpower and resources against it, offering far the better bargain. The Five Tribes were slaveholders, having brought along Negroes they owned when they were deported from the East. Promptly the Confederacy pledged protection of that and other property rights, with indemnities to be paid if it were not provided. Yet tribal economy was not based on slavery, and the common institution was no close bond with the South. It was the influence of trusted Indian agents, mostly Southern sympathizers, that counted most potently—that completely won over the Choctaws and Chickasaws and strongly affected the other tribes. The Confederacy, as the pressure of need increased, promised through its local representatives rights and privileges for which the Indians had been vainly striving for half a century.

Could such promises be kept? Had tribal majorities picked the winning side? So it seemed when word came of a great

Confederate victory at Manassas in the East, followed by a lesser but more important one to the Indians because it was near at hand and a number of red men serving in Arkansas regiments witnessed the prowess of the Gray at the Battle of Wilson's Creek, Missouri, in August 1861.

The Union, reluctant to bring Indians into the conflict at all, at first asked only neutrality of the tribes. When it came to the point of inducements, the Federal Government offered no more than maintenance of the status quo and could not even make that good. The flow of annuities ceased. Forts were abandoned or surrendered by Blue garrisons. In the emergencies and confusion of the first year of the war and in view of Confederate strength in the territory, probably no effective action was possible at the time. Yet it was dangerous to risk losing the allegiance of the Five Tribes from whose estimated population of 63,000 as many as 10,000 warriors might be mustered.

In spite of the fact that the Five Tribes had been virtually relinquished to the enemy, portions of three of them would lend unexpected support to the Union. Old feuds, originating in the East, still divided both the Creeks and the Cherokee. A schism in the former tribe had given General Andrew Jackson allies to help him subjugate their hostile brethren. Factions formed during the expulsion of the Cherokee from North Carolina, Georgia, and Tennessee persisted and finally split them, like the Creeks, for North and South. Some of the Seminoles were still willing to cast their lot with a nation that had crushed them in two bloody Florida wars. Such internal dissensions and remembered respect for the fighting qualities of the U. S. Army swayed groups that declared for the Union. Yet there was also an undercurrent of loyalty as touching as it is difficult to conceive in peoples not long since conquered and banished from their ancestral homes, a loyalty that would endure through trial and tribulation.

At the outset the able Confederate commissioner, Albert Pike, was apparently successful in carrying all Five Tribes for the South by considerable money subsidies and gifts, including Confederate flags, as well as in rousing the Kiowas and Comanches to attack Union wagon trains to Santa Fe. The Choctaws and the Chickasaws proved ready and steadfast allies, joined by most of the Seminoles despite signs of wavering. A formal vote of secession was passed by the council of the Cherokee Nation in August 1861, and there was then no evidence that it would not continue to bind the whole tribe. The only early opposition was that which was covertly fomented by an aging but energetic sub-chief of the Upper Creeks, Opothleyohola. Some months would pass before old cleavages cracked the red men's solid Gray front, with the Upper Creeks breaking away outright and a Cherokee faction, mostly mixed-bloods under Chief John Ross, swinging back to Union adherence.

So in the long roster of Confederate and Union regiments came to be listed the 1st and 2nd Creek Mounted Rifles, the 1st and 2nd Cherokee, the Seminole Battalion, and others. Hard-drinking Colonel Douglas H. Cooper, C.S.A., led the Choctaws and the Chickasaws. Other commanders were mixed- or full-blood Indians who discarded titles as chiefs for military ones: Colonels Daniel McIntosh, John Drew, and Stand Watie. Lieutenant Colonel Chilly McIntosh, Major John Jumper. Later some of the grades, down to company and platoon command, would be filled by white officers along the organizational lines of Negro regiments. Discipline, though loose, was markedly better than that traditional with Indian bands. Drill consisted of a whooping charge, dismounting, taking cover in timber and firing by squads, then cleaning rifles and awaiting further orders. A Union Indian regiment learned to form fours and march to war chants. For all their limitations in formal warfare, these red men were bred to battle, though most effective when they were used as scouts, raiders, or against each other. Yet on occasions they stood up to and repulsed determined attack by white troops—it often took artillery to break them—and there were instances of gallant rearguard actions, particularly by Stand Watie and his Cherokee regiment.

They were ill-armed by the Union and worse by the Confederacy, plagued by its shortages. Their weapons ranged from rifled muskets to smoothbores and old, almost useless flintlocks, with a number of pistols and revolvers. Not a few tribesmen were reduced to fighting as of yore with bow and arrow and tomahawk. For most of them uniforms were nonexistent or nondescript. Some Union Indians were later issued blue uniforms, either too large or too small (an old Army custom), and high-crowned hats or forage caps; worn perched "on their High Heads of Hair they made rather a

Comecal Ludecrous appearance." The picturesque, copper-skinned horseman in warpaint and feathers survived in the Plains Indians. For mounted riflemen of the Five Tribes martial pageantry was gone with Marlborough and Napoleon.

Eighty-year-old Chief Opothleyohola saw a hostile cordon closing around his loyal Creeks. Faced by a choice between submission or massacre or fighting a way out, he did not hesitate. He marched for Union Kansas in November 1861 with some 4000 of his people—1700 warriors, the rest women and children—carrying the tribal treasury and belongings on wagons and herding cattle. A group of Seminoles and later some Cherokee joined them.

They were not allowed to escape unscathed. Colonel Cooper and a force of 1400 Confederate Indians and Texas cavalry hotly pursued and attacked. Twice the old chief and his warriors fought them off. On a third attempt Cooper's horsemen came charging down on the encampment in a rash gallop over icy ground. Creek rifles toppled riders from their slithering mounts. Battered ranks beat a disorganized retreat. When they warily advanced again next morning, they found the camp empty. Renewed pursuit caught up and brought on another engagement. There the same stout resistance and the fact that Colonel Drew's regiment of secessionist Cherokee refused to fight fellow tribesmen among the Union Indians enabled the fugitives to hold off the enemy for four hours. Cooper gave up and withdrew until he was reinforced by white Colonel James McIntosh with 1380 men including veterans of Wilson's Creek, plus stanch Cherokee under Stand Watie, he who would wear a Confederate brigadier's star.

It was more than the weakening Creeks could withstand. They fled through the snows, their toll of dead rising to 700. Once across the Kansas border, they were safe under the protection of Union arms, but the price of their safety was utter misery. Camped on reservations of alien tribes, mostly from old Northwest Territory, the destitute refugees suffered terribly through the bitter winter of 1861-62 despite the efforts of Federal authorities to provide for them. Failing supplies, inadequate from the start, made it essential that the loyal Creeks be helped to fight their way back to their own lands before another winter set in. But first the territory must be redeemed from domination by the Confederate Army.

The Blue and the Gray and the Red began to converge on Pea Ridge, the high ground overlooking Little Sugar Creek, Arkansas. Below the Southeast point of the ridge stood Elkhorn Tavern for which the Confederates would name the forthcoming battle.

Union General Samuel R. Curtis's Army of the Southwest comprised four divisions: Franz Sigel's two under Prussian-trained Peter J. Osterhaus and Alexander Asboth from Hungary and those of Jefferson C. Davis and E. A. Carr. Artillery and cavalry brought the total to 10,500 men. Odds favored the force of magniloquent General Earl Van Dorn, C.S.A., whose subordinate commanders were Generals Sterling Price and Benjamin McCulloch, veteran of San Jacinto, the Mexican War, and an ex-Texas Ranger. Commissioner Albert Pike, now ranking as a general, was induced to add three of his Indian regiments and a battalion despite his reluctance to use them outside their territory. They raised Confederate strength to nearly 16,000.

The advance of the Indian regiments toward battle furnished an arresting spectacle. At the head of a long, strung-out column of red warriors and Negro freemen or slaves, mounted on ponies or afoot, rolled at the outset of the march an open carriage. In it rode the Cherokee chief, John Ross, in stovepipe hat and frock coat, and beside him, in a startling contrast of dress, General Pike, arrayed as an Indian for propaganda purposes. By some odd quirk he had elected the attire of a Sioux chieftain. Sandy whiskers jutted out from under a full-feathered war bonnet. In his headdress, buckskins, leggings, and beaded moccasins, he presented an appearance as incongruous as that of future Preidents of the United States similarly dressed for tribal adoption. General Cooper led his Chickasaws and Choctaws. Huge, pompous Major John Jumper, an ordained Baptist minister, rode in the van of his Seminoles. The Creeks followed another minister, Colonel Daniel L. McIntosh, whose ringleted locks, mustache, and goatee made him the image of a Southern planter. In his regiment a battalion was commanded by his elder brother, the toothless Lieutenant Colonel Chilly McIntosh. Colonel John Drew's Cherokee showed no more enthusiasm for the fray than they had when they faced the fleeing loyal Creeks; given half a chance, they meant to turn on their fellow tribesmen and desert to the Union side. That they would be unlikely to find any such opportunity could be gathered from the watchful, hostile glances bent on them by the opposing Cherokee faction marching behind grim, squat Stand Watie. During the tribe's expulsion from the East, Watie had very narrowly escaped assassination by Ross's men. He and his tribesmen stood ready to pay off old scores at the first sound of the traditional turkey gobble challenge. Of such was the troubled Cherokee Nation, one of the most remarkable of all the Indian tribes, now a microcosm of the Confederacy —part a wealthy, slave-holding class and part backwoodsmen and small farmers under Watie's leadership.

The Indian contingent, marching to join the Confederate Army before Pea Ridge, would receive no warm welcome from its commander. Although Van Dorn when a U.S. officer had been four times wounded in one battle with Comanches and had served in the Second Seminole War, he somehow remained contemptuous of the red man's fighting qualities. As for the Union attitude, Pike's and Cooper's Indian commands would shortly be dubbed by the Northern press "The Aboriginal Corps of Tomahawkers and Scalpers."

A forced march, fifty-five miles in three days through wet, driving snow, brought the Confederates to the battleground. A wing had swung around the north of Pea Ridge, another wing to the west and southwest. Van Dorn, sick, was exercising command from an ambulance. Rations had dwindled toward the vanishing point and no more were in prospect unless foraged or captured from the enemy. But Van Dorn had reached position for an enveloping attack on the smaller Union Army, assembling south of him, and better still might be able to pinch off part of it before it was concentrated.

Union General Curtis had got there first though not with the most. A good fighting man, Sam Curtis; West Point Class of 1831, veteran of the war with Mexico—coolheaded and a fast thinker in action. He put the divisions of Davis and Carr in line along the bluffs overlooking Sugar Creek, and dirt began to fly as they dug in and emplaced artillery. When the trusted scout, Wild Bill Hickok, the future frontier sheriff, confirmed the approach of the enemy, Curtis sent couriers galloping to call in Sigel's detached divisions before they were cut off.

It was touch-and-go, but by the late morning of March 6, 1862, they all made it except the rearmost units under Sigel himself. Curtis heard guns rumbling as the Gray pinchers clamped on the rearguard. He rushed the newly arrived troops back in countermarch to rescue their comrades.

Franz Sigel was fighting his way through the last ten miles. Despite his military education in Germany, his record as a Civil War general would prove to be far from brilliant. Yet he had the gift of arousing loyalty; his name was enough to recruit regiment after regiment of German-Americans. Poorly led or not, they followed him with the proud boast, "I fights mit Sigel." They lived up to it this day, as the Gray troops attacked. With his cavalry fanned out on flanks and inner layers of infantry, Sigel walled his five guns in the middle of the column and fended off sharpshooters trying to pick off the artillery horses. Doggedly he wedged ahead until the bulk of his division came up and freed him, then took position with them in the Union line.

Confederate bivouac fires flared red against the white snow that night. Pike's Indians, along with some Texas cavalry, took station on the extreme right. Toward morning the Gray lines pulled back, keeping the fires burning to draw the enemy into an envelopment.

Along the front half the Blue regiments moved forward to assault at mid-morning of March 7. It was Osterhaus's command that encountered the Indians. For his German artillerymen it must have been as startling an experience as for the Hessians when they first met Iroquois allies of the Americans in the Revolution.

Osterhaus had advanced west of Round Top when he was suddenly confronted by an outlandish-looking mass of men across a field. He had only time to unlimber a few batteries before he was struck by a wildly whooping charge. The Indians broke his line. For once artillery had failed to shatter the red men's onrush. Cannoneers, panic-stricken, fired only a few wild rounds before the batteries were overrun. Texas cavalry in the van of the charge plunged forward to drive the Federal horse in headlong flight through the ranks of supporting infantry. Stand Watie's Cherokee, dismounted, and Drew's on horseback surged close after them. Elation of victory diverted the minds of Drew's warriors from desertion. "With shouts of laughter they danced around the abandoned 'shooting wagons,' roaring delightedly as they held horse collars around their necks and pranced about with harness chains jingling."

Confederate General Ben McCulloch with the quick draw action of an old Texas Ranger flung his regiments at the Union center. On its right General Carr was hard pressed. He had no Indians to contend with today. That was reserved for later years when as a cavalry leader he would campaign against the Plains tribes through to the end of the Indian Wars. Now the men in gray and butternut brown were all and almost more than he could handle. He had taken the first of three wounds; it was being dressed while he sat his saddle. None of them induced him to leave the field, and he would well earn a brevet for gallantry in action. That stout fighter held the line and sent a call for desperately needed reinforcements for which Osterhaus on the left was also clamoring.

Curtis bolstered them both, but help would have saved neither flank nor the threatened center if they had not clung stubbornly to their ground after recoiling before the shock of the first Confederate assaults.

General Pike was urging his Indians to charge again. They paid no heed, for all control over them was broken as shells from Blue batteries began bursting in their midst. Spurred by their dread of artillery fire, they scattered and took to sniping from trees and behind rocks. Bullets wasted on enemy out of range found some targets when the two Cherokee factions started shooting at each other, Drew's warriors looking for a chance to go over to the Union, Watie's determined to prevent them.

Osterhaus's stanch infantry not only held but charged to recapture the lost guns. Rebel regiments met them head on. But Ben McCulloch, riding with the skirmishers, was killed and soon afterward his second in command, General James McIntosh. Yankee artillery dammed the Confederate flood tide, its impetus spent. The Federals, sweeping back over the regained ground, reported that they found at least eight scalped corpses. Although Confederate authorities scaled the count down to an admission of only three or four instances, the old horror the frontier had felt from early days filled the nation. Some confirmation came later when a Choctaw woman declared that scalps from the field had been mailed to relatives in the tribe. Certainly there was no doubt in the mind of a private of the 5th Illinois who found his brother scalped and next day took nine trophies in retaliation.

Night fell on battered lines, Blue and Gray, still facing each other, not far apart. The toll of dead and wounded was high on both sides, and decision still hung in the balance. Sam Curtis issued orders for a full-scale attack at dawn.

In the battle of March 8 the Indians played little part. Drew's regiment retired and would shortly take off for home. Those who remained were disorganized and irresolute except for Watie's Cherokee and they would fail again to stand under cannonading.

Union troops stormed ridge and tavern with one of those splendid Civil War charges that brighten the pages of history with valor and darken them with tragic sacrifice. Under the thundering guns the Blue ranks rushed forward, flags flying and drums rolling. Other charges in the war would win greater renown but none was more gallantly delivered. It won the field.

The Confederate Army in retreat found one Indian regiment still standing by. Stand Watie kept his warriors in hand and helped cover the withdrawal. For his service that day and on until the end of the war he would richly merit his brigadier's star.

For the Indians Pea Ridge was the pivot of the war, yet fortunes only slowly swung on it. The main armies had still to fight Shiloh and other battles, but their red allies were thenceforth engaged almost entirely in Indian Territory.

In June 1862 a Union force marched south in the first of a series of small campaigns to clear the Territory of Confederate and Indian resistance. It consisted of one Creek and one Cherokee regiment with a strong stiffening of white units; two infantry and three cavalry regiments and two batteries of artillery. Meeting no opposition, it drove through to capture Tahlequah, the Cherokee capital. Drew's warriors at last got their chance to join the Blue; with others they formed the 3rd Cherokee Mounted Rifles, U. S. Army. And the way was now paved for John Ross to bring his Nation back to the Union side which he did the following February.

The undaunted Stand Watie was still to be reckoned with. Subsequently he recaptured Tahlequah and burned Ross's stately home. Leading a determined attempt to invade Kansas, he was turned back only by a full brigade of loyal Indian and Negro regiments. Through the rest of the war his destructive raids vied with those of the Confederate guerrilla, William Clarke Quantrill. General Watie was one of the last Confederate officers to surrender, June 23, 1865.

The previous April at Appomattox a Union Indian Chief had been present at the surrender of the Army of Northern Virginia. This was the altogether remarkable Seneca sachem, Ely Samuel Parker. To further the cause of his people he had studied law, but a Supreme Court decision denied him and other Indians admission to the bar as non-citizens. Turning to civil engineering, he graduated from Rensselaer Polytechnic Institute. On construction work in Galena, Illinois, he formed a friendship with an Army ex-captain named U. S. Grant.

At the outbreak of the war Parker sought to join the Army to which his friend had returned. However, he was curtly refused a commission by Secretary of War Seward. The fight, said the Secretary, must be settled by white men without any Indian aid—a pronouncement destined to be flatly contradicted. Three thousand Indians served in the ranks of the Union Army as sharpshooters, prison guards, and on other duties. The 53rd New York Zouave Regiment was fifty per cent Indian. Parker, finally obtaining a captaincy in the Corps of Engineers, recruited 628 Iroquois volunteers.

At Vicksburg the big, dark-skinned Seneca joined General Grant's staff where he was known as "The Indian." Valued as a competent Engineer, Parker served on with Grant through the Chattanooga campaign and in the Army of the Potomac. In August 1864 he was promoted lieutenant colonel—he would eventually be brevetted a brigadier general, Regular Army—and became Grant's military secretary. As such he wrote many of his chief's orders and letters and he was acting in that capacity at Appomattox when General Lee noticed the swarthy officer in blue transcribing the surrender terms. "After Lee had stared at me for a moment," Parker remembered, "he extended his hand and said, 'I am glad to see one real American here.' I shook his hand and said, 'We are all Americans.' "

Peace saw the Five Civilized Tribes resettled in the ruined homes and farms of their lands. Harder than the lot of the Union Indians was that of the Confederacy's. Along with the South they suffered the rigors of Reconstruction, and they were done with rebellion.

Not so the Plains Indians. From 1861 to 1865 they had been waging fierce warfare of their own with the white man, nor would Appomattox end it.

XVII

"Wagons That Shoot"

FOUR SANTEE SIOUX from the reservation in southwestern Minnesota sauntered into a farmyard on a quiet Sunday, August 17, 1862. Showing no sign of the quarrel in which they had taunted each other with fear of white men, they greeted the farm people and challenged them to a shooting match. When their hosts, firing first, had emptied their guns at the target, the Sioux whirled on them and killed their three competitors and two women.

So began the savage outbreak that cut a 250-mile swath of slaughter and destruction across the state. The shock was the more appalling for its utter unexpectedness. Whites had learned to be wary of the Plains Sioux but not of this seemingly tamed tribe on reservations in settled Minnesota. Numbers were Christian converts including their responsible leading chief, Little Crow. Yet accumulating grievances were tinder for trouble. The Santee had been cheated by traders; their annuity payment was late, and rations issued them were poor or spoiled; their own corn crop had been ruined by cutworms. When they pleaded for food at the Agency store, its proprietor turned them away with a callous refusal: "If they are hungry, let them eat grass for all I care."

That Sunday a Santee council heard the four braves boast of their killings. Little Crow, fresh from church, vainly strove to persuade his excited tribesmen to keep peace. In the end his scruples and prudence yielded to a smoldering enmity he had long suppressed. Let it be war then. Now was the time to strike for freedom, with many young white men away in Union regiments. The all-night council broke up with the launching of an early morning attack on the Agency's store.

Twenty-three whites were shot and stabbed to death, among them the proprietor. His body was found with the mouth stuffed with the fodder he had offered hungry Indians. As massacring spread through the countryside, the bloody old days, from Deerfield to Fort Mims, saw an even bloodier re-enactment. Before Monday was over the corpses of several hundred victims littered the ruins of suddenly raided, unsuspecting villages and farms. Most adult males were slaughtered outright. Women were carried off for violation or slain, according to the savages' whim. In trains of captives, some children followed their mothers; the bodies of others, their skulls bashed in, were tossed into the embers of their homes. There were instances where people were spared by Sioux to whom they had been kind; more often friends were sacrificed to hatred and lust. Families fled on foot, on horseback or in vehicles, the lucky escaping, the luckless overtaken and cut down or burned alive in the hay-filled wagon beds. A heroic ferryman carried fifty people across a river to safety before he was shot while returning for a last load.

Panic-stricken refugees streamed into Fort Ridgely with warnings that all the Santee were on the warpath. Only a local uprising, Captain John Marsh estimated—one that quick action could quell. Brave but inexperienced, he sallied out with forty-seven soldiers and blundered straight into an ambush at the river ferry. Sioux blazed away from the tall grass. Marsh, trying to lead his men across a ford cramped and drowned. Of the twenty-five survivors who managed to regain the fort four would soon die of wounds.

Ridgely was no well-stockaded stronghold such as Leavenworth and Laramie had been in earlier days; in fact, it was barely defensible. Cabins and ravined woods, surrounding its quadrangle of buildings and parade ground, afforded ample cover for infiltrations and assault. Lieutenant Tom Gere, nineteen, left in command, mustered less than fifty men to hold the fort, now jammed with 200 fugitives. It would have been relatively easy prey if Little Crow had been able to persuade his tribesmen to press the initial attack. Instead they were lured away by the prospect of booty in the town of New Ulm from which they were repulsed after heavy fighting. Meanwhile hastily dispatched couriers—Private William Sturgis made an epic ride of 125 miles in eighteen hours to Fort Snelling—brought reinforcements. The garrison's strength had been raised to 180, plus armed civilians, when a stagecoach rolled in with $71,000 in specie, a bitterly ironical arrival. For here was the belated annuity due to the Sioux, the cash whose nonpayment had triggered the outbreak. Now it could be theirs for the taking, and it very nearly was.

Fort Ridgely's hope of salvation lay in the fortuitous fact that it had once been an ordnance post. On its parade ground and in its stores remained an amount of artillery extraordinary for a small establishment: one 6-pounder, two 12-pound mountain howitzers, and several 24s, with ample ammunition and equipment. The cannon might have been left to corrosion or employment as saluting pieces had they not been in the charge of Ordnance Sergeant John Jones. He and two artillery sergeants of the garrison not only saw to maintenance but had drilled gun crews, volunteers willing to learn the service of the piece in order to while away the tedium of post duty.

Guns and crews were ready now at a moment of desperate need. Sergeants Jones, S. C. Whipple, an artillery veteran of the Mexican War, and James McGee placed the cannon to command strategic points, with a reserve stationed on the parade ground.

On August 22, Little Crow assembled his warriors for an overwhelming onset. Fire arrows were launched to set fort roofs ablaze, but a providential rainfall extinguished them. Regardless, the Indians closed in, creeping through the ravines and the high grass of the fields. In their headbands they wore such camouflage as would survive to deck World War helmets: golden rod and oxeyed daisies blending with the prairie flowers. Undetected, they reached the outer defenses—broke through them in a whooping rush—dashed forward to storm the barracks. Refugee women screamed for their men to shoot them rather than let them fall into the Indians' merciless hands. The senior officer, Lieutenant Timothy Sheehan of the reinforcing contingent, rallied his troops for a last stand on the parade ground.

Then the "wagons that shoot," as Indians termed field artillery, went into action. Sergeant Jones wheeled around a 12-pounder and raked the flank of the Sioux onrush. Shattered, the attack recoiled. As warriors massed in other quarters, gunners spun elevating wheels and laid on targets. Whistling shells set afire a barn full of Indians. Blasts of canister scourged the ravines, one of the spreading balls gouging a gash in the scalp of Little Crow himself. A 24-pounder dropped a shell into the Indian camp. With its burst, panic erupted, squaws, ponies and dogs scattering in wild flight.

Despite their dread of artillery, the Indians furiously continued the attack. Sheehan's infantry fell back, their ammunition running low. Artillery came to the rescue again when canister shells were opened and their balls served out to load muskets.

The Sioux put the torch to a big haystack, now dry enough to catch fire. From blazing wisps the fort's woodpiles began to burn. Yelping warriors emerged from dense yellow smoke. They charged Jones's barricaded gun. Under heavy fire the Sergeant depressed the muzzle and gave them a point-blank blast—then elevated to shell snipers in the stables, stores, and ravines. Sergeant Whipple called for a shift of trail of his howitzer to smash an assault trying to swing aside out of its range. Sergeant McGee and his crew manhandled their 24 up beside Jones's piece and double charged with canister. When the Sioux launched their main assault with a strong supporting column, both guns crashed into rapid fire. As red waves ebbed, McGee loaded with shell. The projectile, well fused and aimed, screeched down to split the Indian van from its support. Young Lieutenant Gere remembered how "the ponderous reverberations of the big gun echoed up the valley as though twenty guns had opened, and the frightful explosion struck terror to the savages."

With that mighty detonation Fort Ridgely was saved. Little Crow and his warriors had done their utmost. No more valiant as assault against artillery was ever delivered by Indians. Now they fled across the river, giving up their attempt to storm the fort, yet still far from vanquished.

Back at Fort Snelling Henry Sibley had been commissioned colonel to lead the force mobilizing to crush the revolt. An old fur trader, Sibley knew Indians and possessed some military talent. He drove through to the relief of still-threatened Ridgely and beleagured towns with 1400 volunteers. The Sioux, stubbornly undismayed, well supplied with arms and ammunition, more than 250 captives held hostage, gave him a tough fight. They caught a burial party of 200 soldiers and inflicted almost fifty per cent casualties before Sibley rescued it. His final battle at Wood Lake twice came close to disaster. Little Crow hit his vanguard on both flanks and battered it back in disorderly retreat until Sibley covered it with a rush of five companies. Forming up on a hill, for two hours he fought off repeated charges. One of them, boiling out of a ravine, was repulsed by the fire of two artillery pieces. At last the enemy drew off and scattered in flight.

Realizing their power was broken, the Sioux freed their captives to lighten inevitable punishment for the toll of death they had taken in Minnesota, a toll that had risen to at least 800 and was estimated as high as 2000.

Sibley, promoted to a generalcy, began to hunt down the bands. Many escaped to the Dakotas. Little Crow fled to Canada whence, returning some time later on a small raid, he was shot and killed by a settler. The roundup brought in 2000 Santee who were tried by a court-martial which sentenced 306 of them to death. However, a plea direct to President Lincoln induced him to reduce the penalty for the majority. All who had simply fought in battle were treated as prisoners of war. Thirty-eight, convicted of murder and rape, were hanged in the "largest legal group-execution in American history."

The fate of the Santee failed to dampen the warlike ardor of Plains Sioux, untrammeled, still resisting being herded on reservations. Like their brethren to the east they saw the opportunity the Civil War gave them. No less aware of it was another equally formidable group of tribes rivaling the Sioux as the fiercest enemies the U. S. Army faced in the Indian Wars—the Apaches.

Mexico had long engaged in a feud to the death with Apaches. Her provinces, in reprisal for merciless ravages of towns, ranches, and mining communities, paid bounties for Apache scalps: $100 for a man's, $50 for a woman's, $25 for a child's. After the U.S.-Mexico War the tribes widened their relentless hostility to include American troops and settlers in ceded New Mexico and Arizona. Under a succession of great chiefs—Mangas Coloradas, Cochise, Victorio,

Geronimo, and others—they fought the armed forces of both countries, separately or in combination, back and forth across the border. Not many years elapsed before orders were being issued by Army commanders to exterminate every warrior as the only means of ending the menace.

A grim fighter, the Apache. Wily, elusive, and adept at ambushes. Of incredible endurance, a fine horseman and as capable afoot. Given to fiendish tortures designed to strike enemies with terror of his name: mutilation, including emasculation, of the dead or still living captives; slow fires built on chests; staking down on a red ant hill. No wonder that soldiers facing Apaches infinitely preferred a quick death in battle to capture.

Raids, stepped up through the 1850s, increased with the outbreak of the Civil War. Desolation scarred the Southwest. There the Confederates found no allies as they had among the Cherokee, Seminoles, and others. All white men, regardless of the color of their uniforms, were foes to the Apache. Detachments, pursuing tribal raiders through the desert, were ambushed and beaten back or wiped out. However, it was Union pressure and Confederate supply shortages, rather than Indians, that forced out Gray commands. Withdrawing into Texas, they left the Federals to cope with the inroads that left only the town Tucson and a few forts as hazardous islands of safety in a red sea.

The first Medal of Honor was won in action against Apaches in 1856 by Assistant Surgeon Bernard J. Irwin. That young doctor, born in Ireland, was serving in Arizona with the rank of first lieutenant when the Chiricahua Apaches carried off a boy of a frontier family. Lieutenant George N. Bascom with a sixty-man detachment of the 7th Infantry invaded the mountains to attempt a rescue. They overtook Cochise and his tribesmen, but the chief at a parley refused to free the boy. When the soldiers tried to hold Cochise as a hostage, he broke away and led his warriors in a sudden attack. Bascom, about to be surrounded, dispatched a courier to the nearest fort with an urgent call for help.

Because the messenger reported a number of severely wounded, it was Surgeon Irwin who volunteered to command the reinforcement of fourteen picked men. Mounted on mules, they rode through a heavy snowstorm to a canyon opening on the plain where Bascom's force, hard pressed, was holding out. Irwin at the head of his troops burst out the defile and struck the Apaches in a surprise onslaught that routed them. The surgeon then dismounted, removed instruments from his saddlebags and treated the wounded. Thereupon he took part in a raid that found and destroyed Cochise's village. Though the Medal of Honor had not been created at the time of Irwin's feat, he was awarded it retroactively in 1894 when he was Chief Medical Officer of the Army and about to retire as a brigadier general.

The Apache wars were the setting also for the extraordinary saga of an officer whose resounding deeds in the West were drowned by the thunders of the Civil War's great battlefields.

Albert H. Pfeiffer, born in Holland, emigrated to the United States and had settled in the West when he joined the New Mexico Volunteers. He rose to the rank of captain. On duty at Fort McRae, New Mexico, with his Spanish wife, her two maids, and an escort of six soldiers, he left the post one day for an excursion into the apparently peaceful countryside. Shortly after the captain had gone off for a swim in a nearby stream, shrieks, yells, and shots echoed from the camp. He scarcely had time to climb, naked and dripping, from the water and grab his rifle and cartridge belt before Apaches, who had killed the escort and carried off the three women, were on him. For several hours he fought them off from behind a rock barricade. The scorching sun had burned his skin raw by the time he was able to begin a slow retreat over the nine miles to the fort with the Indians pressing him hard every foot of the way. His steady fire beat them off until a well-aimed arrow pierced his back, jutting out through his stomach. Even then his bullets kept them from closing in for the kill. They rode away, as the badly wounded officer staggered over the last stretch to the fort and gave the alarm.

Troopers mounted up and galloped in pursuit. They could not overtake the raiders but pushed them so closely that they rid themselves of their captives as encumberances. The bodies of Mrs. Pfeiffer and one of the maids were found on the pony trail over the desert; the other maid was still alive and recovered.

The Apaches had made an enemy whose bitterness even they could not outmatch, a formidable fighter whose feats became legendary. Pfeiffer slew a grizzly bear with a knife and with that weapon fought a duel with two Indians, killing both, though severely cut up himself. He carried on his vendetta in solitary scouts through Apache country, often being followed by a pack of wolves. "They like me," he explained, "because they're fond of dead Indian, and I feed them well." The captain's vengeance would cover all Indians as the Navajos were to discover. Although he liked to play a lone hand, he was an able commander of troops. The battle-scarred veteran was a colonel when he was mustered out.

Such tough officers as he and an equally hard-bitten rank and file made up the California Column that fought Indians, chiefly in New Mexico during the Civil War. Consisting mostly of Volunteer regiments from Western states and territories, it was always undermanned for the magnitude of its task; even so, strength was drained off from time to time for Eastern reinforcements. Fortunately it was led by an experienced Indian fighter, Brigadier General James H. Carleton. Eyes steely, a firm-compressed mouth, determined chin emerging clean-shaven from whiskers, Carleton looked and was a man capable of carrying through his assignment despite its handicaps. But for him and the Army of the Pacific, the frontier would have been completely overrun, every white slaughtered, every habitation left a smoking ruin. Along with the scalps of settlers and their families, of mail carriers and stagecoach drivers and station keepers, the Apaches raked in considerable booty: mounts and herds, arms and ammunition, and a windfall of $50,000 in gold dust when they massacred a party of thirteen miners.

Troops in Blue fought the Apache, as they must, on his own terms, ambushing and being ambushed. The toll of dead on both sides mounted by twos, threes, and scores into hundreds.

Almost never was it possible to bring the raiding tribes under Mangas Coloradas and Cochise to pitched battle. In July 1862, however, the Army and the Indians met head on. Carleton's California Column marched to clear the territories of remaining Confederate forces, speed their retreat and drive them into Texas. From five to seven hundred Chiricahua and Mimbreño warriors lay in wait for the vanguard as it approached southeastern Arizona Apache Pass through which ran the road from Tucson to El Paso. High-walled, ideal for ambush, the Pass's strategic value was heightened by the fact that it contained springs which were the only water supply for a day's march on either side. How perilous a place it was the graves around its now abandoned stagecoach station testified.

Captain Thomas F. Roberts, 1st California Infantry, led the advance guard, followed at an interval by the first section of the wagon train under veteran Captain John C. Cremony. The main column was far in the rear. Men licked parched lips. Since leaving Dragoon Springs on the 40-mile march to the Pass, they had had only a cup of coffee apiece to sustain them. Most canteens were empty now, and thirst was raging.

Desert dust rose in stifling clouds, stirred by boots of three companies of infantry, hoofs of the mounts of a cavalry detachment, and the wheels of two mountain howitzers. The services of those cannon, as of artillery generally, fort and field, at critical moments in the Indian Wars, have been little noted and appreciated. About this time massed Union batteries on Malvern Hill in far-off Virginia were blasting back a Confederate assault as, a year later, they would break Pickett's charge at Gettysburg. Robert's two howitzers would serve as splendidly in the forthcoming combat in the Pass.

They rolled on in the marching column, their bronze tubes mounted on prairie carriages. The mountain howitzers at 5 degrees elevation could hurl a 6.9-pound shell 1000 yards, as well as firing spherical case (shrapnel) and canister at ranges of 800 and 250 yards respectively. This modern type of prairie carriage used a separate limber, accompanied by a caisson, a two-wheeled, shafted cart. Carriages sometimes doubled as ambulances, carrying wounded. The howitzers were also being constructed for disassembly with the parts carried on mule-back as pack artillery and thus able to operate over steep, rugged terrain which defied wheeled vehicles.

Forward rumbled the two stubby-barreled cannon that day on the approach to Apache Pass. Models of 1836 or 1841 cast in the Boston foundry of Cyrus Alger, their like would roll on through American history into the Second World War to climb precipitous trails into the Italian mountains, trails where no other field artillery could follow. Cannoneers led the horses and walked beside the carriages, now and then greasing a hot axle or halting perhaps to bind up a cracked wheel with rawhide. They stared up, estimating ranges, at the canyon rims. Looked as if they could be raked though at maximum elevation which would be risky, for the "hows" had a considerable recoil, tough on the carriage when muzzles were raised high.

Beady eyes of unseen Apaches warily watched the advancing artillery. Likely this was their first encounter with "wagons that shoot"—that "shoot twice," as they described them because of the report of the propelling charge, then the detonation of the bursting shell. Rifles between the rocks and from pits covered them.

Points out, Roberts entered the Pass with proper precautions, aware of its danger. Silent in ambush Mangas Coloradas, Cochise, and their warriors let him traverse two thirds of the defile's length. As the Blue column neared the stone station of the Overland Mail, short of the springs, a storm of bullets and arrows plunged down on it from both sides of the battlemented gorge. With no targets visible—the enemy was firing from behind rock barricades—the troops recoiled in countermarch to the entrance and re-formed.

Skirmishers forward! The shouted orders and bugle calls seconding them were welcomed by men whose throats were raw with alkali dust. Though the odds against them amounted to seven to one, they must fight their way through at all costs. It took them an hours-long struggle to wedge a way back to the stagecoach station. While losses were still slight, the springs lay 600 yards farther where ground sloped up to a divide. And the Apaches, rifles peering down over natural rock breastworks, were determined to bar them from that vital water.

Then Captain Roberts ordered his artillery into action. Hastily the howitzers moved to the fore. In the rush one overturned, a mishap to which the too-narrowly based prairie carriages were prone. A fusillade from above scattered its crew. The cannon lay on its side, abandoned and useless.

Artillery's mission is to support other arms, but now it was cavalry that supported it. Sergeant Titus B. Mitchell and six troopers ran forward and righted the gun, its crew returned to man it, and both pieces opened up. Shells burst among the Apaches. "We were doing all right," one of them later told his captors, "until you began firing wagons at us." With the Apaches scattered in flight, the way to the springs was open. Sixty-three Indian dead, shell-fire casualties, were later admitted by the Apaches; only three were killed by musketry. Once again cannon had saved the day. The American loss was surprisingly light—two killed, two wounded—probably because the Indians overshot like many marksmen firing down from heights.

Captain Roberts pitched camp, mounted guard, and made ready for combat again on the morrow. He would face another fight then but it would be brief and minor, with the howitzers once more clearing the way, and the rest of the Pass safely penetrated. Meanwhile he decided to send a warning message back to Captain Cremony. The dependable Sergeant Mitchell, another sergeant and three troopers drew the perilous mission.

Watching Apaches saw their chance to recoup somewhat for the prey they had lost and to catch the supply train before it was alerted. Hardly had the little detail of cavalrymen emerged from the Pass when Mangas Coloradas with fifty warriors galloped after it in hot pursuit.

The Indian Wars furnished no scene more stirring than a running fight between cavalry and mounted redskins. At the gallop Mitchell and his men fired carbines and revolvers over saddle cantles. Bullets and whizzing arrows answered as the Apaches narrowed the gap. A sergeant was hit but kept his seat. Three troop horses went down, flinging their riders clear. Comrades picked up two of the troopers, mounting them behind them, and galloped on to outdistance their pursuers. But Private John Teal, some 200 yards behind the others, was lost in the dust cloud.

Teal stood alone in the desert beside his dying horse. He crouched down at the head of the poor creature which licked his hands before it breathed its last. Apache lives would pay for this favorite mount of his. He was ready when the warriors came galloping back and commenced circling him. From behind his horse's body, he opened fire with his carbine, fortunately no issue muzzle-leader but a breechloader, now cavalry equipment.

"They knew I also had a 6-shooter and a saber," Teal would relate in his report, "and seemed unwilling to try close quarters. In this way the fight continued for over an hour, when I got a good chance at a prominent Indian and slipped a carbine bullet into his breast.

"He must have been a man of some note, because soon after that they seemed to get away from me, and I could hear their voices growing fainter in the distance. I thought: this is a good time to make tracks, and divesting myself of my spurs, I took the saddle, bridle, and blanket from the dead horse and started for the camp. I have walked eight miles since then."

Thus the gallant cavalryman ended his report. Although the equipment he lugged across the desert could have been surveyed as expended in action, he was taking no chances on that. Too often Private Teal had seen such items, lost by soldiers, charged against them on the payroll. Also it was easier to find a new mount than a saddle, and no trooper likes to foot it. So Private Teal reported ready for duty, less only a horse. The exploit of his stand proved greater than he then knew, for it was later learned that the huge Apache he had drilled with a carbine shot was Mangas Coloradas himself. It was months before that formidable chief recovered from the wound he had forced a Mexican doctor to treat on threat of death and was able to lead his warriors again.

The following year Mangas Coloradas was decoyed to a parley and made prisoner. Colonel J. R. West looked down on him as he lay beside a campfire and told the two night sentries in the hearing of another soldier: "Men, that old murderer has got away from every soldier command and left a trail of blood five hundred miles along the old stage line. I want him dead or alive tomorrow morning. Do you understand? *I want him dead!*" As the colonel left, one of the guards heated his bayonet in the fire and plunged it into a leg of the chief. The moment he jumped up he was shot to death. Treachery was not always the province of Apaches alone.

Under other chieftains the implacable hostility of the Apaches continued unrelaxed. It carried far past the Civil War and on into the late 1880s, and then the last bands would only be tracked down and conquered through the use of their own tribesmen serving as Army scouts.

XVIII

Descent Into Hell

COLONEL CHRISTOPHER CARSON, 1st New Mexico Cavalry, mustered troops for another campaign against the Navajos in the winter of 1863-64. Its final objective would be the Canyon de Chelly, the "Gibraltar of Navajodom," that great gorge which, an officer had once warned, no command ever should enter. Though partly penetrated, it remained a mystery and a menace. A lieutenant of Carson's command, staring down into the chasm's awesome depths, would summon up his Latin to brand them *descensus averni.*

It was characteristic of Kit Carson to be undaunted by his mission. Through the Mexican War the renowned scout had served as an Army courier and guide and since as an Indian agent. This was his country, the home of his close-knit family. What if this quiet-spoken man, clean-shaven, long hair combed close to his head, looked more like a minister of the Gospel than a soldier? He knew Indians and how to fight them. It mattered nothing that "guardhouse lawyers" occasionally got around him like thirsty troopers whose canteens were always filled with liquor. Carson called in and mildly scolded the sutler. "John, don't you know it's agin regulations to sell whiskey to enlisted men of the post without the written order of the commanding officer?" Thereupon the sutler showed him a foot-high stack of countersigned orders for quarts of molasses which had been traded in for stronger liquid. No more did it matter that orthodox tactics were not in the colonel's book; for such, if needed, and to take care of paperwork Carson detailed an experienced officer as his military adviser.

A Volunteer, Colonel Carson, like most of his command. Of such was the bulk of the troops, submerging the small Regular Army, in conflict with Indians or Confederates. They were men of a different stamp from the green, short-term levies of the earlier Indian Wars. These, for the most part, were seasoned frontiersmen, well adapted to the hard campaigning they faced.

The march on Chelly was designed to end the stubborn resistance of the Navajos, to round them up and confine them to the Bosque Redondo Reservation. For the past two years General Carleton, with Carson as his right-hand man, had harried and hunted down the tribesmen. Though ill-supplied with firearms and not expert bowmen, though the hands of other tribes, Apaches, Utes, and Pueblos, were turned against them, the Navajos were no easy conquest. More or less with impunity they attacked army outposts and supply trains and extensively raided herds. Gradually numbers, persistence, and destruction of resources began to prevail over them. Bands were wiped out, women and children captured. Trapped warriors surrendered. Yet Canyon de Chelly remained. Until the Navajos' confidence in it as a stronghold and place of inaccessible refuge was destroyed, they would never yield.

In January, Colonel Carson took the field against it. His column consisted of 650 infantrymen and cavalrymen, accompanied by two mountain howitzers, Ute and Mescalero Apache scouts, and an ox-drawn supply train. With that force he was expected to subdue some 10,000 Navajos.

In the early easy going, marching men roared out the campaign song written by a soldier of the 1st California Volunteers, a chant set to music by the bandmaster. One of its eight verses ran:

Come dress your ranks, my gallant souls, a-standing in a row.
Kit Carson he is waiting to march against the foe.
At night we march to Moqui o'er lofty hills of snow
To meet and crush the savage foe, bold Johnny Navajo.
Johnny Navajo. O, Johnny Navajo!
We'll first chastise, then civilize bold Johnny Navajo.

But soon the "lofty hills of snow" left no breath for singing. The panting oxen slowly struggled through it, retarding the rate of march to five miles per day; twenty-five of them died of exhaustion in a 25-mile stretch. Cavalry horses weakened as grain gave out; some collapsed and had to be shot. Now and then there were skirmishes with the enemy who made only brief stands before fading back toward

Chelly. They left unprotected their fields and such cattle as they were unable to drive off.

Carson did what had to be done to starve the Navajos into submission, following a scorched-earth policy like Sullivan's against the Iroquois. Peach tree orchards were hewn down, irrigated fields of wheat, corn, beans, and pumpkins devastated, flocks of sheep and goats seized. A swath was cut that left the enemy few food resources except those in Chelly. And at last the Blue column closed in on the canyon itself, detachments breaking off to advance on its entrances and other means of access as well as along the rims. That thorough commander, Colonel Carson, left nothing to chance if he could help it.

From one rim young Lieutenant John Van D. DuBois peered into the chasm, then began to lead his men and pack mules down an appallingly steep trail.

"The descent was truly terrific," he recorded and must have shuddered from the memory as he wrote. "We were four hours getting down the 800-foot depth. Mules fell distances from twenty to forty feet. Two were killed and several only saved by their loads which prevented them from striking the rocks in their fall. Looking up it seemed as if there were no escape. The stream was running in the cañon, though often, the Indians say its bed is dry. Tall pines looked like bushes when contrasted with the sides of this *descensus averni*. Men and animals on the top, as seen from below, were like mites in the sky."

Simultaneously Carson forced the western gateway with more troops. They thrust on through the canyon, the Navajos falling back before them. As a group endeavored to make their escape by a side entrance, they were struck by a detachment of fifty soldiers commanded by Sergeant Andreas Herrera, a first-rate noncommissioned officer often cited in reports. With that outlet blocked, the red men again filtered toward the rear. There was no chance for them to win free by scaling the cliffs, for Blue columns on both rims were watchfully paralleling their retreat. Their last and only route to freedom now lay through the eastern entrance.

But Kit Carson had taken care to provide for that, and a force under the redoubtable Captain Pfeiffer, nemesis of the Apaches, was swinging around to the east. If that able officer arrived in time, Chelly would be sealed off, and pincer jaws clamped on the Navajos.

Pfeiffer, his men, and pack train made it in a tough forced march in severe cold. Pick-and-shovel pioneers with his advance guard opening a way through snowdrifts, he wedged into the canyon and forged forward. Mules broke through the ice covering the stream, the belly of one of them split by jagged edges. Pfeiffer pushed on. Now the canyon echoed to ringing shots and whistling arrows. From ledges and from caves in the cliff sides the Navajos desperately defended their stronghold. Whooping and cursing in broken Spanish, they flung every object at hand down on the heads of the troops. Above him the captain sighted a squaw hurling rocks and logs as furiously as the warriors. His mind seared by the memory of his murdered wife, he leveled his rifle and squeezed the trigger without compunction. The body of the squaw crumpled, as other accurate fire dropped several braves. Resistance died away and ended.

Midway in the canyon the two columns met. Remarkably, they had suffered no casualties. With the legend of Chelly's invincibility vanished the fighting spirit of the Navajo tribe. Captures were swelled by mass surrenders until more than 8000 were corraled under guard for removal to the Bosque Redondo Reservation on the Pecos River in eastern New Mexico.

"The Long Walk." So the Navajos would term their journey into exile, as the Cherokee had called theirs "The Trail of Tears." The lengthy column of twos and threes—men, women, and children—with horses and sheep and mule-drawn wagons moved sadly. Even the soldiers guarding it were touched by pity, and their mood was expressed when the bard, who had written the expedition's marching song, added a verse.

They are gatherin' in fast,
In each valley and plain,
To remove from the land
They shall ne'er see again.
And their cry of deep sorrow will sadly echo,
When they take a last look at their loved Navajo.

Sympathy and understanding shone plain the pages of General Carleton's report to the Indian Department.

"The exodus of this whole people from the land of their fathers is not only an interesting but a touching sight. They have fought us gallantly for many years; they have defended their mountains and stupendous canyons with a heroism which any people might be proud to emulate; but when it was their destiny, as it has been that of their brethren, tribe after tribe, to give way to the insatiable progress of our race, they threw down their arms. As brave men and fully entitled to our admiration and respect, they have come to us with confidence in our magnanimity; with the belief that we are too powerful and too just a people to repay that confidence with meanness or neglect. They hope that in return for having sacrificed to us their beautiful country, their homes, the associations of their lives, the scenes rendered classic in their traditions, we will not dole out to them a miser's pittance in return for what they know to be a princely realm."

Bosque Redondo, not to be irrigated until half a century later, was miserably adapted as the home of a pastoral people. Hunger and disease soon began to take heavy toll of the Navajos. While they were still under Army control, General Carleton did all he could for them, putting his troops on half rations and sparing food to prevent their wards from starving. Many Navajos died before the Indian Department returned them to their own country in 1867 and gave them new flocks and herds, and the tribe began its progress toward a happier future as shepherds, blanket weavers, and silversmiths.

XIX

Carnage by The Creek

THE BODIES OF A SETTLER, his wife, and their two children, scalped, their throats cut, and otherwise mutilated, were placed on public display in Denver, Colorado, in the summer of 1864. Here was ghastly evidence that the Cheyennes, along with the Sioux and Arapahoes, were back on the warpath they would seldom quit for years to come.

Death at the hands of Indians had long been a familiar spectacle in the West. Crumpled heaps in blue or homespun

—a soldier killed in line of duty, an emigrant who had run his risk and lost. Charred remains in the smoking ruins of a ranch house, whitened bones on the prairie. Yet to not a few Denver townsfolk the corpses exhibited were a novel and shocking sight. It was distressing enough to learn of women and children carried off as captives. Their cold-blooded murder was beyond the pale and it was to provoke bitter retaliation in kind.

The Plains tribes, taking natural advantage of the Civil War's drain of manpower from the West, were raiding far and wide. Besides prey already within striking radius of those hard-riding horse Indians, more was presented them when emigration increased greatly in 1864. Many wagon trains contained men seeking "to get shunt of" the draft for Union armies. In avoiding the hazards of military service they met a worse fate. Scores and hundreds were shot or lanced by red raiders, while surviving families disappeared into captivity, the women taken into warriors' lodges as squaws, the children adopted into the tribe.

Troops, spread thin to protect trails and settlements, fought throughout the year over broad areas. In April, a hundred troopers of the 1st Colorado Cavalry with two howitzers had battled four hundred Cheyennes in western Kansas, beating them off when the Indians lost heavily in a rashly daring charge on the battery. Sioux who had wiped out a military escort, would fare better when they eluded pursuit by a cavalry command for 120 miles, then lay in wait and ran off all their enemy's mounts. Disgusted troopers burned their saddles and trudged the weary distance back to Laramie.

War parties about to be cornered parleyed for peace. They surrendered their old men, women, and children and turned in broken-down ponies and old, unserviceable guns. Then the young bucks resumed hostilities. Wrote a disillusioned Army officer: "There was no confidence to be placed in any of these Indians. They were a bad lot. They all needed killing, and the more they were fed and taken care of the worse they became."

By the summer of 1864 Indians were in control of all lines of communication east of Denver except the Santa Fe Trail. Colorado mail had to be detoured via Panama and California. The price of goods soared. Denver considered itself to be in a state of siege, for the settler and his family had been slaughtered in its near vicinity. Every able-bodied citizen was armed and drilled, with women and children assembled at night in the most defensible buildings. Frantic appeals were made for Colorado troops to be returned from the Union armies and for help from New Mexico and Arizona forces under Carleton—calls that could not be answered. One-hundred-day volunteers were mustered to meet the emergency which, many believed, would develop into disaster unless swift and drastic action was taken. Never, people declared, would the country be safe until every Indian was exterminated. The old doctrine that the only good Indian was a dead one would be restated a few years later by General Sherman in the following dispatch to General Grant. "We must act with vindicative earnestness against the Sioux, even to their extermination, men, women, and children. Nothing less will reach the root of the case."

In command of the Colorado district was Colonel John M. Chivington. He had entered the ministry and served as a missionary to Indians, then fought Confederates in New Mexico. Now he and his men, some of them also veterans, were about to exact the Biblical vengeance of an eye for an eye, a tooth for a tooth.

With authority from superior headquarters Chivington organized a campaign and, in November 1864, marched with 750 cavalrymen, two thirds of them recruits, a number of infantrymen and several pieces of artillery. At sunrise on the twenty-ninth they came suddenly upon a large encampment of Southern Cheyennes under Chief Black Kettle, their 130 lodges pitched on the south bend of Sand Creek, a tributary of the Arkansas River. The two hundred warriors and five hundred women and children made no attempt to flee. The tribe had done its share of recent raiding, as would be testified by the dresses of white women and fresh scalps found in the camp, but now it wished peace. Black Kettle hoisted an American flag over a small white one on his lodge pole.

No emblems could save them. Chivington launched a three-pronged attack, with one column swinging around to cut off the pony herd. Rifle fire crackled, punctuated by booms of the howitzers. Some of the Indians escaped up the creek bed, but many rallied to make determined stands in the sand hills. Troops poured a furious fire into them, their targets any and every Indian, regardless of age or sex. Women and children were shot down without compunction. Few prisoners were taken. The dead were scalped, a hundred of those grisly trophies to be exhibited in Denver. For almost two hours the Cheyennes held. Then the two howitzers shattered and routed them. A five-mile running fight, continuing until dusk, strewed the prairie with more bodies. The Indian loss was three hundred killed, about half of them warriors, the rest women and children. Two squaws and five youngsters were the only prisoners. Casualties of the troops amounted only to seven killed and forty-seven wounded, seven of them mortally.

Colonel Chivington was at first acclaimed, then castigated for the bloody retribution he inflicted. He was ordered to face a court-martial but mustered out before it convened. According to the consensus of opinion, the attack was justified but not its manner. "To the abstract question, whether it is right to kill women and children, there can be but one answer. But as a matter of retaliation, and a matter of policy, whether these people were right in killing women and children at Sand Creek is a question to which the answer does not come so glibly." So ran a view in a controversy still argued.

"May God grant that Indian fighting may never make me a brute or harden me," a lieutenant of the Regiment of Mounted Riflemen had prayed. But he, too, in the course of his service came to amend his petition, though he retained a certain sympathy for the red man. "Poor devils, it makes one sad to think how they are driven from mountain to plain and back again at the will of any agent of Uncle Samuel," he wrote. "But then again, when their cruelty to prisoners and constant robberies are considered against them, an honorable war is too great leniency."

Sand Creek and its like, along with the far greater number of massacres by Indians, stand as somber pages in the unending history of total warfare. Yet the centuries-long struggle between white man and red records many a passage-at-arms chivalrously fought by foes worthy of mutual respect.

Deeper in the Southwest war was being hotly waged in that month of November 1864, though only combat was heated. Choice of a winter campaign avoided the scorching sun and burning thirst of the desert but imposed its own penalties.

It rained, it blew,
It friz, it thew.

In the bitter cold all ranks resorted when possible to *spiritus frumenti* in the surgeon's kit or to personal supplies. One officer remembered being so nearly frozen that several flasks of whiskey and a hot toddy seemed as weak as water.

Fifes shrilling "The Girl I Left Behind Me," they marched out of the little forts or the towns once ruled by Mexico with backward glances at Army wives or languorous Spanish señoritas. Perhaps the column was headed by a veteran officer who had seen his first service in the Mexican War. Behind his back disrespectful young juniors might be referring to him as "a kind of old fellow whom superior age had unfortunately placed in command . . . of great physical energy but deficient reason, cramped in his understanding and warped in his judgment." He in turn might put the cocky young shavetails in their place with such a remark as: "Mister, your ability is unquestionable but unfortunately you know it." To that the subaltern would make an unspoken retort: "Well, isn't West Point study a system of self-reliance—not only to know but to know you know?"

And they *did* know, most of them. Young lieutenants, who had fought Indians before them, were generals now in the Union or Confederate armies. Where columns today were marching into the Southwest, the celebrated 2nd U. S. Cavalry had ridden before them, mounted on Kentucky-bred horses, gallant in its plumed Kossuth hats and brass shoulder scales to turn saber cuts, its uniforms braided with cavalry yellow. The regiment's officers during its plains service had been Colonel Albert Sidney Johnston, Lieutenant Colonel Robert E. Lee and Majors George H. Thomas and William J. Hardee, with Earl Van Dorn, Kirby Smith, John B. Hood, and Fitzhugh Lee in company commands. In blue or gray they had become a glittering galaxy on Civil War battlefields.

The 2nd Cavalry had fought Kiowas and Comanches in 1859 and '60 and sometimes even the 2nd had been outfought, taking losses and losing prisoners. Both Thomas and Hood bore the scars of wounds inflicted by those redoubtable tribesmen. As the 2nd had crossed sabers with Kiowa and Comanche lances, so must its successors. Those long weapons, often decked with white women's scalps stretched on hoops, the long hair their pennons, now stood ready before tribal lodges around Adobe Walls in northwest Texas.

It was Colonel Kit Carson, "as simple as a child, as brave as a lion," who led the expedition from Fort Bascom. The veteran frontiersman's courage had often been proven; his simplicity, mostly in manner, was no longer being taken advantage of by troopers with a penchant for trading his signed orders for molasses for whiskey. He kept the force that followed him well in hand: 325 New Mexico and California mounted volunteers, artillerymen manning two mountain howitzers under the command of an infantryman detailed as a gunner officer, Lieutenant George H. Pettis; 75 Ute and Jicarilla Apache scouts, an ambulance, and 27 wagons laden with 45 days' supplies, Carson, conqueror of the Navajos, was determined to locate the hostiles and bring them to battle. He was about to find plenty of them.

In brisk weather, growing colder, the column commenced a march of 200 miles down the Colorado River. Snowstorms blanketed and impeded it, but it made steady progress and by the fourteenth day, November 24, was approaching the old trading post of Adobe Walls on the Canadian River when scouts rode back to report Indians in that neighborhood. Carson ordered a forced and silent all-night advance; no talking, no smoking. The enemy must be run down without chance of escape.

A halt and brief rest before dawn. Quiet word passed. Stand to horse. Mount up. Men in blue, whitened by heavy frost, swung into saddles. Indians, Kiowas and Comanches, emerged from the haze ahead. Muffling air was rent by war whoops, the crackle of rifle fire, and the twang of bowstrings. The cavalry drove ahead, skirmishing for several miles. A large cluster of lodges loomed up before them. Bugles blared the charge. Blades, rasping from scabbards, reflected the first rays of sunrise. Troopers leaned forward, legs gripping leather, and pounded down on the village at a thundering gallop.

From 170 lodges more warriors erupted, buffalo robes flung from bare, war-painted bodies. They ran for their lives but not far. A flight of a few miles and they rallied.

Vaulting on to their ponies, firing along their necks, or leveling lances, they countercharged the blue horse. As the cavalry formed up to meet the red onslaught, Carson and some of his men discarded overcoats they would not be able to find in later chilly hours.

A look at oncoming warriors heavily outnumbering him, and the colonel turned to his artillery commander. "Throw a few shells into that crowd over thar," he directed.

"Battery, halt," Lieutenant Pettis ordered. "Action right! Load with shell."

Crews manned and laid pieces, their field of fire cleared by the cavalry now fighting dismounted in the tall grass.

Pettis shouted: "Number one, fire! Number two, fire!"

The howitzers flamed, banged and bucked back in recoil. Cannoneers manhandled them, muzzles smoking, back into battery, swabbed and rammed in new charges. Charging warriors rose in rope stirrups with dismay as the first shells burst over them, then cowered low on pony backs. Two more rounds and they scattered in yelling flight. Cheering soldiers relaxed and began to bolt a breakfast of raw bacon and hardtack.

They were given no time to digest it. Down on them from another large village, three miles east of the first, swept a cloud of 1000 whooping Indians at a breakneck gallop. Kit Carson's scouts, none equal to him in his scouting days, had not looked far enough. They had found Indians for him —too many of them.

Rifles spurted crimson through the sere grass. The howitzers, served at top speed, spoke again and again. Despite the cold, sweat streaked battle-grimed faces, and throats were dry with that fear of imminent death a soldier suppresses but will not deny.

Now Indians, circling to the rear of the troops, fired the grass. Soldiers gasped as the thick smoke, mingling with the bitter, acrid powder fumes, billowed over them. The choking rearguard closed up on the battle line at the double.

Repeatedly the warriors charged. A shell plunged through the galloping mount of a Comanche. In its death throes the animal pitched its rider twenty feet in the air to land sprawling and senseless. Two tribesmen raced for him, leaned low from their ponies' back, each grasping him by an arm, and dragged him off to safety amid a spate of bullets. Yonder in the red mass a chief, probably Satanta of the Kiowas, raised a bugle to his lips. As clearly and shrilly as the best cavalry "music," he answered every call sounded by soldier buglers with a countersignal—"Retreat" echoing a summons to advance from the other side, and vice versa. Blue ranks wavered in confusion.

All Carson's cavalry were now fighting dismounted except for the horseholders, each struggling to control three linked mounts of comrades. Troopers and Indian allies barely managed to hold off the enemy though the colonel, setting grass fires of his own to cover the movement, concentrated his force on higher ground clear of most of the smoke.

It was the two mountain howitzers, decisive as they had been at Apache Pass, that saved the day. The "wagons that shoot" blasted charges sometimes surging up to within a few yards of their muzzles. Scourged by canister and bursting shells, the red waves ebbed. Carson drove through the rout over a field, strewn with a hundred Indian dead and many wounded, to the first village which was ransacked of finely dressed buffalo robes, gratefully appropriated by the overcoatless. A quantity of cavalry equipment and several dresses of white women also were found. The lodges then were put to the torch.

Ammunition low, men and horses staggering with fatigue —they had fought without intermission from sunrise to sunset—there was no choice for the little army but to retreat. While its loss in killed was remarkably light, the twenty-one wounded overflowed the ambulance, and a number suffered rough transportation on the gun carriages, lifted off when the howitzers were unlimbered to cover the retreat then put aboard again. Hard pressed by what seemed to be the whole Kiowa and Comanche nations at their heels, the troops were not far from disaster before they succeeded in fighting their way back to their wagon train and finally regained Fort Bascom. But the blow struck had broken Kiowa and Comanche power for a time, though the tribes would not succumb to conquest for another decade.

XX

Salute

April 1865, and Lee surrendering the Army of Northern Virginia while Grant's military secretary, Lieutenant Colonel Ely Parker, a Seneca sachem, transcribed the terms of capitulation. The Civil War was virtually at an end. Not so the Indian Wars. The Senecas had long since yielded to such conquest as one of them was now witnessing. Tribes of the plains, the desert, and the mountains of the West still maintained their fierce resistance. There would be no peace until close to the turn of the century.

Arms went unstacked. Troops, a portion of the great armies of the Union, mustered again at the frontier posts. Veterans and the younger men, who would carry on for them, once more took the field in the long continued Indian Wars, wars which had only passed their middle span, wars that bequeathed the Old Army's gallant heritage and tradition to those that followed it.

A soldier, speaking a tribute the nation must echo, stood at the graves of fallen comrades and rendered them a last salute.

"By losing their lives they gave freedom to thousands of travelers who seek new homes amid the western wilderness."

Three volleys in farewell. A bugle sounding Taps, its poignant notes lingering to merge with the stirring summons of the Call to Arms. Tread of infantry, clatter of cavalry, and rumble of artillery as the U. S. Army marched again to war.

Selected Bibliography

Abel, Annie Heloise. *The American Indian as Slaveholder and Secessionist.* Cleveland: The Arthur H. Clark Co., 1915.

———. *The American Indian as Participant in the Civil War.* Cleveland: The Arthur H. Clark Co., 1919.

American Heritage. Files.

Anburey, Thomas. *Travels through the Interior Parts of North America.* 2 vols. Boston and New York: Houghton Mifflin Co., 1923.

Arnold, R. Ross. *Indian Wars of Idaho.* Caldwell, Idaho: Caxton Printers, 1932.

Bandel, Eugene. *Frontier Life in the Army, 1854-1861.* Glendale, Calif.: The Arthur H. Clark Co., 1932.

Barce, Elmore. *The Land of the Miamis.* Fowler, Ind.: The Benton Review Shop, 1922.

Barnhart, John D., ed. *Henry Hamilton and George Rogers Clark in the American Revolution.* Crawfordsville, Ind.: R. E. Banta, 1951.

Beatty, Lt. Erkuries. *Journal in the Expedition against the Six Nations under General Sullivan.* Pennsylvania Archives, XV. Harrisburg: E. K. Meyers, 1890.

Beers, Henry Putncy. *The Western Military Frontier, 1815-1846.* Philadelphia, 1935.

Bellah, James Warner. *A Thunder of Drums.* New York: Bantam Books, 1961.

Biographical Sketches of the Generals of the Continental Army of the Revolution. Cambridge, Mass.: John Wilson & Son, 1889.

Boatner, Maj. Mark M., III. *Army Lore.* Japan: Kyowa Co., 1954.

———. *The Civil War Dictionary.* New York: David McKay Co., 1959.

Britton, Wiley. *The Civil War on the Border.* 2 vols. New York: G. P. Putnam's Sons, 1899.

———. *The Union Indian Brigade in the Civil War.* Kansas City, Missouri: Franklin Hudson Publishing Co., 1922.

Brooks, Elbridge S. *The Story of the American Soldier.* Boston: Lothrop Publishing Co., 1889.

Brooks, Noah. *First across the Continent: The Story of the Exploring Expedition of Lewis and Clark in 1803-4-5.* New York: Charles Scribner's Sons, 1901.

Callahan, North. *Henry Knox.* New York: Rinehart & Co., 1958.

Campbell, William W. *Annals of Tryon County; or, The Border Warfare of New York, during the Revolution.* New York: Baker & Scribner, 1849.
Carleton, Lt. J. Henry. *The Prairie Logbook.* Chicago: The Caxton Club, 1949.
Carrington, Col. Henry B. *Battles of the American Revolution, 1775-1781.* New York: A. S. Barnes & Co., 1876.
Catlin, George. *Letters and Notes on the Manners, Customs, and Condition of the North American Indians.* New York: Wiley & Putnam, 1842.
Clark, George Rogers. *Papers, 1771-1781 and 1781-1784.* Collections of the Illinois State Historical Library, vols. 8 and 19. James Alton James, ed. Springfield, Ill., 1912 and 1926.
Clarke, T. Wood. *The Bloody Mohawk.* New York: The Macmillan Co., 1940.
Cleaves, Freeman. *Old Tippecanoe.* New York: Charles Scribner's Sons, 1939.
Colton, Ray C. *The Civil War in the Western Territories.* Norman: University of Oklahoma Press, 1959.
Commager, Henry Steele, and Morris, Richard B., eds. *The Spirit of 'Seventy-Six.* 2 vols. Indianapolis: The Bobbs-Merrill Co., 1958.
Company of Military Collectors & Historians. *Journal.* Files.
Connelley, William Elsey. *Doniphan's Expedition and the Conquest of New Mexico and California* (incorporating the diary of Col. John T. Hughes). Topeka, Kan.: Gammel's Book Store, 1907.
Cook, Frederick. *Journals of Military Expedition of Major General John Sullivan against the Six Nations of Indians in 1779.* Auburn, N.Y.: Knap, Peck, & Thompson, 1887.
Cooke, Philip St. George. *Scenes and Adventures in the Army.* Philadelphia: Lindsay & Blakiston, 1857.
———. *Cavalry Tactics.* 2 vols. Philadelphia: J. B. Lippincott Co., 1862.
Crane, Stephen. *Works.* vol. 9. Wilson Follett, ed. New York: Alfred A. Knopf, 1900, 1926.
Cremony, John C. *Life among the Apaches.* San Francisco: Roman & Co., 1868.
Crockett, David. *Autobiography.* New York: Charles Scribner's Sons, 1923.
Croghan, Col. George. *Army Life on the Western Frontier.* F. P. Prucha, ed. Norman: University of Oklahoma Press, 1958.
Crook, Gen. George. *Autobiography.* Martin F. Schmitt, ed. Norman: University of Oklahoma Press, 1946.
Cross, Maj. Osborn, and George Gibbs. *The March of the Mounted Riflemen.* Raymond W. Settle, ed. Glendale, Calif.: The Arthur H. Clark Co., 1940.

Cunningham, Frank. *General Stand Watie's Confederate Indians*. San Antonio, Texas: The Naylor Co., 1959.
Darnell, Elias. *A Journal . . . of Kentucky Volunteers, 1812-1813.* Philadelphia: Grigg & Elliott, 1834.
Dawson, Henry B. *Battles of the United States on Sea and Land.* 2 vols. New York: Johnson, Fry & Co., 1858.
Debo, Angie. *The Road to Disappearance.* Norman: University of Oklahoma Press, 1941.
Denny, Maj. Ebenezer. *Military Journal.* In Publications of the Historical Society of Pennsylvania, vol. 7. Philadelphia: J .B. Lippincott Co., 1860.
Digby, Lt. William. *The British Invasion from the North.* James Phinney Baxter, ed. Albany: Joel Munsell's Sons, 1887.
Douglas, Marjorie Stoneman. *The Everglades: River of Grass.* New York: Rinehart & Co., 1947.
Downes, Randolph Chandler. *Frontier Ohio, 1788-1803.* Columbus: Ohio State Archeological Society, 1935.
Downey, Fairfax. *Indian-Fighting Army.* New York: Charles Scribner's Sons, 1941.
———. *General Crook, Indian Fighter.* Philadelphia: The Westminster Press, 1957.
Drake, Samuel Adams. *Burgoyne's Invasion of 1777.* Boston: Lee & Shepherd, 1889.
Draper, Lyman C., ed. Collections of the State Historical Society of Wisconsin. Madison: The Society, 1849-1903.
Du Bois, Col. John Van Deusen. *Campaigns in the West, 1856-1861.* Tucson: Arizona Pioneers Historical Society, 1949.
Dunn, J. P., Jr. *Massacres in the Mountains, a History of the Indian Wars in the Far West, 1815-1875.* New York: Archer House, Inc., 1886.
Dyer, Lt. A. B. Letter (Santa Fe, Feb. 14, 1847) to Dr. Robert Johnson, Richmond, Va.: *New Mexico Historical Review,* Oct. 1947.
Elkins, Capt. John M. *Indian Fighting on the Texas Frontier.* Amarillo, Texas: Russell & Cockrell, 1929.
Eliott, Charles Winslow. *Winfield Scott, the Soldier and the Man.* New York: The Macmillan Co., 1937.
Ellis, Edward S. *The Indian Wars of the United States.* New York: Cassell Publishing Co., 1892.
English, William Hayden. *Conquest of the Country Northwest of the River Ohio, 1778-1783, and Life of Gen. George Rogers Clark.* Indianapolis: The Bobbs-Merrill Co., 1896.
Fairbanks, George R. *History of Florida.* Philadelphia: J. B. Lippincott Co., 1871.
Fisher, Sydney George. *The Struggle for American Independence.* 2 vols. Philadelphia: J. B. Lippincott Co., 1908.
Fiske, John. *The American Revolution.* 2 vols. Boston and New York: Houghton Mifflin Co., 1891.

Fitzpatrick, John C. *The Spirit of the Revolution.* Boston and New York: Houghton Mifflin Co., 1924.
———. *The Writings of George Washington from the Original Manuscript Sources.* 39 vols. Washington, 1931-1944.
Force, Peter, ed. *American Archives.* 9 vols. Washington, 1837-1853.
Foreman, Grant. *The Five Civilized Tribes.* Norman: University of Oklahoma Press, 1934.
———. *Indian Removal.* Norman: University of Oklahoma Press, 1932.
———. *Advancing the Frontier, 1830-1860.* Norman: University of Oklahoma Press, 1933.
Forsyth, Gen. George A. *The Story of the Soldier.* New York: D. Appleton & Co., 1916.
Fowler, William W. *Woman on the Frontier.* Hartford: S. S. Scranton & Co., 1884.
Frost, John. *The Book of the Army of the United States.* New York: D. Appleton & Co., 1845.
———. *Indian Wars of the United States.* Auburn, N. Y.: Derby & Miller, 1852.
Ganoe, Col. William Addleman. *The History of the United States Army.* New York: D. Appleton & Co., 1942.
Giddings, Joshua R. *The Exiles of Florida.* Columbus, Ohio: Follett, Foster & Co., 1858.
Glisan, Rodney. *Journal of Army Life.* San Francisco: A. L. Bancroft & Co., 1874.
Green, James A. *William Henry Harrison: His Life and Times.* Richmond: Garrett & Massie, 1941.
Grinnell, George Bird. *The Fighting Cheyennes.* New York: Charles Scribner's Sons, 1915.
———. *The Cheyenne Indians.* 2 vols. New Haven: Yale University Press, 1923.
Hadden, Lt. James M. *A Journal Kept in Canada and Burgoyne's Campaign in 1776 and 1777.* Albany: Joel Munsell's Sons, 1884.
Hafen, LeRoy R. and Ann W. *Relations with the Indians of the Plains.* Glendale, Calif.: The Arthur H. Clark Co., 1959.
———. *Powder River Campaigns and Sawyer's Expedition.* Glendale, Calif.: The Arthur H. Clark Co., 1961.
Hafen, Leroy R., and Young, Francis Marion. *Fort Laramie and the Pageant of the West.* Glendale, Calif.: The Arthur H. Clark Co., 1938.
Halsey, Francis Whitney. *The Old New York Frontier.* New York: Charles Scribner's Sons, 1901.
Hamilton, Holman. *Zachary Taylor, Soldier of the Republic.* Indianapolis: The Bobbs-Merrill Co., 1941.
Hildreth, James. *Dragoon Campaigns in the Rocky Mountains.* New York: Wiley & Long, 1836.

Hitchcock, Maj. Gen. Ethan Allen. *Fifty Years in Camp and Field*. New York: G. P. Putnam's Sons, 1909.
Hollon, W. Eugene. *The Lost Pathfinder: Zebulon Montgomery Pike*. Norman: University of Oklahoma Press, 1949.
Howe, H. "McDowell's Story." In Ohio Historical Collection, vol. 2.
Huddleston, F. J. *Gentleman Johnny Burgoyne*. Indianapolis: The Bobbs-Merrill Co., 1927.
Hughes, Col. John T. Diary. (*See* Connelley.)
Hulburt, Archer Butler. *Military Roads of the Mississippi Basin; the Conquest of the Old Northwest*. Cleveland: The Arthur H. Clark Co., 1904.
Hunt, Aurora. *The Army of the Pacific*. Glendale, Calif.: The Arthur H. Clark Co., 1951.
———. *Major General James Henry Carleton, 1814-1873*. Glendale, Calif.: The Arthur H. Clark Co.
Hyde, George H. *Rangers and Regulars*. Columbus, Ohio: Long's College Book Co., 1952.
Irving, Washington. *The Adventures of Captain Bonneville, U.S.A., in the Rocky Mountains and the Far West*. New York: G. P. Putnam's Sons, 1852.
Jacobs, J. R. *The Beginning of the U.S. Army, 1783-1812*. Princeton, N.J.: Princeton University Press, 1947.
James, Marquis. *Andrew Jackson, the Border Captain*. Indianapolis: The Bobbs-Merrill Co., 1933.
Johnson, Sir John. *Orderly Book of Sir John Johnson during the Oriskany Campaign, 1776-1777*. Albany: Joel Munsell's Sons, 1882.
Johnson, Brig. Gen. R. W. *A Soldier's Reminiscences*. Philadelphia: J. B. Lippincott Co., 1886.
Judd, A. N. *Campaigning against the Sioux*. Watsonville, Calif.: Press of the Daily Pajaronian, 1906.
Kelleher, William A. *Turmoil in New Mexico, 1846-1868*. Santa Fe: The Kydal Press, 1952.
Kreidberg, Lt. Col. Marvin A., and Henry, 1st Lt. Merton G. *History of Military Mobilization in the United States Army, 1775-1945*. Dept. of the Army Pamphlet No. 20-212. 1955.
Lamb, Roger. *An Original and Authentic Journal of Occurrences during the Late American War*. Dublin: Wilkinson & Courtney, 1809.
Lancaster, Bruce. *From Lexington to Liberty*. Garden City, N.Y.: Doubleday & Co., 1955.
Lancaster, Bruce, and Plumb, J. H. *The Revolution*. New York: American Heritage Publishing Co., 1958.
Lane, Lydia Spencer. *I Married a Soldier*. Philadelphia: J. B. Lippincott Co., 1910.
Lefferts, Charles M. *Uniforms of the American, British, French,*

and German Armies in the War of the American Revolution. New York: New York Historical Society, 1926.
Lester, Charles Edwards. *The Life of Sam Houston.* New York: J. C. Derby, 1855.
Lewis, Oscar. *The War in the Far West.* Garden City, N.Y.: Doubleday & Co., 1961.
Lockwood, Frank C. *The Apache Indians.* New York: The Macmillan Co., 1938.
Logan, Gen. John A. *The Volunteer Soldier of America.* Chicago and New York: R. S. Peale & Co., 1887.
Lossing, Benson J. *The Pictorial Field-Book of the Revolution.* 2 vols. New York: Harper & Brothers, 1851.
Mahan, Capt. A. T. *Sea Power in Its Relations to the War of 1812.* 2 vols. Boston: Little, Brown & Co., 1919.
Manring, B. F. *The Conquest of the Coeur d'Alenes, Spokanes, and Pelouses.* Spokane, Wash.: John W. Graham & Co., 1912.
Metcalf, Lt. Col. Clyde H. *A History of the United States Marine Corps.* New York: G. P. Putnam's Sons, 1939.
Millis, Walter. *Arms and Men.* New York: G. P. Putnam's Sons, 1956.
Monaghan, Jay. *Civil War on the Western Border.* Boston: Little, Brown & Co., 1955.
Montross, Lynn, *Rag, Tag and Bobtail, the Story of the Continental Army, 1775-1783.* New York: Harper & Brothers, 1952.
Molte, Jacob Rhett. *Journey into Wilderness.* Gainesville: University of Florida Press, 1953.
New York State and the Civil War. New York Civil War Centennial Commission. Albany, October 1961.
Nickerson, Hoffman. *The Turning Point of the Revolution.* Boston and New York: Houghton Mifflin Co., 1928.
Oehler, C. M. *The Great Sioux Uprising.* New York: Oxford University Press, 1959.
Okison, John M. *Tecumseh and His Times.* New York: G. P. Putnam's Sons, 1938.
Palmer, Brig. Gen. John McAuley. *America in Arms.* New Haven: Yale University Press, 1941.
Parkman, Francis. *The Oregon Trail.* Garden City, N.Y.: Doubleday & Co., 1946.
Parton, James. *Life of Andrew Jackson.* 3 vols. New York: Mason Brothers, 1861.
Pelzer, Louis. *Marches of the Dragoons in the Mississippi Valley.* Iowa City: State Historical Society of Iowa, 1917.
Pike, Cpl. James. *Scout and Ranger.* Princeton, N.J.: Princeton University Press, 1932.
Powell, E. Alexander. *The Road to Glory.* New York: Charles Scribner's Sons, 1915.
Prucha, Francis Paul. *Broadax and Bayonet; the Role of the United States Army in the Development of the Northwest,*

1815-1860. Madison: State Historical Society of Wisconsin, 1953.
Roddis, Capt. Louis H. *The Indian Wars of Minnesota.* Cedar Rapids, Iowa: The Torch Press, 1956.
Rodenbough, Gen. Theo F. *From Everglade to Cañon with the Second Dragoons.* New York: D. Van Nostrand, 1875.
Richardson, Rupert Norval. *The Comanche Barrier to South Plains Settlement.* Glendale, Calif.: The Arthur H. Clark Co., 1933.
Riegel, Robert E. *America Moves West.* New York: Henry Holt & Co., 1930.
Rosebush, Waldo E. *Frontier Steel.* Appleton, Wis.: C. C. Nelson Pub. Co., 1958.
Sabin, Edwin Legrand. *Kit Carson Days.* 2 vols. New York: Press of the Pioneers, 1935.
St. Clair, Arthur. *Papers.* 2 vols. William H. Smith, ed. Cincinnati: Robert Clark Co., 1882.
Sargent, Winthrop. Diary. In Ohio Archeological and Historical Society Publications, vol. 33.
Scott, John Albert. *Fort Stanwix and Oriskany.* Rome, N.Y.: Rome Sentinel Co., 1927.
Seymour, Flora. *Indian Agent of the Old Frontier.* New York: D. Appleton & Co., 1941.
Sipe, C. Hale. *The Indian Wars of Pennsylvania.* Harrisburg: The Telegraph Press, 1929.
Smith, Justin H. *The War with Mexico.* 2 vols. New York: The Macmillan Co., 1919.
Spaulding, Col. Oliver Lyman. *The United States Army in War and Peace.* New York: G. P. Putnam's Sons, 1937.
Sprague, John T. *The Origin, Progress, and Conclusion of the Florida War.* New York: D. Appleton & Co., 1847.
Starkey, M. I. *The Cherokee Nation.* New York: Alfred A. Knopf, 1946.
Steele, Maj. Matthew Forney. *American Campaigns.* 2 vols. Washington: Byron & Adams, 1909.
Stegens, Frank E. *The Black Hawk War.* Chicago, 1903.
Stone, William L. *The Campaigns of Lieut. Gen John Burgoyne and the Expedition of Col. Barry St. Leger.* Albany: Joel Munsell's Sons, 1877.
———. *Life of Joseph Brant—Thayendanegea.* 2 vols. New York: George Dearborn & Co., 1838.
Sweeney, Lt. Thomas W. *Journal, 1849-1853.* Arthur Woodward, ed. Los Angeles: Westernlore Press, 1956.
Tebbel, John, and Keith Jennison. *The American Indian Wars.* New York: Harper & Brothers, 1960.
Thacher, James. *A Military Journal during the American Revolutionary War.* Boston: Cottons & Barnard, 1827.

Thornbrough, Gayle, ed. *Outpost on the Wabash, 1787-1791.* Indiana Historical Society Publications., vol. 19.

Thwaites, Reuben Gold. *How George Rogers Clark Won the Northwest.* Chicago: A. C. McClurg Co., 1903.

———. *Rocky Mountain Exploration.* New York: D. Appleton & Co., 1914.

Tipton, John. "Tippecanoe Journal." *Indianapolis News,* May 5, 1879.

Trevelyan, Sir George Otto. *The American Revolution.* Part 3. New York: Longmans, Green & Co., 1907.

Tucker, Glenn. *Poltroons and Patriots, a Popular Account of the War of 1812.* Indianapolis: The Bobbs-Merrill Co., 1954.

———. *Tecumseh, Vision of Glory.* Indianapolis: The Bobbs-Merrill Co., 1956.

Underhill, Ruth M. *The Navajos.* Norman: University of Oklahoma Press, 1956.

U. S. Department of the Army. *The Medal of Honor of the United States Army.* Washington: Government Printing Office, 1948.

———. The Infantry School. *Selected Readings in American Military History.* 3 vols. Washington, 1953.

———. *R.O.T.C. Manual. American Military History, 1607-1953.* Washington, 1953.

U. S. Department of the Interior National Park Service. *Historical Report on Fort Bowie, Arizona.* Robert M. Utley. Santa Fe, 1962.

U. S. War Department. *The War of the Rebellion: Official Records.* 130 vols. Washington, 1880-1901.

Upton, Bvt. Maj. Gen. Emory. *The Military Policy of the United States.* Washington: Government Printing Office, 1917.

Van Tyne, Claude H. *The War of Independence.* Boston and New York: Houghton Mifflin Co., 1929.

Wallace, Ernest, and E. Adamson Hoebel. *The Comanches, Lords of the South Plains.* Norman: University of Oklahoma Press, 1952.

Wallace, Willard M. *Appeal to Arms.* New York: Harper & Brothers, 1951.

Ward, Christopher. *The War of the Revolution.* 2 vols. New York: The Macmillan Co., 1952.

Ware, Capt. Eugene F. *The Indian War of 1864.* New York: St. Martin's Press, 1960.

Wayne, Anthony. *A Name in Arms.* Richard C. Knopfied, ed. Pittsburgh: University of Pittsburgh Press, 1960.

Wildes, Harry Emerson. *Anthony Wayne.* New York: Harcourt, Brace & Co., 1941.

Wellman, Paul I. *Death on Horseback.* Philadelphia: J. B. Lippincott Co., 1947.

Wesley, Edgar Bruce. *Guarding the Frontier.* Minneapolis: University of Minneapolis Press, 1935.
Wilkinson, Gen. James. *Memoirs of My Own Times.* 3 vols. Philadelphia: Abraham Small, 1816.
Willett, William M. *Narrative of the Military Action of Colonel Marinus Willett.* New York: G. C. & H. Carvill, 1831.
Williams, T. Harry. *Americans at War.* Baton Rouge: Louisiana State University Press, 1960.
Wilson, Frazer Ells. *Arthur St. Clair.* Richmond: Garrett & Massie, 1944.
Wisconsin Historical Collections. Files.
Woodward, Arthur. *Lances at San Pascual.* San Francisco: California Historical Society, 1948.
Wyllys, Rufus Kay. *Arizona, the History of a Frontier State.* Phoenix: Hobson & Herr, 1950.
Young, Col. Bennett H. *The Battle of the Thames.* Filson Club Publications, no. 18. Louisville, Ky.: John P. Morton Co., 1903.
Young, Otis E. *The West of Philip St. George Cooke, 1809-1895.* Glendale, Calif.: The Arthur H. Clark Co., 1955.
———. *The First Military Escort on the Santa Fe Trail.* Glendale, Calif.: The Arthur H. Clark Co., 1952.

The Dramatic Saga Of The
Greatest Of All The Indian Tribes

THE CHEYENNE WARS

By Joseph Millard

A MONARCH AMERICANA BOOK

For decades the Cheyenne Indians endured abuses from the white settlers without spilling a single drop of white blood in well-merited reprisal. Finally, goaded beyond human endurance, they turned on their tormentors with all the pent-up ferocity of their savage natures. Hungry, homeless and driven, the Cheyennes repeatedly defeated overwhelming forces of well-equipped troops, to win the accolade: "The finest natural cavalry on earth."